99 Jobs

Also by Joe Cottonwood

FOR GROWN-UPS

The Naked Computer
Famous Potatoes
Frank City (Goodbye)
Clear Heart

FOR CHILDREN AND GROWN-UPS

The Adventures of Boone Barnaby
Danny Ain't
Babcock
Quake!
Four Dog Riot

POETRY

Son of a Poet

99 Jobs

Blood, Sweat, and Houses

JOE COTTONWOOD

2013

© Joe Cottonwood, 2013
All Rights Reserved

Editing and text design: Susan Walker
Author photograph: David Minard
Printer: CreateSpace

ISBN 978-0615909448

Published by Clear Heart Books
La Honda, California

Contents

About Labor

Working-Class Hippie

Rookie

The Road Not Taken

What's My Crime?

Diary of a Small Contractor

The Good Life

Plenty

Everybody Lives Somewhere

You Fix the Toilet

Acknowledgements

About Labor

Screwdriver, Melted

Saturday, February 11, 1989

Jack wants me to wire an illegal rental he's building behind his house in Mountain View. He's a Lockheed space engineer on medical disability. I get the sense that the disability is in the psychological realm. Like, he's half crazy. It's in the eyes.

He wants a bid, but I tell him I can only do this on a time-and-materials basis at forty dollars an hour. Cash.

He seems stunned. "I've never paid forty dollars an hour to anybody in my entire life."

I don't budge. I'm not cutting my rates on an illegal job for a crazy man. He shakes his head and paws his boots along the gravel and finally agrees. Good. I need the money.

As I work, Jack loosens up. He tells me his two boys, now at UC Berkeley, want to be an artist and a bass guitarist. "All that schooling." He shakes his head.

It's a cold day. I'm wearing three shirts plus a hooded sweatshirt. Metal is frigid to the touch as I open his electrical panel and flip the main

1

switch. Then, stupidly, without testing for voltage, I insert a screwdriver and—ZAP! FLASH!

The screwdriver smokes, half melted. An ozone smell.

That could've been my finger smoking, half melted. Or my heart. The circuit breaker was defective—it didn't turn off. I push it again. This time it clicks off—but later, when I try to push it on, it won't go. Jack has to go to Orchard Supply Hardware and pay ninety-nine dollars for a new Zinsco 100-amp breaker, which doesn't please him. "That's a dollar an ampere," he says incredulously.

That's two dollars a year for my life, I'm thinking. Never trust a switch. Test, then touch.

The day never warms. In fact it gets colder. A raw wind. I crawl under the house pulling wires. I drill holes, drive staples, climb ladders. Freezing fingers strip the insulation, twist the copper. To stay warm I work fast, but even so it's a twelve-hour day. I have a vision of my father, shaking his head. All that schooling.

No regrets. You make your choices.

It's $480 for labor, $120 (rounding down) for materials. Jack says, "I'm going to deduct a hundred dollars for that circuit breaker."

I say, "It was already busted or else it would've shut down the first time I flipped it. That thing could've killed me."

"The hell you say."

"Jack, I'm getting pissed."

Still, he hesitates.

I say, "You'd better hope nobody tells the Mountain View Building Department what you're doing here. An anonymous tip. That's all it takes."

Jack rubs his chin. His eyes dart about. Then he counts out six Ben Franklins.

Some jobs you like. Some, you bear. Some days it's a tough world. And you're part of it.

Junior Electrician

September 1968

I got hired to change light bulbs. The maintenance department at Washington University in St. Louis advertised for a junior electrician, and I showed up.

My job was to walk around campus with a cardboard box of fluorescent tubes on one shoulder and an 8-foot stepladder on the other. I was the guy who made all the clanking noise in the library setting up the ladder, opening the casement, dropping twenty-year-old dust on your table when you were trying to study.

Washington University had a large campus. Changing light bulbs was a full-time job.

Franklin showed me what to do. He'd been promoted to senior electrician. I was his replacement. Franklin was about my age, maybe a year older. I was white; Franklin was medium brown.

First day, in the stifling St. Louis heat, walking across campus to our assigned building, Franklin asked me how I'd spent my summer.

"Long story," I said.

"Go ahead," Franklin said, stopping in the shade of a tree. "We got all day."

I gave Franklin a brief synopsis of my summer. It included being turned down for a summer job at Jack in the Box (thank God); hitchhiking to California and somehow winding up in a hippie commune in Big Sur; hitching back; a Hells Angel; a man who owned seven brothels; a stolen truck; a night alone in the middle of the desert; a drunk cowboy; a day in the Winnemucca, Nevada, jail; a Mormon missionary; hopping a freight train; joining my girlfriend in Colorado and driving her beat-up old VW bug to a ghost town in New Mexico and then to Vancouver, Canada, and then across Montana to Madison, where at a party we met Miss Wisconsin, who was tripping on LSD; and then to Chicago just as the National Guard was pouring in for the Democratic National Convention; and then to Washington, DC, to see our parents; and back to St. Louis. And so here I was. "What about you, Franklin? How'd you spend your summer?"

"Right here," Franklin said.

And there it was: I was working my way through college; Franklin was just working.

We started in Dunker Hall. Franklin parked the ladder under a fixture, climbed up, opened the casing, and began my training on

3

everything there is to know about changing a fluorescent tube. Two minutes later Franklin said, "Okay, you got it." I wasn't allowed to replace ballasts or cut any wires—that was a job for a senior electrician.

Next, Franklin showed me where to hide from Boss Man: a little storage closet tucked into a wall of the English department. The closet was about four feet high and eight feet deep—just big enough to hide inside. Franklin said that when he had my job he used to go in there and stay all day.

There was no light in there. It was a wooden box. You close the door and you might as well spend your day in a coffin. Actually, a coffin would be better: at least it would have bedding.

I preferred doing a day's work, so I said, "Um, not today, but thanks, Franklin."

"Can I ask you something?" Franklin was scratching his chin.

"What?"

"Why do you want a beard?"

"Girls like it," I said. Not true, actually, but it was an easy answer.

"Girls. Huh." He turned and started walking. "Follow me."

He took me to the art school building—Bixby Hall, I think—up to the top floor where, in a hallway, there was a metal door to an air vent. Franklin held the door open. "Go on," he said.

"Why?"

"Live models," he said. "Naked." Franklin climbed right into the air vent.

"I dunno, Franklin . . ."

"Would you shut up and get in here?"

I followed. What can I say? Adventure beckoned.

The air vent was about three feet across the bottom, two feet high, sheet metal. It smelled like stale dust. It rumbled and creaked and boomed like thunder when you moved. (And it was probably full of asbestos, but who knew at the time?)

"You have to slide yourself real easy," Franklin whispered, and he started squeezing along this tunnel that was angled slightly downhill. Cautiously, I followed.

Probably everybody in the building could hear us moving around up there.

The tunnel made a transition from rectangular to round. At the bottom of the round section was a circular metal grate. This grate, Franklin said, looked out over the art studio. Franklin was on his stomach, slowly sliding feet-first down toward the grate. I was a few feet behind him, facing forward. I was wondering how Franklin expected to see anything if his feet were where his eyes needed to be.

4

At about this point it dawned on me that Franklin had never actually done this before. He was just trying to impress me.

The last ten feet or so was at a slightly steeper angle, and that's where Franklin lost his grip. The metal was slick and there was nothing to grab.

Franklin went booming feet-first down that air tunnel and came up hard against the grate. There was a *clunk* and then a POP. All this time I was leaning forward trying to grasp Franklin's outstretched hands. Franklin was desperately looking up at me and waving his hands around toward me and couldn't see that the grate had popped off. He was starting to slide out.

Now imagine you're in the art class. You're sketching, sculpting, doodling. It's one of those big, airy studios with skylights and a high ceiling.

You hear this odd noise.

You look up, and this big metal grate comes popping off the wall twenty feet above you. You scramble out of the way. There's a crash and a clatter and a WUNK WUNK WUNK as the grate hits the floor and settles to rest.

You look up again and see two feet sticking out of the air vent, kicking wildly. Suddenly—this is where I finally catch hold of Franklin's desperately flapping hands—the feet zip back inside the vent. You hear a *rumble rumble rumble* as Franklin and I scramble back up the vent and into the hallway. You run out of class to see what is going on. You run up the stairwell just as two dusty guys are running down a different stairwell with all the adrenaline that comes from sheer terror.

Franklin and I ran all the way across the parking lot. We ran up the grandiose front entry steps to Brookings Hall. We ran across the glorious grass of the quad. We ran back to the English department, where we opened that little wooden door and climbed into that hard, dark space and shut the door and lay there with the box of fluorescent tubes between us.

Never have I been so glad to spend an hour in a coffin. A dog wandered into the building and started sniffing at our door. You could hear students and professors walking by. Just outside the closet a conversation developed between a grad student and a whiny-voiced professor, and it became clear that they were having an affair, that neither of them was enjoying it, and that it was going to end badly for both of them.

Nobody caught us. Officially, that is. Larry, the gray-haired master electrician, seemed to always be suppressing a smile as he ordered us around. After the incident Larry usually assigned Franklin and me to opposite ends of the campus.

Before the year was up, Franklin got drafted. On his last day all the electricians chipped in and gave him an envelope of cash, about a hundred bucks, as a going-away present. It was a tradition there. Franklin gave me his old pair of linesman's pliers with a nick in the handle where it had touched a live wire that sent him jumping.

I never saw him again. I lost the pliers when somebody stole my tool box.

Many years later, visiting Washington, DC, with my kids, I touched Franklin's name on the Wall.

Franklin was my first buddy in the trades.

The Gorilla Method

Sunday, February 26, 1984

I didn't go into plumbing for the glamour. Still, I have my limits: I don't do septic tanks.

So I call Buck.

I've already dug out the top of the tank and opened the lid. It's your basic 1,500 gallons of stench. This particular tank is overflowing.

Buck ambles up the hillside carrying no tools. Buck is a boxer. He's built like one and he walks like one: sort of jerky, as if it's hard to hold back those powerful muscles. I respect Buck, but I'm cautious with him. There's an air of the outsider about him. He always seems to hold something back, not only muscles, but something at the core that nobody should mess with. Something angry.

Buck used to be our local honeydipper, the guy who pumps out septic tanks and hauls the sewage away in a tanker-type truck. Buck couldn't stand how much the county was charging to empty his "honey." For a while he had an arrangement with a local farmer to dump the sewage on one of the farmer's fields. The farmer was happy for the fertilizer. Buck was happy to put it to use. Unfortunately the county found out and stopped the operation.

Buck was disgusted. So he sold the truck. I told him—in fact, everybody told him—"Just raise your rates, Buck. If you don't, somebody else will. We need a pumper. We'd rather it was you than some guy from San Jose." But Buck couldn't stand the idea of charging so much money. So he quit.

Today he's wearing blue jeans and a hooded sweatshirt. "So it's blocked?" he says.

"Yes. Have you got a tool for that?"

"I use the gorilla method." On his knees, Buck peels off his sweatshirt. He leans over and plunges his hand inside the tank up to his armpit. His face is just an inch from the surface. He grimaces, clutching something, and pulls with all his might. Shoulder muscles bulge.

I'm thinking: to be a boxer, a good one, you need to know how to focus on just one thing. You shut out the pain, the noise. You shut out the shit.

Suddenly it gives. There's a swirl of water. Buck nearly loses his balance while a wave of effluvium laps up to his neck.

Buck straightens up on his knees. In his hand is a basketball-sized glob of roots and human waste, dripping. Meanwhile, sewage is rushing into the drain line, sinking lower in the tank.

Buck heaves the glob into some weeds. "I think we got it," he says.

I appreciate the "we."

I'd pay him a half day's wage for what he just did. He only wants an hour. He washes with cold water from a hose. Then he ambles back down the hillside, heading toward Apple Jack's, our local tavern.

Let's appreciate the Bucks of the world. They keep it flowing.

The Speculation of Ladders

Friday, October 25, 1985

New clients. A comfy old ranch house. An elderly couple wants me to build a platform in the garage, above the Lexus. They want to store suitcases and Christmas decorations up there.

To look around, I climb a ladder.

The old woman is wearing a flour-dusted apron over a calico dress. She says to her husband, "Eugene, you'd better move the cat dish from under the ladder. We wouldn't want the man to fall on it and hurt himself."

Not budging and in no hurry, white-haired Eugene stares first at the loft area. Slowly he lowers his eyes to the floor. "If he falls," the old man says, "he'll hit the beam up there and break his neck. Then he'll hit the water heater and the washing machine. He'll be dead long before he reaches the cat dish."

"Oh," his wife says. "All right then."

The cat dish remains, unmoved, under the ladder.

Woodpeckers

Friday, March 27, 1987

The voice in the phone says, "We have woodpeckers."

"Uh, excuse me?"

"Woodpeckers are making holes in the side of our house."

Her name is Pepper. She lives in Portola Valley Ranch, which is not a ranch but a highly regulated subdivision where you have to submit plans to the homeowners association before you can paint your mailbox. Or kill a woodpecker.

Pepper greets me at the front door. She is petite, pretty. No eye contact. She leads me through the house taking unusually short steps.

Standing on the rear deck, I see that the woodpecker holes are in an awkward spot that will be difficult to reach, even with a ladder. I'll have to build a scaffold. As I explain the job, I notice that Pepper's eyes are wandering in two different directions.

Aha. Of course. She's blind.

Pepper explains that the male woodpecker makes holes in the cedar-shingle siding, hoping to attract a female. To discourage him, I must hang cut-up pieces of garden hose. The hose pieces look like snakes, supposedly. Snakes eat eggs. The female won't be attracted. The male will move on.

This is the upper middle–class solution to woodpeckers. The blue-collar solution would be to blast the little beasts with a shotgun. Which, most likely, would not be approved by the homeowners association.

"Do they look like snakes to you?" Pepper asks.

"Not exactly," I say. "But I'm not a woodpecker."

"The birds. Are they pretty?"

"Very handsome," I say. The topknot is an exuberant red; the body, a busy black and white. They seem brilliant and hardworking both.

Pepper is a lovely woman wearing a wedding ring. Delicate freckles. She could only learn your face through her sensitive fingertips. Her lipstick is slightly awry. Don't even think about it.

This house, this protected neighborhood, is a safe place to be blind.

Balancing on my scaffold of ladder, plywood, and 2×4s, I replace shingles in the siding and install rubber hose "snakes" on the roof and discover more holes up there, some with acorns stuffed inside. I jam metal flashing under the shingles, a little surprise for the next jabbing beak.

Scarlet-headed birds are calling, swooping, clinging to oaks. They tap-tap-tap on the house next door where a cleaning woman is playing loud rock and roll. Carpenters up the street are shouting, cursing, joking—and also playing loud rock and roll.

It's hot on the roof, but the view is nice: native grass and scattered trees, a well-ordered, rustic tidiness. I'm shirtless, in raggedy shorts that catch on a nail and rip across the butt. Doesn't matter; she can't see.

A patrol car, private security, stops on the street. A man peers at me through mirrored sunglasses. I wave from the roof. He stares a moment longer, then drives on.

I write Pepper a bill that she can't read. She says her husband will mail a check. I exceeded my estimate, but fortunately the extra roof work gives me cover.

"Thanks so much," Pepper says. "I'll see you to the door. Oh. Wait." She smiles.

I like this woman, her sense of humor, her ease with herself.

As I drive away, the security car follows until I reach the main road.

People—very nice people—live here to get away from peckers like us: The cleaning woman, the carpenters, our raucous rock and roll, our mating dances. We intrude with our bright feathers and do the work that needs to be done. Then, not by shotguns but by mirrored shades, rubber snakes, we get the message: We must leave.

Impaled

Thursday, October 5, 1995

I'm installing ceiling hooks for a therapy practice.

It's attic work on a sunny day, probably 120 degrees up there. Dust hangs in the air. I plow through spider webs and shove itchy insulation aside.

As I'm balanced on my knees over a joist, tightening a nut, my sweaty hand slips from the wrench and comes down hard on something sharp.

Ow!

In the beam of my headlamp is a nasty chunk of wood broken from the top of the joist. Like a grainy dagger of Douglas fir, it is about four inches long, coming to a point at one end. The point is embedded in my right palm with the wood hanging down, pulled (painfully) by gravity.

Cautiously, I try to tug at the wood. It won't come out. When I pull at it, I see stars.

I crawl back to the trap door, step carefully down the ladder. Holly, one of the therapists, sees my hand and blanches.

"Ack!" she says.

"Little accident," I say. "Could you try to pull it out?"

"It'll rip you apart!"

"Just try. Please."

She pulls gently at the stick of wood. Won't budge.

I see stars.

"I'll drive you to the emergency room," Holly says.

"Not yet," I say. "I want to finish first." I start climbing to the attic, still impaled, the piece of wood clattering (painfully) against the side of the ladder.

Holly calls after me: "You almost fainted when I pulled on that thing."

"Thank you for trying."

"You'll bleed all over the attic. The ceiling down here will turn red."

"I'll clean it up."

One thing about me: pain makes me stupid.

Crawling across joists, I nearly faint again.

Okay, I get it. I crawl back to the trap door and come down the ladder. Holly is standing there, scowling at me. "Get in my car," she says.

"I'll drive myself."

"You can't drive!"

But I do. The truck has a stick shift. Changing gears, I see stars. Instead of the emergency room, I drive to the Palo Alto Clinic where I have medical coverage and a family physician who knows me. Of course, you're supposed to make an appointment weeks in advance.

There are three receptionists in the family practice department. It's a busy place with a waiting room full of people. My face is smeared with sweat and dirt and cobwebs. I step to a desk and say, "Excuse me. I'm sorry. I don't have an appointment, but is there any chance I could see Dr. Wisler?"

I hold up my hand for the receptionist to see. Blood is trickling down the chunk of wood and dripping onto the floor.

All three receptionists bolt from their desks, running in different directions.

A minute later one of them returns and says, "Dr. Wisler is seeing a patient and is supposed to go on lunch break after that, but he says he'll see you on his break. Now let's get you out of here."

Everyone in the waiting room is staring at me and my chunk of wood and the little puddle of blood at my feet. I suppose it looks like somebody attacked me with a wooden stake. Like I was fighting a vampire.

I follow the receptionist to Dr. Wisler's office, where I take a seat in an armchair. The receptionist places towels on my lap to catch the blood.

After about fifteen minutes Dr. Wisler arrives with a nurse. For some reason he doesn't move me to a treatment room but operates on me right there in the office, holding my hand over a towel draped over the blotter of his desk. The nurse squirts antiseptic while the doctor dislodges bits of skin. I'm seeing stars the whole time.

Dr. Wisler seems to be enjoying himself.

"I'm sorry to make you miss lunch," I say.

"This is better than lunch," he says.

The nurse and I exchange a look. She shrugs.

The whole operation takes a half hour. My hand is wrapped in white gauze.

Dr. Wisler orders me to take the afternoon off and to keep the hand elevated above my heart.

I drive home steering and shifting with my left hand. Once, when I was hitchhiking, I saw a one-armed man do this in a Volkswagen bug. You have to lean forward and press your shoulder against the steering wheel while you reach across to move the shifter, mounted on the floor. You tend to swerve each time you shift, so you change gears as little as possible.

At home I take a lengthy bubble bath, my favorite recreational activity. My bandaged hand stays above water on the edge of the tub. While soaking, I read a book of poetry by William Carlos Williams. He was a doctor, so it seems appropriate.

My daughter (age seventeen) comes home from high school while I'm still bathing in bubbles. Talking through the door, she reminds me that when she injured her ankle, she was told to keep the ankle above her heart for a few days. Being a dancer, she could do that.

Tomorrow I'll go back to that attic. I hate to leave a job unfinished.

About Labor

Thursday, November 16, 1995

I'm sleeping. Early morning, dark outside. The phone rings and it's Steve, an old client. He's frantic: "I'm supposed to have a new roof installed tomorrow. The tear-out guy exposed some rotten sheathing yesterday, and for a bunch of stupid reasons the roofing company can't repair it today and my whole house is exposed to the weather. Please, *please*, if you can repair the sheathing today, they could install the new roof tomorrow before the rains come. You can bill me directly."

"Okay."

"And while you're up there would you please install a cricket— whatever that is? The roofer recommends it. You know what a cricket is?"

"Yes." A cricket is like a little gable, or saddle, to prevent debris from piling up against the chimney.

"And by the way, sorry if I woke you."

So I cancel my scheduled job and instead spend the day going up and down a ladder for Steve. Fourteen steps up. Fourteen steps down. I'm schlepping wood, nailing. Tough on the knees.

For the morning I'm alone.

Around noon a delivery truck arrives. A man with a walrus mustache climbs my ladder and starts cursing. With indelicate words he curses this rustic cabin, which he likens to violent acts committed on one's mother. He curses the narrow dirt driveway, which he likens to poverty-stricken liquid human waste. He curses the fact that he can't get a boom or a crane or a forklift "way out here" in the orifice at the end of the alimentary canal "of nowhere." Most of all he curses that he'll have to carry several thousand pounds of phallus-sucking human excrement on his shoulder up the fourteen rungs of my ladder, load after load.

Then he smiles and turns chatty. Standing with his belly against the gutter, Walrus says he used to be a commercial fisherman, so he knows hard work. "Crabbing is good pay, but nineteen-hour days of physical labor, it takes a price from you."

After a few minutes of smiles and chatting he goes down the ladder and comes back up with a small box on his shoulder. With an ingratiating smile, belly against gutter, he says, "Hey, will ya just set this down for me?"

I take the box from his extended hands—and nearly drop it. My back gives a twinge. It's a box of nails, fifty pounds of steel. He smiled me into

15

a con. Sure, the job would take half the time if he could hand me all his fifty-pound bundles, but he's the one getting paid for it. We serve different bosses.

"That's all," I say. "Sorry, but I've got a back."

He frowns. "I've got a back too," he says. But he's stuck with the job, and he knows it.

No hard feelings. It was worth a try.

Walrus guy cheerfully carries the shingles by himself while telling me in installments with each trip up the ladder about his seventy-four-year-old mom who's had five heart operations, three triple bypasses, plus she has diabetes and gets dialysis. He thinks she's great. I think of my tax dollars at work.

At the end of the day, the county building inspector arrives in his white Jeep. Fortunately I've just finished. Cricket built, sheathing in place. The roof is naked, skylights removed, two-inch air gaps like zebra stripes between each board. Fine furniture below, draped with sheets against the dust.

I've dealt with this inspector for years. He has white hair, a clear gaze, a soft spot for babies. Standing in the mud at the base of the ladder, looking up, he says, "Tell me about it."

From the roof I say, "One-by-four sheathing. Five and a half on center. Two nails per rafter. Eight-penny galvanized."

"Good. You pass."

Walrus guy calls down from the roof: "Don't you want to look at it?"

The inspector waves his hand at the ladder. "I'm sixty-eight years old," he says.

Walrus guy says, "Hey, man. You could retire."

The inspector signs the job sheet, then hangs the clipboard on a nail by the chimney. "When you retire," he says, "you die."

Walrus guy comes halfway down the ladder, points to a roll of 30-pound felt paper at the feet of the inspector and says with a smile, "Would you mind handing that up to me?"

The inspector suggests that the walrus perform a sexual act upon himself.

It's quitting time. A day's work, a day's pay fully earned. The inspector, hands in pockets, walks slowly to his Jeep. A few drops of rain are starting to fall. Walrus carries the last roll of felt paper up the ladder. I gather my tools.

The sky is suddenly black.

Oh, man.

Somebody goofed at the weather center. It's a downpour.

We scramble, me and Walrus. Hustling without a word of discussion—it's not my job, but it's not his either—we unfold sheets of blue plastic tarp and anchor them with bundles of shingles. Our feet slip on the wet plastic. It's dangerous. Slide off, fall fourteen feet, you'll be broken.

The inspector has climbed the ladder. As I wrap plastic around the chimney, he braces my leg with his hand.

We get drenched.

A few grunts but no bickering. Because, in the end, we all serve the same boss.

In the foggy cabs of our two trucks and one Jeep, heaters blasting, hair dripping, we drive our separate ways to our separate homes.

Skateboarder

September 2001 to March 2002

Mordecai tells me about some famous skateboarding movie (which I've never heard of) that shows footage of him.

"So you're a pro?" I ask.

"In my dreams." He laughs and rolls his eyes.

I'm wary, but I hire him. I can always use a teenage helper. It's mid-September 2001. My youngest son has just started college back East, leaving an emotional hole in my soul like a tiny suggestion of that smoking ruin in Manhattan.

For the first two days Mordecai takes directions and works hard, with his shoes untied and his pants hanging low. He can't stand still. He's a hothead, but somewhere within he's a nice Jewish boy.

It's a termite job. We're tearing out siding and spraying boards with borate.

Mordecai's father calls me after the second day and asks if his son is being useful.

"He's good," I say. "I like his hustle."

"Hustle!" The father laughs. "That's a benign way to describe it."

On the third day Mordecai goes home for a lunch break. While I'm eating my sandwich, the phone rings. It's Mord: "Sorry, Doctor"—he often calls me Doctor—"but I'm leaving for Oregon. They're picking me up in fifteen minutes."

He's just been invited to tour with some professional skateboarders. A week later he's back.

"How was it?" I ask.

"Sweet," he says. And we resume the work.

It's one of those jobs that just keeps growing. A small termite repair develops into replacing the roof on a garage, building a deck, stairs, and a fence, a long string of jobs. Mordecai stays with me for that whole depressing winter after 9/11.

I'm happy to have a companion, erratic as he is. Mordecai takes the occasional week off—on ten minutes' notice—to go skateboarding in Tahoe or L.A.

You come to know somebody through how they work. When I spray transparent stain onto house siding, I start at one corner and make my way methodically down and across to the opposite corner. Mordecai sprays scattershot in wiggles and circles, seemingly at random, until the entire wall is coated.

I say, "We need to make sure each board gets an even coat."

"I get it even," Mordecai says. "I'm a compulsive perfectionist."

Nope. Neither. But I don't say anything.

Though fearless on a skateboard, he's nervous about "sketchy ladder work." So I start a scaffold job by myself, ripping out siding twenty feet above the ground. After watching for a few minutes, Mordecai comes up too. From then on he's fine, full of questions and restless energy.

Inanimate objects such as 2×4s are "bad boys," as in "Do you want me to nail this bad boy up now?"

On a day when we're working on my own house, I tell him to saw off the end of a 1×6 that's sticking out too far at the base of my chimney. "I've been meaning to cut that board for twenty years," I remark.

Later I learn that Mordecai has been quoting me to his parents and friends like I was some weird old geezer: "I've been meaning to cut that board for twenty years." He thinks I'm hilarious. Another time, again working on my own house, I tell him, "Pull off that rotten piece of siding, then take a five-minute break while I puke." The damage behind the siding isn't as sickening as I'd feared, but the quote spreads all over town.

I show Mordecai how to lay bricks, and he starts building a pathway. I leave him alone all day, without supervision, while I deal with another job. In the evening, Mordecai gone, I find an uneven, sloppy mess of brick. Compulsive perfectionist? This looks like the work of an impulsive slob.

Once before, I told a carpenter he had to tear out something he'd spent all day building. He screamed at me for an hour, then stomped off the job and never came back.

In the morning I begin by telling Mord: "I'm sorry; I guess I didn't give you enough instructions."

He squints at the brickwork. "Sucks, huh?"

"You'll have to break it up and try again."

"Okay, Doctor."

Cheerfully, on the second try he gets it right. And then, after work, he goes home and announces to his parents that he wants to build a brick pathway all around their house.

He has instant but transitory enthusiasm, moving from one new skill to another as quickly as he can learn.

Somewhere along the line I discover to my surprise that this boy I've been treating as a teen is actually a college graduate with an evolving desire to go to law school. The plan seems to grow in direct proportion to the time he spends on skateboarding trips. I think he's discovering that it's a young man's sport and that at age twenty-two he's no longer young. Or indestructible. He's also getting seriously involved with a certain young woman, which may also make skateboarding seem like a less than perfect lifetime plan.

Mordecai asks me how I became a contractor. I explain the process, ending with the state licensing exam. That night Mordecai goes home and tell his mother, a schoolteacher, and his father, a doctor, that he's decided not to go to law school. He's going to take a one-day class and become a contractor.

His parents are less than thrilled, though somewhat amused. He's forgotten, or didn't hear, that to become a contractor you need four years of experience in the trade plus a series of classes, then a big exam. Law school, at three years, is faster.

The winter passes. By equinox the wildflowers are spectacular, while the weather is unpredictable. Late March, I take a two-day job that balloons into two weeks, the kind of hard carpentry that makes my body hurt all over. Fortunately I have Mordecai.

In Afghanistan US troops are slaughtering the Taliban. In La Honda my wife and daughter are preparing for my daughter's wedding. Insignificantly, in Menlo Park, Mordecai and I are installing signposts and a decorative fence in front of an office building. It's a cold day with dark clouds rolling over the mountains in the west. There are occasional blasts of wind and quick splats of hard rain. Appreciating him, at this moment I choose to tell Mordecai that I'm giving him a raise from ten dollars an hour to twelve.

Looking embarrassed, Mordecai coughs—he's been coughing a lot lately—and says, "I should have told you. I've got a new job. I'm starting Monday."

Today is Friday. It's his typical short notice.

From digging post-holes, standing in mud, we're saturated with the smell of damp earth.

"Actually," he says with another cough, "I was supposed to start two weeks ago. I told them I wanted to stay with you. Finish up. It's for the park service. I'll be doing construction."

"What are they paying?"

"Fifteen an hour. With benefits." He coughs again, and when he removes his hand from in front of his mouth, the palm is spattered with blood.

"Go home. Right now."

"Are you firing me, Doctor?"

"Of course not. You're coughing blood. Go home, have some chicken soup, and go to bed."

I continue alone, getting drenched in an icy shower. And suddenly it's all so clear: what a cheapskate I am. And how he must value working for me. I was paying ten dollars without benefits when he's worth fifteen with bennies to the labor market out in the real world. And yet he stayed with me, didn't want to leave even when he had a better job, even when he was coughing blood.

He wasn't mocking me, quoting that stuff about "meaning to cut that board for twenty years" or "take a five-minute break while I puke." The kid admired me, latching onto a role model as only the young can do.

It's scary being that important to somebody. Maybe it's better that I wasn't aware. And yet I should have known. I've taken that role again and again, hiring teens (or those I thought were teens), training them not so much for carpentry as for life, witnessing the magic of creation, that look of pride when they see what they've built. And then they're gone, and I go on.

Leather Tool Belt

Monday, April 24, 2006

First thing in the morning the phone rings and it's Stan.

Uh oh.

I repaired his kitchen faucet yesterday, and when a client calls you at 7:15 a.m. after a plumbing job it usually means trouble. Spectacular, spraying, floor-flooding trouble. Actually, it's only happened to me once, but for the rest of my life I'll have PTSD—plumbing trauma screwup damnation. Thirty years later I still dream about it.

But not today. Stan says, "I just want to thank you for coming to my place on a Sunday." Stan is one of my core clients. I have a key to his front door. Heck, I installed his front door and the lockset that controls it. In fact I drew up the design for the entry and created a sand-blasted pattern for the glass.

Stan is an insomniac, so I guess I'm lucky he didn't phone me at 3 a.m. He's still talking: "You know, I look around this house and see all the nice things you put in, and I just want you to know that you've made this a great place to live, and I appreciate it."

Which is nice to hear except that it's almost like an elegy. He's an old man. Yesterday Stan was dropping hints that he wasn't making any long-term plans. He's a wealthy real estate developer, my polar opposite in politics, but we respect and trust each other—which you could say about all my core clients. I hope he's okay.

My day's task involves setting up planter boxes and generally sprucing up the entry to an office building. After a week of rain it's a sunny day. I'm attaching a flower box to a stucco wall—hammer drill, molly bolt, spirit level, caulk—when suddenly I see myself as if viewed from afar. The feeling washes over me like a wave: I love this work, this simple but skilled puttering in a pleasant place in cheerful weather. *All the nice things you've put in.*

At one point there's a commotion. A bearded man in layers of old clothing is walking down the center of Menlo Avenue followed by a Menlo Park police car with flashing blue and red lights. Staggering slightly, the man ignores the cop car and the oncoming traffic. He's homeless, crazy, and high. He veers from the street and walks straight toward me. Two policemen approach on foot, grab the man, and place him in handcuffs while the man looks directly in my eye and shouts, "Look at me! This is what happens!"

Do I know this guy? I don't think so.

Back home, my son Will has come for dinner and brought a couple of friends. Will lives in San Francisco now. He plays a new song he's recorded which begins, "I am a carpenter, and I'm trying to get back home." It's an autobiographical song mentioning the successful careers of his brother and sister while he is still a struggling musician working as a carpenter. All true. In the chorus there's a line, "Got these carpenter's bags slung over my shoulder; My father used to wear them before he got older."

Ouch.

Also true. I gave him my old leather tool belt when I could no longer cinch it around my expanding waist. I'm taking fewer jobs because, yes, I'm getting older. Look at me. This is what happens. I do have a new belt with built-in lumbar support and a nice holster for my drill, but it's made of some kind of nylon polyester crap, and I've never warmed to it.

Will apologizes for making it sound as if I'd retired and for saying I'm too old. "I had to do it for the song," he says.

I understand altering facts in pursuit of truth. I should; I'm a writer. And I understand the other thing, the underlying, unspoken message of the song: A carpenter is a failed musician. Or a failed writer.

A writer who is still mounting flower boxes.

I've lost weight. Maybe the old belt would fit.

"Hey, Will. Can I have the old tool belt back?"

Then look at me. What happens. Peace.

Working-Class Hippie

B-Sharp Karma

April 1969

To me Rob seemed the hippest guy in St. Louis—cool without effort. He never put me down, but I always knew my place. Like, one time, soon after meeting Rob, I made what I thought was a safely cool comment about Sam Cooke, calling the pop singer a sellout to white culture. Rob just went "Mmm," as if pitying me, and he shook his head, saying, "There wasn't a dry eye on the North Side the day Sam Cooke was shot." So not only was I disagreeing with Rob, I was disagreeing with the entire black population of St. Louis. It was intimidating. Embarrassing. Uncool.

Another time we were talking about draft resistance. I had applied to be a conscientious objector. My local draft board had already rejected the application. I'd filed an appeal.

"You'll lose," Rob said. "Then what?"

"Jail," I said.

"Prison," Rob corrected. I was the naive suburban muffin. Of course Rob knew the difference between jail and prison. And of course I didn't.

Rob was short, black, and built like a basketball. He subsisted on a diet of White Castle hamburgers, bought by the dozen. He was a poet, a playwright, and a sometime student.

Rob was working through a greasy bag of White Castle hamburgers. Rubbing one finger over his goatee, he winced at some thought he was having and said, "You don't want to go to prison."

"Of course I don't *want* to," I said. I thought I was a pretty tough guy, actually. Idealistic and strong enough for five years in the pen.

"Prison would *break* you," Rob said, wincing again.

Somehow I'd been thinking of it as a five-year sabbatical spent meditating and reading books.

Rob was shaking his head. "Mm-*mmm*."

And so I had a change of plan. I might go to Canada, or I might end up in Vietnam. But prison was no longer an option. Rob could do that to me: summon his street cred, speak a few words, and change my life.

I had a student job at the university maintenance department. I was a junior electrician with the permanent assignment of wandering around campus replacing burned-out fluorescent tubes. Rob thought my light bulb–changing job was hilarious. With his local contacts, he picked up small handyman jobs and usually made more money in one hour than I earned in a shift.

One day Rob came to me needing help. A woman had asked him to move a bed out of her apartment on the third floor. The bed was too large to fit out the door and down the flights of stairs.

"Couldn't we just take it apart, carry it out, and then reassemble it?" I asked.

"Glued. Antique," Rob said. "They hauled it up on a rope through a double window. That's how we'll get it out."

So we walked over to the woman's apartment, Rob with a rope coiled over his shoulder. On the way—because we happened to be passing—we stopped at the White Castle on Delmar Boulevard. There was a white guy in front of us ordering five burgers. "No, wait," he said. "Make it ten." He turned around, saw us behind him, the rope on Rob's shoulder. He was tall, thin, red-haired, freckled. He smiled. With twinkling eyes he asked, "Who you gonna lynch?"

"Some old bed," Rob said. "Heavy as a Buick. Hey—you happen to know anything about knots?"

"The Buick knot? I thought you'd never ask."

Rob doubled over in laughter. I didn't see how it was that funny. But have you ever seen love at first sight? This meeting was like that.

"I'm Theodore," the guy said. "My friends call me Ted."

"And your enemies?" Rob asked.

"The Odor."

"I'm Rob."

"And your enemies, Rob?"

"I got no enemies."

Ted and Rob were the kind of people who drew your attention in a crowd. They had harmonizing charisma. Rob's was sharp and solid, drawing on black urban soul. Ted's was goofy and broad, drawing on white pop exuberance.

So the three of us downed some burgers, and the two of them smoked a joint—and then another—and an hour later we showed up at the woman's apartment. Stephanie Friedman. She was a bit too young to be called a shrew, but she was heading there in a sexy kind of way. She was selling the bed because it reminded her of the ex-husband. She was sucking a Benson and Hedges 100, pacing, an ashtray full of thin filters smeared with scarlet lipstick.

The buyer would be arriving any minute and we were two hours late and the bed was worth $1,500. Rob was charging thirty to move it to the sidewalk.

First we carried the mattress and box springs down the flights of stairs.

I had a bad feeling. While Ted and Rob tied Buick knots around the sideboards of the bed frame, I examined the old wood. Walnut, I'd bet. There were cracks around all the joints. The glue was dead.

"We could take it apart," I said. "It's already—"

"Don't you dare," Stephanie said.

"Okay," I said. "I believe the agreement was for thirty dollars?"

Stephanie grimaced. For some reason she'd taken an instant dislike to me. And I to her. But she opened her purse, glared at me, and handed three ten-dollar bills to Rob.

Ted, Rob, and I lifted the massive walnut frame and staggered to the open window. We'd removed the bottom slats of the bed so all we held were the four sides. Angling the headboard out first, we dented the top of the window trim and knocked a floor lamp that Stephanie caught as it was falling.

"Careful," she said.

"This *is* careful," Rob said, panting.

With a groan, and then a rush of ticking noises, the frame flattened upon itself—like squashing a box. The headboard separated. It hit the sidewalk with a sound like a splash.

The remaining, folding, sides of the bed wrenched out of our hands. The weight pulled Rob, still holding the rope, stumbling toward the window. He stopped with his feet braced against the wall, and I grabbed the rope, and the foot of the bed, now dangling outside the window, popped loose and sailed, spinning like a lazy Frisbee, to land at the edge of the parking lot.

Meanwhile the two sideboards had gone vertical and slipped right out of their Buick knots, plunging like spears into the petunia garden.

I leaned out the window, transfixed by the wreckage, the rope still in my fists. It was only a few seconds, but when I leaned back inside, I was alone with Stephanie Friedman. Rob and Ted had disappeared.

She was speechless.

"Uh, sorry," I said, unconsciously bunching the rope against my chest. "I'll . . . uh . . ." I ran down the stairs.

Outside there were splinters and fragments of walnut among the grass. Rob and Ted were nowhere to be seen.

I could guess where they'd be.

Sure enough, they were sharing a bag at White Castle. When they saw me, they broke out in laughter. "You even saved the rope," Rob said, and he handed me the thirty dollars. "Man, it's all yours. I never woulda thought to ask in advance."

Ted asked, "Did you know?"

"Not what I expected," I said. "But the karma in that place was . . . was . . ."

"Shit," Ted said.

And from then on *shit karma* was a private joke, sort of a password among us. But also from then on I saw less and less of Rob. He and Ted had been instantly tight. They became roommates, Mr. Cool and Mr. Clown, each a connoisseur of ways to get high.

Then one day Ted the prankster, acting alone, broke into an ROTC building, painted slogans inside, and got caught. Destruction of military property. A felony. Mug shots. Lawyers. Goofy Ted. Who'd have thought?

And Rob—who'd never been more than thirty miles from St. Louis and spoke no foreign language—got offered some kind of playwriting fellowship in Sweden of all places, starting next year. How's that for cool?

It seemed as if some great hand was reaching into the campus and plucking us, one by one, into the real world.

Meanwhile, I got fired from my job.

The Washington University maintenance department—including Larry, my boss—expected me to work through school vacations. I disagreed. After Christmas, Larry chewed me out royally. He warned me about spring break. When I returned after Easter, Larry called me into his office with what was known in the department as the Beckon of Doom.

Larry was mad. "You can't just disappear when you feel like it. You're an employee."

"I'm a student," I said.

"I was hoping you were a man."

That stung. "Just let me work this one day," I said.

"Why?" Larry asked.

"I want to go out on a good note."

"D-flat?" Larry asked. He could be a stern boss but he had a sense of humor.

I signed out the master key, slung a box of tubes over one shoulder, a ladder over the other, and I set out. In a normal day I might work two or three buildings and replace twenty or thirty tubes. Expectations were low, and I met them.

On this final day I replaced 156 tubes. I worked fourteen buildings. For my final act I went to Brookings Hall. With the master key I unlocked the tower. Brookings Hall is the face of Washington University. In the center of the building is a lovely archway, and above the archway are four stone towers, the kind you'd expect on a fairy castle. Nobody was allowed up there. Spiral stairs wound upward and opened to a small turret with a magnificent view.

The breeze ruffled my hair. It was April. The sun was low in the west. Brookings and its towers cast long shadows to the east. Beyond the shadows stretched the green swath of Forest Park. Farther away, beyond the crumbling factories and gray offices of downtown, rose the stainless-steel rainbow of the Gateway Arch.

When I had arrived as a freshman in 1965, the Gateway Arch had been under construction. Each day I would stand in the breezeway of Brookings and check for progress, and each day the two edges of the arch were closer together, section by section, a stunning piece of construction, a defiant act of beauty.

I was near the end of my senior year. As the Arch had grown and become a part of the life of St. Louis, so in a small sense had I.

People passed through the breezeway below me and down the wide entry steps, chatting, unaware of my presence above.

Now two figures were descending the grand Brookings stairs side by side. One was tall and thin; the other was built like a basketball. So—news flash—Ted was out on bail. I felt a twinge of jealousy. Shit karma. Part of me had always wanted to be Rob's best buddy, and Ted had just walked right in.

None of us knew it, but the campus was heading for a year of tragedy, the burning of a building, arrests, the killings at Kent State, a complete shutdown of classes, and a canceled graduation. Today, though, all lay calm in a cooling breeze. The long shadows of the city, the gleam of the Arch, the Laurel and Hardy partners descending the stairs, all seemed at peace. It was a season of hope. Of new growth. And suddenly I realized—as I should have from the start—that I must return those thirty dollars to Stephanie Friedman. I was obliged. If I could find her. If I could face her.

I climbed down from the tower. In the maintenance building the radio was playing Sam Cooke, "You Send Me." And I thought at that moment: Sam, you *do* send me. Honest you do.

I returned the master key, reported my totals on the form they shove at you after each shift. Larry raised his gray eyebrows. Nobody had ever replaced 156 tubes in one day.

"So am I leaving on a good note?" I asked.

"B-sharp." Larry was never effusive with praise. "Good luck," he said.

We shook hands. "Thanks." I held his hand. "Really."

"Really what?"

I couldn't say what I suddenly knew: I loved this stupid job that no longer was mine; I loved this old city that soon I would leave. I loved growing up. "Thanks for so much."

Pissing Out the Door

May 1970

In 1970 my old friend Gretel and her new husband, Mason, bought some nearly inaccessible, mostly vertical land and started building a geodesic dome in the Rocky Mountains.

This was an utterly cool thing to do.

I helped them for a few days as they were erecting the basic geodesic frame, bolting triangle to triangle, higher and higher toward what was to be the last, triumphal piece at the top.

It was less than a glorious topping, actually, because the different edges didn't align the way they were supposed to. Slight errors of construction at the bottom became magnified at the peak. I remember tugging on ropes and pushing on poles, trying to bring the pieces together, fighting that wonderful rigidity for which domes are famous.

A lot of folk helped. Imagine the barn-raising scene in the movie *Witness*, but instead of the Amish substitute hippies, instead of Pennsylvania farmlands substitute the Colorado Front Range, instead of the soaring background music substitute news reports of four students shot dead at Kent State.

Then we all faded away, leaving Mason and Gretel with years of hard work.

It leaked, of course. Domes are notorious for that. The driveway was like a bobsled run, and you needed four-wheel drive in the best of weather, so Gretel and Mason wintered in Boulder and camped in the dome during the summers.

They built an outhouse with a spectacular window view. On a clear day, I swear, you could sit on that throne and see all the way to Kansas.

It was a rugged life. The weather could be merciless. Day after day you'd see Gretel up on the roof, sealing leaks. Inside, the dome was spacious, spirit-lifting, a magnet that gathered friends for food, music, and talk of how to sabotage Nixon, how to stop the stupid war.

Mason bought a 1947 Dodge coupe so they could cruise the mountains in high style. A chipmunk lived in their wall. A porcupine hung out in the basement and would eat the plywood, loving the glue. Sometimes it waddled to the outhouse, so if you went there at night you'd have to stand at the window and shoo porky out the door with a broom.

They built that outhouse, by the way, on top of an old mine shaft, which gave them a bottomless pit and also served to discourage anybody from returning to exploit the mineral rights, which Gretel and Mason did not own.

Mason was friendly, charismatic, sometimes crude, and he had a few demons. He proclaimed one particular philosophy that seems to have universal appeal, and I've heard it repeated many times in many places—among men. Women, oddly, don't seem to agree. What Mason said was: "A man should live in a place where he can take a piss out his own back door."

Dewey

Saturday, February 24, 1973

He had a shaggy mop of reddish-blond hair and a bushy mustache. He looked to be about my age—twenty-five. He walked into the garage where I was setting up tools and asked, "You a carpenter?"

"Sorta." I was touching these tools for the first time in three years. Since graduating from college, I'd been working as a computer operator.

"You make furniture?"

"Sometimes," I lied.

Which is how I got the job of building a chest of drawers. Dewey was my downstairs neighbor. We shared a stucco box that was basically a three-car garage. My wife and I lived above the garages; Dewey lived behind them.

Dewey had scavenged six drawers that somebody had left out on the street. My job was to build something—anything—that would house the six drawers. He wasn't going to tell me how it should look because, he said, "You wouldn't want some clown tellin' ya what to do."

Our garage box home was located a block from Highway 101 in a neighborhood of struggle: Cooley Avenue, East Palo Alto. We were bathed in traffic noise and diesel exhaust. There was the occasional drug-war murder, but the rent was as cheap as it ever gets in California.

Dewey had two cats: one with a limp, one with no tail. The no-tail cat liked to climb the ivy and stare into my second-floor kitchen window. One night after taking a shower, my wife walked into the kitchen while toweling herself and saw a pair of eyes staring in at her—and screamed. I told this story to Dewey, who seemed to have decided to spend the afternoon in my garage, and he said, "That's Nilsson. Yeah, he's kinda friendly that way."

Dewey kept a blue 1961 Chrysler in the middle garage and used it as an office. There was a two-drawer file cabinet in the back seat. He'd created and sold several posters that were popular in college dorms. He'd also published a book of sketches. Every page was a cartoonish drawing, and every image was some variation of a penis.

"Some people say I have a phallic obsession," he said, "but I don't know where they get that idea." He said he had a second book ready—drawn in a different style. Then he said, "Do you mind if I talk to ya? I'll try not to be too depressin'."

"You're not depressing."

"I just killed Sinatra."

33

"Who?"

"Gray cat? Limp? Fed her some downers and she went to sleep peaceful. Purrin' till she stopped breathin'. I just buried her in that garden there." He pointed to the house next door. "Don't tell the girls."

Two female graduate students—the girls—lived discreetly, quietly in the house next door. I wondered if one of them would try planting flowers soon, turning a spade of earth and finding a surprise.

"There's a gallery in Frisco wants to show my stuff," he said.

"Cool! Are they—like —?"

"Dongs? Naw. New style. I'm goin' up there tonight. Put on my best blue jeans and all. Get the final word."

"Good luck."

"I quit the post office."

"You were a mailman?"

"That was after I quit the clown profession. Actually, maybe mailman was the same profession, new venue. Anyway, I quit yesterday. You heard of Dewey Paints?"

"No."

"Chain of paint stores in Denver. My father owns it. Named for me. Or me for it. Me and the stores, we both started about the same time. I'm supposed to run it when I grow up." He laughed. "When can you make the drawer thing?"

"I have to get some wood." Also, though I didn't say so, I'd need to quickly study a book about furniture-making.

Sunday, February 25, 1973

I began building the cabinet for Dewey.

Woodworking soothed my soul. The street became my workshop. With the garage door open, I cut plywood on the sidewalk. The flow of life on Cooley Avenue was like an impromptu theater—vaudeville, updated—and I became one of the acts. It was a neighborhood of transience. Rentals.

From a house down the street a trio emerged: Dewey, holding hands with a woman on one side and a little boy on the other. The woman was round-faced, red-haired, with shiny skin and a ready smile. She gazed up at Dewey with unabashed fondness. The boy, also red-haired, was unsteady, lurching. One of his legs was twisted. Dewey walked slowly so the boy could keep up.

In front of the garage, the woman said, "Bet you thought I was gonna invite you to stay for dinner, ha ha."

"Gotta let me go, Beep." Dewey knelt while transferring the boy's hand to the woman. "Keep on truckin', Beep," Dewey said, and he tousled Beep's hair.

Woman and boy walked slowly away.

"How'd it go with the art gallery?" I asked.

"Sucked," Dewey said. Without a glance at the cabinet I was building, he stalked around the side of the garage to his rear door.

Half a block away, boy and mother had stopped, turned around, and Beep was waving.

I waved, subbing for Dewey. With the sun at my back, all the boy could see would be my silhouette.

Holding hands, boy and mother walked into their squat little house. Next to the house was a chain-link fence, and beyond the fence was the belching, roaring freeway. Face it: Cooley Avenue was for the cash-impaired. For most residents, it was short-term—or so we hoped. A ramshackle purgatory.

I knew something about Beep's condition, metatarsus varus—known as pigeon toe—because I was born with that condition. Sometimes mild cases cure themselves as the body grows up. My less mild case required putting my leg in a cast (with everlasting side effects). A serious case requires surgery. Beep's was a serious case.

Poverty can seem romantic when you're young, especially when you know it's temporary. When your boy needs surgery, the romance fades.

Sometime during the night I heard the clatter of glass bottles. A motor started in the garage below our bedroom. A behemoth car pulled out and drove away.

Monday, February 26, 1973

In the morning as usual, Nilsson the cat was staring into the kitchen window. On the sidewalk was a garbage can full of empty wine bottles. On top, four bottles had handmade labels that said:

> TO OUR ESTRANGED MASTER
> FROM MRS. CLOWN AND BEEP.

Dewey's garage door was open. Gone was the gas-hog tail-finned monster Chrysler with a file cabinet in the back seat.

I was putting the final touches on the chest of drawers when the woman with the shiny skin stepped into the garage. The boy was not with her.

"Will you feed the cat?" she said. She had a friendly smile.

"Nilsson?"

"He left it behind, didn't he?"

"He *left*?"

"Gone to sell paint in Denver," she said.

"Yes. He left the cat."

"It belongs to Beep. But it keeps coming back here. Which is a lot better than wandering out on the freeway." She noticed the wine bottles in the garbage can. Wincing, she ran her fingers over them. "He really means it," she said sadly. "Letting go."

I drummed my fingers on the top of the cabinet. "I was building this for Dewey."

"He couldn't have paid you, anyway."

"He *conned* me?"

"No. Please don't think like that. Dewey is a hopeful person. That's why he was a mailman."

"Um, how is that . . . ?"

"He was better as a clown. Except the money part."

She contemplated the empty bottles on top of the garbage can. "Bye-bye," she whispered. "No grudges."

I felt like a cat staring into her window.

She turned to me. "Thank you for waving to Beep," she said.

"Oh," I said. "Cute kid."

"Not everybody thinks so."

"Dewey does."

She smiled. A sunbeam. "Bless you." Her face became serious. "Dewey wasn't the father. Please don't think—whatever. It's not simple."

I never saw Dewey again. In fact, after that day I don't believe I ever saw Nilsson again. Or Mrs. Clown. I heard she moved back home to Napa County and reconciled—somewhat—with her parents. And Beep had the surgery.

Thirty-eight years later I still have that first cabinet I built. Sturdy, crude, it's stuffed with my socks and sweatshirts and, in the bottom drawer, an errant blessing, one empty wine bottle with a handmade label.

Yoo-hoo!

Sunday, May 6, 1973

"Yoo-hoo!" Fingers tapped on glass. "Hello! Yoo-hoo!" A little white-haired woman was at the cabin window.

I'd been staining shelves. Wiping hands on my T-shirt, I stepped outside. I'd never in my life heard somebody actually use the word *yoo-hoo*.

She bobbed up and down like a bird. "Oh at last—I was beginning to wonder if anybody—would you tell me—we're lost . . . Where are we?"

Good question. I'd recently moved into a place called Wagon Wheels, an odd little bohemian paradise, a cluster of broken-down cabins near Stanford University. We were in a pocket of cheap rent and hippie lifestyle surrounded by wealth and academia. If you have to live in poverty, think location, location, location.

The woman smelled of rose-petal powder in abusive quantity. Still bobbing up and down she said, "We're thoroughly lost. The Sharon Heights Country Club—the clubhouse—we had directions but we couldn't find it."

Leaning against a white Bentley sedan, quietly mouthing a pipe, stood an old man wearing a white suit. The woman wore a pastel dress with pearls and a fruit-basket hat. They might have stepped out of a croquet party in the 1920s.

I tried to give directions. "Keep going down this road. Make a left at the second traffic light. Then you're on Sand Hill Road. Go about two miles . . ."

The woman clasped her hands. "Do you have a car?—we'll follow—we'll reward you—we'll drive behind—we'll make it well worth your while—we're late, you see—we'll pay you handsomely—"

I'd never in my life heard somebody actually say *pay you handsomely.*

I said, "Just make a left at the second traffic light, and about two miles—"

"Now which way—do we go right or left—did you say there was a traffic light?"

"Continue down this road. At the second light—"

"Are you an artist?" She was studying the cherry oil on my T-shirt and bare legs.

"No, ma'am. I'm a carpenter."

"Oh. What a pity." She shook her head. "Well. Could you drive in front—we'll reimburse you—it's my birthday—they're giving me a party—it started at six."

It was already seven fifteen.

"Follow me," I said.

She clapped her hands and—I swear—jumped in the air. "Oh goody," she said.

My Volkswagen wouldn't start until I opened the hood and unstuck the throttle. Now my fingers were black with engine grease. I drove slowly along Sand Hill Road. The Bentley followed at a distance and then stopped at the side of the road. I parked and walked back to them.

They were out of the car. The man was pointing with his pipe. His voice seemed to say, "Whoosh whoosh whoosh." Then he folded his arms and sucked on the pipe, waiting for something. He looked like an owl.

"He thinks he recognizes it—that building back there," said the woman. "We were here once before—everything looks different now— there weren't all these houses—this road—"

"That's not it," I said.

The owl whooshed and pointed again with his pipe at an office building, newly built.

The woman stood on tiptoe and cupped her hands over Owl's ear. *That's not it!* she shouted.

We climbed back in the cars.

I knew where the golf course was. You can't miss it. But I'd never noticed a clubhouse. Turning off Sand Hill Road, Sharon Heights turned out to be a fantasy land of dainty landscapes, swans floating on a sculptured lake, a manufactured waterfall. But no clubhouse. The road turned a corner and came to a sudden dead end.

I was wearing rags. On the radio: "The World Is a Ghetto." My car was a junker with a GET NAKED bumper sticker. People who live in places like this hire security guards to keep out people like me. The woman was clutching a handful of dollar bills. "Take this," she said.

I refused.

"Ask somebody," she said.

We drove back through the surreal landscape to Sand Hill Road where I spotted a barefoot girl struggling to push a shopping cart uphill. I called from my car, "Where's the entrance to the Sharon Heights Country Club?"

"How the crap would I know?" she said.

"What did she say?" the old woman called from her Bentley.

"She said it's this way. Follow me."

38

We drove up Sand Hill Road for the second time. When we passed the empty office building, the Bentley stopped again, Owl whooshed and pointed his pipe, I shook my head, the woman tried to press her dollar bills into my hand, I refused, and we drove on.

I found it.

How could I have missed it?

We stopped in the parking lot. I could hear music from the clubhouse, some Carpenters song. A man in a topcoat and top hat walked toward us, grinning, with a handful of balloons. People were staring at me, frowning. For some reason, when I awoke that morning I hadn't dressed in club whites. The woman offered money. I refused. She insisted: "Please. You must."

Finally, to make her happy, I took two dollars. "Happy birthday," I said.

"You're welcome," she said.

Jim the Plumber

Monday, May 13, 1974

Around 1 a.m. the dog starts barking and won't stop. Finally I get out of bed and find steaming water spreading over the linoleum from the kitchen to a hole in the floor by the front door, where it pours down to the termites and fungus below. The water heater has burst. The dog felt it was worthy of note.

In the kitchen, bare-ass and groggy, I search for a way to shut off the water and find none. Out behind the house I turn off the valve for the entire cabin. Back in the kitchen I can find no shutoff for the gas, so, naked, I return outside with a Crescent wrench and turn it off out there. Then back to bed.

It's a rental, a cheap cabin on the verge of collapse. Not my problem. In the morning the landlady calls Jim the Plumber.

These are the days of redneck–hippie wars, so I'm cautious as Jim arrives in his truck. More cautious when I see the American eagle tattoo on the back of his hand.

Jim greets me with clear eyes and an honest smile. "How ya doin'?" he asks, taking off his denim jacket and draping it on the steering wheel. Immediately he makes friends with my dog, a semi–German shepherd who is skeptical of strangers. "What's his name?"

"Quinn."

"Hi, Quinn."

They have an affinity, Jim and Quinn.

"One of these guys saved my life once," Jim says, scratching the dog's chin. "Lost his."

"What happened?"

"Aw, it ain't nothin'." Jim looks away toward the cow pasture across the street. When he looks back at me, his eyes are clear, his smile is genuine. "Let's get to work."

Jim doesn't mind if I watch. In fact, he enjoys the company.

The old heater sits unbraced on a wobbly floor next to the old gas stove. "You're lucky this tank didn't topple over and kill ya," Jim says.

We're friends by now. Jim's an affable man. He likes the fact that I want to learn about plumbing; I like that he uses the word "topple." That, and his Okie accent. He seems so comfortable in his job. Unlike me, Jim has found his slot in the world and seems happy to be there.

40

"If it don't land on ya, it breaks the gas line." Jim glances at the cabin. "Three minutes, max, this shack is a ball of flame." For just a moment, Jim seems to flinch.

He replaces the 20-gallon heater with a 30-gallon model and straps it to the wall with metal plumber's tape. He replaces the old, rigid copper gas tubing with flexible brass. "Useta be we got clean gas from down around L.A. Now it's from Texas and it leaves junk in the pipe. Texas gas eats the copper. Some chemical reaction." He shakes his head as if longing for the old days. He must be about my age, which is twenty-six.

Jim installs three safety valves we'd lacked before: gas shutoff, water shutoff, and pressure temperature relief valve. "If it's worth doin', it's worth doin' right," he says. "Musta been a moron installed that old thang."

"I think it was the landlady's husband."

"Well hush my mouth."

As a last act, he cleans up with a paper towel. "If my daddy saw me leave a job with fingerprints on the heater, he'd be rollin' in his grave."

I help Jim load the old heater in the back of his truck. Among the toolboxes are three empty whiskey bottles.

At the cab, Jim reaches to the dashboard, then tosses half a ham sandwich to the dog. Stenciled on the door are the words:

FRIENDLY
QUALITY

Removing the jacket from the steering wheel, Jim shrugs it over his shoulders. On the back of the denim is an embroidered map of Vietnam, bright red, and the words:

WHEN I DIE I'LL GO TO HEAVEN
I'VE ALREADY BEEN TO HELL
25TH INFANTRY PLEIKU 1966–67

Jim gets behind the wheel. Quinn stands on hind legs, forelegs on the driver's window. A hand reaches out, rubs the dog's ears.

"Peace to ya, Quinn," Jim says. Then he's off to the next job.

Herbert Hoover's Bench

July 1974

Jan Anderson was my landlady. I was her handyman. She'd been on the planet since 1892. We called her Jan when she was friendly and Mrs. Anderson when she was acting like a landlady.

One day Jan showed me a bench. Or at least, she said it was a bench. All I saw was a rotten pile of wood. "Can you fix it?" she asked.

"No. It's too far gone."

"Herbie Hoover gave it to me."

"Herbert Hoover? The president?"

"This was after he got fired."

Jan had run a taxi company. When Mr. Hoover left office, he settled in Palo Alto. Upon his arrival in California he called for a taxi. Jan sent her best driver, a man who was polite and reliable, and the driver never came back. Hoover hired him as chauffeur.

Jan and Mr. Hoover met frequently. She owned a peanut factory next door to the taxi company, and Mr. Hoover used to wander into the taxi office with a bag of fresh roasted nuts. "Want some?" he'd always ask. He loved peanuts, but he was not an interesting man. "Not a conversationalist," Jan said.

Jan grew up among the fruit orchards and dirt roads of the Santa Cruz Mountains near Los Gatos. She rode a donkey to school. Some days the donkey would stop at a creek, bend down for a drink, and then buck her off into the water. Furious, she would chase the donkey, which would stay just out of her reach all the way home.

Jan grew up fast. At age eleven, she confided to me, she was "fully developed," and grade school was a humiliation. She transferred to a new town, lied about her age, and graduated from high school at age fifteen. She wanted to be a pharmacist but found that nobody would respect a female in that field. She found few opportunities for a woman to do anything except make babies, at which, she said, she was a failure. With peanuts and taxis she found some success.

To me she seemed a piece of living history. She remembered the 1906 earthquake—it ripped her house into three pieces. These days, a widow, she lived at the edge of the Stanford golf course on land that Leland Stanford had been "furious to discover he didn't own," she said with satisfaction. She rented cheap cottages and invited tenants over for whiskey sours and conversation. I happily obliged.

"Did Herbert Hoover flirt with you?" I asked.

"No." She sighed.

"Did you flirt with him?"

"Well of course!" Even at age eighty-one Jan was a coquette, especially after a couple of whiskey sours, sometimes batting her eyes at me. Once, after a third whiskey sour, she showed me two nude photos of herself, taken by her husband on a hill near Half Moon Bay. She'd placed hands in strategic places and smiled warily at the camera. Quite the babe. Now, with failing body and bad cooking, she could still summon the come-hither smile but carried the permanent smell of urine and burnt cheese.

Jan told me that Herbie's wife, Lou Hoover, used to call for a taxi about once a week, and she always asked for car number seven.

One day Jan pulled the driver of No. 7 aside and asked, "Why are you Lou's favorite?"

The driver just smiled. "I'll never tell."

After Lou died, the driver revealed that Lou used to smoke in the taxi. He'd give her a pack of cigarettes and drive her around for an hour while she smoked. He also bought beer for her, which she drank in secret at home. Herbie wouldn't have approved.

"So that's the worst you have on the Hoovers?" I teased. "His wife smoked cigarettes and drank beer?"

"Sometimes what's normal is the scandal," she said.

"What do you mean?"

"Scandal is what people are ashamed of. Some things are accepted, so they aren't tittle-tattle."

"Like what?"

"Herbie had a sign posted at his ranch: *Help wanted. No Japs or Negroes need apply.*"

"He had a ranch? I thought you said he had a house in Palo Alto."

She looked at me darkly. "Now you're the expert on Hoover?"

"No, ma'am."

"He loved peanuts." She ran hands through white hair, once blonde. "Can you take me for a ride?"

"Where do you want to go?"

"A little hill I know. Near Half Moon Bay." She smiled like a kitten. "There's something I want to show you."

"I can't today. Sorry. Did you ever ask Mr. Hoover to take you to that hill?"

"Once."

"What did he say?"

"Same as you: 'Not today.' He was a gentleman. Anyway, if he'd said yes I don't know what I would have done."

"You might have kissed him. Just for fun."

"I might have. And then we'd have tittle-tattle, he and I. Everybody should make some gossip. So what can you do for this bench?"

"Burn it."

"Everything rots." She sighed. "I'm next."

"Not yet. There's still time to make some gossip."

"Go ahead. Burn the bench." She winked. "And some day, you'll take me to that hill."

"Yes, ma'am. Some other day."

The Airplane Room

Thursday, March 20, 1975

Today Rose and I are driving north to San Francisco in our Volkswagen Squareback stuffed with mattresses and tools. We've just made the down payment on a wreck of a house on Lincoln Way, across the street from Golden Gate Park, one block from the Pacific Ocean. Our plan is to fix the place, then rent it out. We are young, childless, energetic.

As we arrive we find Tim, a man who was supposed to move out, still there. "I'm waiting for a tent," Tim explains. "It should be delivered today."

Tim is a man with a plan: to hitchhike to Maine by way of Los Angeles with tent, sleeping bag, backpack. Having hitched several times myself across the USA without tent, without sleeping bag, without backpack, I think Tim's got a sound plan.

Another tenant, Bob the Idaho smokejumper, is gone and so is the stove. "I told him not to take that," Tim says, and he helps us unload the mattresses and tools.

Then Sonny arrives. As an enthusiastic carpenter, Sonny is my mentor, a term that would amuse him. He's also a bona fide hippie, a term that definitely amuses him.

After the obligatory baptism of living in Haight-Ashbury, Sonny lived in a school bus in the hills above Palo Alto on a bucolic, anarchic piece of land known forthrightly as The Land. Dozens of hippie squatters were living there rent-free, erecting imaginative cabins, tree houses, tipis. On my initial visit to The Land I stepped out of my car and saw, first thing, two naked women up on the roof of a barn, repairing shingles. Right away I liked the place.

Since everybody at The Land had to construct their own dwellings, it bred an ethic of handy hippies who developed into a network of self-taught, innovative tradesmen. They discovered that they could make good money doing outlaw construction for the more enlightened and nonconforming population of Palo Alto.

In 1974, in the school bus at The Land, a daughter was born to Sonny. Life changed. He, his daughter, and his wife moved into a cottage next to mine at Wagon Wheels, a rustic little spot near the Stanford golf course.

Without Sonny's encouragement and promises of help, Rose and I never would have had the nerve to buy this, our first house.

After a quick cruise through the rooms, Sonny decides we should insulate and panel the third-floor loft, a space that we call the "airplane room" because it has a soaring, airborne feel and a view of the ocean. Off we go in Sonny's doddering old pickup, down Highway One, with the sun shimmering over the waves, green grass, mountains, an hour's drive to Big Creek Lumber, which sits atop a bluff over the ocean. It's Sonny's favorite lumberyard. Immediately it's my favorite too. We get a deal on rough-sawn redwood 1×6s from an old guy with a giant, many-gabled nose. From the lumberyard we can see a whale breaching below.

We return slowly up Highway One in the creaky, overloaded truck. Tim greets us at the house. His tent still hasn't arrived. He helps us unload dripping-wet redwood planks into the garage. Leaving Tim in charge of the house, I treat Sonny at an Armenian cafe; then we drive back to Wagon Wheels.

I try to settle up with Sonny. He says, "No, no. Today I'm just a friend helping out."

I say, "Tomorrow you're working for hire."

"Tomorrow. Yeah."

Sonny's pay for that first day is one Armenian dinner. Soon I will learn that it is nearly impossible to give Sonny anything or to pay him for a day's work.

Friday, March 21, 1975

From Wagon Wheels I set out with Sonny in his trusty old truck. Starting in Belmont and working south, Sonny guides me through a bewildering array of building supply stores. We end at McLeod Glass in Mountain View—not to buy glass but to haul away their old pallets, which Sonny regularly harvests for their wood. Sonny is a first-class scavenger. On the way home we stop at a yard sale and buy a rattan hanging-basket chair, which looks like a cocoon, for three dollars. It'll be perfect for the new house. Sonny is an indefatigable cruiser of yard sales.

Back at Wagon Wheels, Rose and I again cram our Squareback with supplies, including a pile of redolent cedar. At 10 p.m. we drive through a wild storm in our packed car. Quinn, our eighty-pound semi–German shepherd, rides on Rose's lap because there is no other space. He's panting, ambivalent, his ears twitching: sometimes the ears are pricked in excitement, other times the ears are tucked, cowering from the squalls. He hates rain, loves puddles. With foggy windows, interior scented by cedar and dog breath, we drive to the house on Lincoln Way where Tim, by golly, is still waiting for his tent.

Tim and Quinn bond immediately, a good sign. Otherwise, the house is a haunting disaster: drafty, dark, cold. Most of the light fixtures are missing, so we walk around with flashlights. Quinn chases a rat and discovers to his surprise that these city rats fight back.

A gale is blowing. It is our first inkling of the downside to living right next to the ocean. Water is pouring through the roof into the airplane room where we planned to sleep. Steady little waterfalls are splashing down the steps from the attic into the hallway.

Like a mysterious ghost, Tim sleeps in the basement. He can't seem to explain where his tent is coming from or how it will be delivered.

Rain is blasting at the windows. My wife and I have each taken two weeks off from our jobs with the plan to camp out in this house and get it rehabbed and ready to rent. As a stream of rainwater cascades down the stairs and spreads in pools over the curling hardwood floor, Rose and I stare at each other in disbelief.

The dog loves the puddles.

Saturday, March 22, 1975

Far beyond midnight we corral water and spread pots to catch drips. We mop with bed sheets we had planned to sleep on. At last we collapse on a bare mattress in a cold bedroom with the dog curled beside us, sharing our warmth.

Saturday I'm up at dawn, wild with the energy that comes of desperation. Over wet streets I run out for donuts, then drive to Sears and am waiting at the door when it opens to buy two ladders and a roll of heavy plastic. Then from a corner store I buy ten pounds of Oreo cookies and a case of Anchor Porter, and from another retailer outside the corner store I buy a lid of marijuana. Not for myself, mind you. I've invited my friends—and, more importantly, Sonny has invited his friends—to come lend a hand at the house. A weekend work party.

Back at Lincoln Way, Tim goes up on the roof with me. Tim is a sailor and turns out to be a daredevil as he scoots over the crumbled rooftop laying plastic and nailing wood battens. While up there we get pelted by another quick squall.

Sonny arrives after visiting a few choice garage sales. For Sonny, cruising the sales is a sacred Saturday-morning ritual. Today he's scored a vintage light fixture, old brass. A gift to the house.

We tear out a toilet and then rip up the bathroom floor. Friends and visitors set to work scraping paint. We discover that some previous owner painted and then plastered (badly) over lovely clear-heart, old-growth redwood planks in the living room. What a crime! Unbelievable.

Sonny repairs the kitchen floor.

Tim and I tack insulation in the walls of the attic. I entertain Tim with some hitchhiking stories from the redneck–hippie wars of the '60s, reminding him that the rest of the country isn't as friendly as San Francisco—such as the time I was kidnapped and then kicked out of a Jeep forty miles from nowhere in the middle of a Nevada desert, or the time a drunk cowboy drove me into a ditch, or the day I spent in a Winnemucca jail cell because the guy who'd picked me up was an AWOL soldier driving a stolen truck, or the kids in the bed of a farm truck riding ahead of us who tossed a brick through the windshield and nearly killed the driver and me.

Frenchie, who lives next door, stops by and gives us 180 pounds of concrete. He's moving to New Zealand where he says life is dull but happy. He's bare-chested on a cool day. He's an ironworker. From France.

Meanwhile, unbeknownst to Frenchie, Frenchie's wife stops by. Painted and powdered and nearly as bare-chested as Frenchie, she asks if they can rent the house when it's ready. She's from Sweden but flings several choice American words about the landlord who is evicting them.

When she's gone, Sonny says, "Don't rent to them." Sonny the anarchic squatter is now protecting my interest as a property owner.

Sonny's raggedy friends are swarming over the house. Finally some friends of ours drop by. About ten years older than us, they are a couple raising children in Palo Alto, living a more conventional lifestyle. We know them through a square-dancing group. One of my quirkier fixations has always been a love of square dancing. As a side benefit, it keeps me in touch with a group of people I wouldn't otherwise meet. The bureaucratic husband seems somewhat grumpy to be here, outside his comfort zone, but his librarian wife listens with enthusiasm as I describe the renovation. She says, "You're young and beautiful and I know whatever you do will be wonderful." There's a touch of envy in her voice.

We are plugging in to the endless cultural mix and musical energy of San Francisco, a crossroads at the edge of a continent. Idealism is normal. Hair is exuberant. Art is vibrant. Beauty is habitual.

By sundown we're exhausted. It's the equinox. Sonny goes to an equinox party at The Land, back in the mountains where he used to park his school bus. We're invited, too, but it's a long trip for a party. A native Californian, Sonny loves to drive.

In a clawfoot tub I bathe the fiberglass out of my body. Rose and I drink wine and go to bed early, sleeping in the now-insulated airplane room. We hear rain lashing at the walls. The plastic holds. Tonight we are dry.

Sunday, March 23, 1975

Sunday morning I work with Tim, lugging a radial arm saw and piles of heavy, wet lumber up to the attic. Tim is helping me in exchange for letting him remain in the house. He's twenty-nine, a vagabond from upstate New York, married and divorced in Maine, and still somehow strangely naive. He never says so, but I think he has a child back there. He spent two weeks over Christmas on a constant party binge in Tahiti. He says, "There was a lot of good action there."

"What does 'good action' mean?" I ask.

"Women," he says.

To me Tim is starting to seem creepy. To my wife, he's downright scary. Ever since I regaled him with hitchhiking horror stories, he's been withdrawn and moody.

While we work, Tim's long-awaited tent is mysteriously delivered.

Sonny arrives at noon. We eat lunch, and without a word Tim departs. I see him out of the corner of my eye heading down the steps to the front door, and then he's gone. A loner on a trip to Maine and perhaps to a reunion with his child. A sad man.

Sonny says, "I bet he's going straight to the bus terminal downtown. Three days on a Greyhound."

After lunch I continue working in the attic, installing the redwood 1×6s in a diagonal pattern over the insulated walls. It's fun work, but I make two mistakes. First, Sonny comes up to help.

"I think I've got it covered," I say. It seems like a one-man job. "How about if you go install the cedar paneling in the bathroom."

Sonny's face, usually so open, freezes. I don't pick up the signal. Mistake number one. I have yet to learn that Sonny doesn't always express his feelings, especially the negative ones.

Late in the afternoon I come down from the attic and find Sonny sitting in the bathroom, whittling. I take his photo. He doesn't look up.

"Something wrong?" I ask.

"Two weeks of shitwork," he says. "And you took the fun job."

"It's paneling," I say. "And you're paneling the bathroom."

"We could've done them together."

It would be more efficient if we worked separately, each paneling a different room at the same time. But it would be more fun to work together, and to Sonny that's the whole point.

I apologize.

Sonny tells me he found a box of old weather-beaten cedar shingles in the basement. They'd look great covering the plaster wall next to the one I'm paneling with redwood.

"Let's do them together," I say. And we do.

Bone-weary at the end of a long weekend, Sonny suggests we get together with some of his friends. Back in the Haight-Ashbury days Sonny parked his school bus on Fell Street and hung out with a group dubbed the Fell Street Gang. Soon I'm naked in a sauna on Market Street with Sonny, among six naked men and women of the gang. It's another aspect of Sonny that I will soon grow used to: casual group nudity.

As for the redwood paneling, mistake number two won't become apparent for several weeks. When I finally install a furnace in the unheated house, the sopping-wet redwood paneling—selected by Sonny at that marvelous lumberyard above the ocean—dries and shrinks, exposing quarter-inch gaps of shiny foil insulation between each board. A rookie error. Sonny is a self-taught carpenter whose ideas and enthusiasm sometimes exceed his grasp. Just like me. And for every slip-up he does a hundred things right. I wish I could make that claim for myself.

Even with the inevitable blunders, the house is looking good. With the steady sound of surf coming through the window glass, the green of Golden Gate Park across the street, the scent of saltwater in the breeze, beams of sunlight off the ocean, sitting on a mattress on the floor of the airplane room is like sitting at the center of an unfinished heaven.

Saturday, April 5, 1975

You can't build a house without spilling some blood. Construction accidents usually come late in the day when people are tired. The blood is not always your own.

Late in the afternoon on Lincoln Way, Sonny goes down to the basement for more lumber and forgets to close the door. His almost-one-year-old daughter, Holly—the world's happiest kid—has been merrily cruising around the house in a walker, a circular device with wheels in which she can hold herself upright and "walk" by wheeling herself about. In the walker Holly tries to follow Sonny to the basement—and tumbles down the stairs in a crashing of metal and screams and a solid thump on the concrete floor. Then silence.

Awful silence.

She's cracked her skull.

Never again do I want to see that look on a mother's face, the look of Sharon as she lifts her broken daughter.

And yet we are lucky.

After horrible hours at the UC Medical Center we learn that yes, it's a skull fracture, but she'll be okay. Sharon sleeps for two nights beside her daughter in the hospital, surrounded by children having heart surgery, children dying of cancer, children with horrible disfigurements,

50

attended by parents who force cheerfulness and then run to the bathroom to vomit in the sink. Sharon gets so frazzled that finally, with the Fell Street Gang, we perform an intervention and drag her out for an evening of Irish coffees at a bar.

Holly, meanwhile, has a fine time. She loves parties, and that's how the constant care and swirl of sick children seem to her. To a one-year-old, a hospital can seem a merry place.

Sunday, April 6, 1975

It's time to decamp. As the last act before leaving Lincoln Way late on a Sunday night, I coat the bathroom floors with varnish. I'm all alone for this final chore, alone with the mixed smell of new lumber, drying paint, fresh varnish.

Folding drop cloths, sweeping floors, dipping brushes in paint thinner in the strangely silent house, I feel I'm cleaning up after a party. The work in the house was something of a two-week whoop with streams of visitors, mostly friends of Sonny and Sharon, mostly hairy and colorful, full of energy and enthusiasm, who would chat or help with a chore or try to drag me away to a sauna or a bar or a nude beach.

After cleaning, I go out to the back yard where I can flick the last of the paint thinner out of the brush and into the weeds.

As fog blows fluttering, star-like mist, the air seems like magic. We'd been talking about the spirit of the house. Part of it is right here in this yard. For one final moment I stand surrounded by the windows of neighboring houses and flats, little frames of city life.

In one frame a man in bright red pajamas is munching cookies and ironing a shirt, his every move followed by an old collie dog diving for crumbs.

Suddenly a light comes on in a ground-level window, a basement apartment. There is no curtain, no frosted glass, just a few strands of beads. A man hurriedly strips off every stitch of clothing and starts pedaling furiously on an exercise bike. I can hear it hum. Behind him a woman enters the room and likewise removes every stitch of clothing—in this case, a single robe. Then she switches off the light. The bike continues humming.

All this in half a minute. I flick the last drops out of my brush. How I love this city, this energy, these pockets of intimate privacy tumbling one over another.

We have done much of what we set out to do. We took a sad shell of a once-proud structure built in 1913 and restored some dignity with a few enhancements. We discovered and salvaged as much original wood as possible, scraping, sanding, oiling, buffing. We turned a dusty, drafty

51

attic into the airplane room, a warm and rustic suite with views of the ocean and Golden Gate Park. Our money budget was slightly exceeded. Our psychic budget was severely overrun.

All of which is now part of the spirit of this house.

About midnight, I drive south along the Great Highway by the Pacific Ocean. A 20-foot ladder is tied to the roof of the Volkswagen Squareback. At my side is a box of jelly donuts.

The ocean breeze hums aluminum tones through the ladder.

Next to a sand dune, I stop for a cheerful hitchhiker who has a bushy white beard. While stopped, I check the ropes holding the ladder.

"You brought your stairway to heaven," the old guy says.

The hitchhiker is your basic San Francisco derelict: half blind, half deaf, fully inebriated. An old salt in bad health. He gladly accepts a jelly doughnut and then half-recites, half-sings a poem—or song—harmonizing roughly with the humming ladder. He seems to be composing on the spot. It's about an Irishman who falls off a ladder and is offered a glass of water.

> Tell me, sweet lass, in a job so risky,
> How far must I fall for a glass of whiskey?

I drop the jolly folksinger among the house-boxes of Daly City. I'll never see him again. Now I wonder: To what subdivision of heaven will the old man climb?

March 22, 2011

Lincoln Way would become an ongoing adventure of repairs and rentals and strangeness. In 1978 we sold it without ever living there, without making any profit from the rental, but we came out ahead. Under Sonny's tutelage I made a leap in my construction skills. And Rose and I became members of Sonny's amazing network of friends.

Holly came out fine. She continued living next door to us at Wagon Wheels. When Jesse, my first child, was born, Holly adopted him as if she were the big sister.

Life goes on. Sonny became a specialist at installing doors. Eventually we lost touch, but recently I found him. He lives in a boat on the San Francisco Bay. Though our paths no longer cross, I remain bonded to him—and to Holly, and to Sharon—from those intense days of work and play and that awful moment on the stairs. Some moments last a lifetime.

Holly is a grownup. Like all of us, her life has had its ups and downs. You might say Holly fell down another staircase into a bad crowd. And picked herself up again. Now she has a bright and shining daughter. This daughter attends the same alternative grade school that Holly and my son Jesse attended together—and so does my grandson, who is a couple years younger than Holly's daughter. Twice a week I pick up my grandson at school, and often I see Sharon picking up her granddaughter at the same time. How patterns repeat.

How lives intertwine.

Another accident of construction.

On March 22, 2011, the property on Lincoln Way was sold to somebody for about ten times the price I got for the place. The house has evolved into something more modern. Over the years most of our salvaged woodwork has once again been covered with paint or plaster. To balance it they've upgraded the old strip oak with glorious new hardwood floors. The airplane room is no longer paneled with redwood and cedar, nor is it called the airplane room but rather "the large master bedroom with sitting area and beautiful ocean view." They've added larger windows, drywalled everything, and painted it white. It looks great, actually, and much more appealing to your average home-buyer than the hippie/craftsman style we favored.

Traces of our work remain. The listing bragged about the kitchen with its "butcher block counters and vintage gas range." I installed those counters and that range, which was vintage even then. They were in the spirit of the house. The counter—and I'm sure this is unknown to the buyer or seller—was built out of exotic Asian hardwoods salvaged from motorcycle packing crates.

As I was installing that kitchen counter, I remember interviewing a teenager named Kit who wanted to create a stained glass window to install over the front door.

Kit was living at The Land. Sonny had brought her to meet us. He said she was a gifted young artist who needed a break, someplace to start.

In fact she seemed incredibly young.

"Are you in high school?" I asked.

"I graduated myself."

"What's that mean?"

"Pacific High School? In the mountains? Near The Land? It's a tiny alternative school nobody ever heard of. You graduate when you decide you're ready." Looking around the house, loving the changes we were making, she said she wanted to blend the nearness of the ocean and the calm of the park without shutting out the city or the light "in the spirit of the place."

She was fresh, naive, and my wife had a good feeling about her. Without seeing any of Kit's work—in fact she had no installed work—we gave her a hundred dollars and said, "Make something."

Above the entry, that stained glass window is still there, the last hippie touch.

Black & Decker Worm-Gear Saw

Tuesday, April 15, 1975

Sonny says if I want to be a genuine carpenter, I need a worm-gear saw. And he's found one. Together we drive in Sonny's old truck to an industrial area of San Jose where he finds a guy working out of a garage.

Sonny, always friendly, says, "Hi. I'm Sonny."

The guy avoids our eyes. "Pleasedameetcha," he mumbles, wiping greasy fingers on a rag, then briefly shaking hands. He has a black mustache and hair that needs a brush.

He's got two worm-gear saws for sale at this moment, each a rebuild. "That's what I do," he says. "Fix 'em and sell 'em."

"Where do you get them?" I ask.

He frowns, looks away.

Oops. Some things you aren't supposed to ask. I don't want to buy a stolen saw, but these tools are freshly rebuilt with bright new copper windings on the motors. If you want to steal construction equipment, you don't grab the broken stuff.

My instant character judgment is that this mumbly dude is good at his work, shy with people, has a shady past, but has found his niche. He can handle salvaging tools but not much else.

It's a choice between a clean-looking silver Skilsaw for eighty dollars or a roughed-up old Black & Decker for seventy. New, they sell for a hundred and twenty-nine.

Sonny asks, "Which is better?"

Mustache Guy picks up the Black & Decker. "Looks like piss because it's older. And yeah, it's heavier. Nobody wants it, but they built 'em better back then. Steel. No aluminum. I put new windings. Forget the paint job. Paint don't cut. I make more money on the Skil but, honest to God, this is stronger."

"I'll take it," I say. Rebuilding that Black & Decker, I sense, was a work of love.

He wants the check made out to *cash*. He never tells us his name.

Wednesday, March 20, 1996

I used—and abused—that saw for the next twenty-one years. I built decks, rooms, entire houses in weather good and bad, cutting lumber good and bad, pushing that saw just as hard as I pushed my own body. In other words, I worked the crap out of it.

Near the end, the top handle came loose and would lift off when I was in the middle of guiding a cut. Then the blade went out of alignment, putting extra load on the motor. The blade guard jammed and broke off, turning the tool into a lethal weapon. And at last—on March 20, 1996— when I was ripping timbers, the motor started bubbling, and the saw died in a cloud of smelly black smoke.

Some tools you're fond of, you give nicknames. Some you just operate. That old Black & Decker was a solid worker, and I maintained it—or near the end, failed to maintain it—without sentiment.

I didn't throw the machine away, because my son Jesse wanted it. In college he studied to be an engineer (and a philosopher). In the summer he was a counselor at a summer camp. He took the dead saw to Plantation Farm Camp where, in a stroke of genius, he'd invented a popular activity in which he and his campers would take apart old, broken machinery. They'd handle the parts. Pull springs. Turn gears. Touch the grease and sawdust and dirt. Spread little pieces over a concrete floor. With a sense of wonder and play, they became familiar with human industrial ingenuity.

As a final act, the campers took turns with a sledge hammer. Gleefully, they smashed everything to bits. Jesse knew just what kids wanted.

In that final dismantling, as in Mustache Guy's long-ago rebuild, the old Black & Decker received more respect than I'd given it in twenty-one years. I wish I could have joined in that final smashing: a celebration, a last rite. What a glory.

A Working-Class Hippie

Summer 1975

"I hear you need a housepainter."

"Who told you?"

"Word is out." He was a short guy, ugly (in my opinion), long-haired, oily. "I'll do it."

His name was Dog and he'd do the entire exterior for $350 if I supplied the paint.

I had two other estimates. A nonunion painter had quoted $750, while a union man had said $1,650. "You've got it," I said.

"I'll need a fifty-dollar advance," he said.

"Okay," I said.

He seemed surprised as I pulled out the money. He placed the bills between the pages of a paperback copy of *Siddhartha*. Then he returned the book to his back pocket. Apparently it was his wallet.

The next day he brought a fistful of color chips, and we selected paints. "Last night I had a dream about painting this house," he said. "I'm excited."

Dog began sanding and prepping outside while I waxed and buffed floors inside. It was an old house in San Francisco, wrecked and neglected, which I had salvaged.

When I returned early the following morning, I found Dog in a sleeping bag on the bare floor of the living room. "Is this okay?" he said, getting up naked.

"Not really. I've got tenants moving in next week."

"My girlfriend kicked me out. Can you give me a progress payment?"

"No." But I treated him to breakfast at the Beach Boy Coffee Shop. He told me he was born Doug, but even as a baby everybody had called him Dog. "I always had a snout," he said.

He admired the fact that I was a writer. At that point I had one self-published novel that had sold about fifteen copies. Nobody had heard of it. Or of me.

"At least you're somebody," Dog said.

"You're nobody?" I asked.

"I'm just a working-class hippie."

After a week Dog had painted the bottom floor of the house. I gave him a hundred dollars and invited him to the housewarming party. He never showed up. In fact, he disappeared for two weeks.

The new tenants were a sculptor, a student at San Francisco State, and a disc jockey at KSAN. They all knew Dog. "Don't worry," they told me. "He'll be back."

And he was. He explained the absence: "Somebody gave me a free ticket to the Rolling Stones concert. I got loaded, natch. I got a ride home with some guy I didn't know. I must've passed out in the car. He gave me a concussion and stole all my money and dumped me on some rocks by the bay. I spent the night in the hospital. When I went home my girlfriend kicked me out because she says I'm loaded all the time and she's tired of it. I guess I sorta started beating on her. Her roommate called *her* boyfriend, and he came over and kicked the shit out of me. I spent the night in jail. Then I didn't feel like painting for a while."

Dog painted the exterior off and on all summer. Occasionally he'd ask for a progress payment and soon exceeded his original bid. He did good work—when he worked. One day I paid him fifty dollars and he came back the next day needing fifty more. "What happened?" I asked.

"I'm a compulsive gambler," he said.

After starting in June, Dog was still painting in September when I invited him to go to a zoning hearing with me. The planning commission was considering a proposal to downzone the neighborhood so that no more apartments could be built. About 200 people were there. Most of the public testimony was opposed to the change, geezers saying their life savings were tied up in the property and they needed to tear down the ugly old houses and replace them with pretty pink apartments. I stepped up to the microphone and said, "I'd like to say a word in defense of old houses. I think they're beautiful. Six months ago I bought an old house on Lincoln Way. It was a wreck. I've spent the last six months putting all my time and money and love into it, and it's beautiful. I think there are other people like me who would like to buy these houses."

I got warm applause. Then they took a vote, and the pink apartments won.

Afterwards I asked Dog how he liked my little speech. "Didn't much hear it," he said. He explained that he'd been playing footsie with "this chick with eyeglasses and a clipboard" who was sitting beside him, and he'd tried to pick her up with his newfound interest in zoning law. Somehow she wasn't impressed.

Finally, in October, he was done. I gave him a final payment and said goodbye. He was leaving town, going back to New Jersey. Dog was feeling sentimental. There were tears in his eyes. He said the tenants—the sculptor and student and DJ—had thrown a surprise party for him last night, attended by "a chick I've been wanting to ball for three years. Well,

I went home after the party. I was totally wrecked. At three o'clock she comes knockin' on my door."

"No offense, but just what," I asked, "do women find attractive about you?"

He pressed a fat rolled doobie into my hand. A parting gift. "I dunno," he said. "Maybe because what they see is what they get. I like them. No bullshit. And I give 'em stuff."

I had no doubt that one day he would accidentally impregnate somebody. I wondered what would become of that puppy.

The next day he boarded a Greyhound for a trip across the country. He had a job lined up filling vending machines in Atlantic City.

I gave the doobie to my neighbor Sonny, who took it to a party and passed it around. "Nobody can remember what happened," Sonny told me. "That was great shit."

I heard from the tenants that Dog met a woman on the bus and stepped off with her in Chicago. After one postcard, none of us ever heard from him again. He disappeared into the random maw of America. A nobody. A working-class hippie.

Rookie

The Rookie

September 1976

You have to start somewhere. You have to be the rookie. They give you the worst tasks, and they test you. There's no other way.

A neighbor told her boyfriend-of-the-week that I was looking for a job. Pierce, the boyfriend, was a construction foreman. He strutted over to my cottage and knocked on my door.

Pierce was a tall, skinny guy with curly blond hair. A pompous bastard. He let me know first thing that he'd studied architecture at Yale. Then he interviewed me:

"Have you ever worked on a construction crew before?"

"No."

"Do you have construction experience?"

"Some. I rebuilt a couple of houses."

"By yourself?"

"Mostly."

"Do you have a Skilsaw?"

"No."

"Then I can't hire you."

"I have a power saw. Not a Skil."

Pierce smirked. "Can I see it?"

I showed him my Black & Decker worm-gear saw.

Pierce said, "I didn't know Black and Decker made a worm-gear saw."

59

"That's what everybody says."

"Doesn't Black and Decker make hobby tools?"

"This is tougher than a Skil. It's a bulldog."

"Looks like you worked the crap out of it."

"Uh huh." I didn't mention that I bought the bulldog used, when it was already beat-up from years of work. It made me look more experienced.

"Okay, can you start tomorrow? Bring the bulldog."

So most of the interview was about the saw, not me. If I'd had a sidewinder saw, Pierce wouldn't have hired me. In 1976, on the west coast, if you were serious about carpentry, you had a worm-gear, usually a Skil. It was like a law.

Pierce made the right decision to hire me—I'm a hard worker—but for the wrong reason—the Black & Decker. He flaunted Yale credentials, then invoked—not quite successfully—worm-gear machismo. As a rookie carpenter I'd be working for a rookie foreman.

First day, I worked with Jim, a short guy built like a pickle. Friendly. Jim had a dusty old Plymouth station wagon with a surfboard sticking out the rear window.

Jim was not far from being a rookie himself. He'd started a week before me. Together we spent the morning hauling pressure-treated 2×10s in the hot sun. "Rasty wood," Jim called it. The greasy poison soaked into our T-shirts and cutoffs while smearing our exposed arms and legs. We hammered the rasty 2×10s upright to a frame, constructing the world's ugliest garden fence. The two-bys made it massive; the toxic ooze had a lethal smell. I suppose it looked gardenish, though, being green.

We broke for lunch. Jim told me he used to have a leather and glass shop in San Luis Obispo, "a bitchin' little town if you like small towns and don't mind everybody knowin' every time you take a shit or who you're fuckin'." Jim said he'd had a show in Aspen, selling his leather and glass. He came back to California—something about a surfing contest—but soon would be moving back to Colorado for an architectural job in Glenwood Springs.

"You're an architect, Jim?"

"Got the degree. Kept me in San Luis for five years."

Unspoken was the fact that right now Jim was working as an entry-level carpenter, probably for the same wage as me, five bucks an hour. I wondered how much architecture-trained Yalie Pierce was earning.

"Glenwood Springs, I'll mostly be emptyin' wastebaskets," Jim said. "Fetchin' donuts. But at least they're architects."

"Not much surf in Colorado."

"They got snow."

I asked, "Is everybody on this job an architect?"

"Are you?" Jim asked.

"No."

"Then I guess not everybody."

After lunch a man drove up in a Jeep Wagoneer. He was dressed in a pinstriped shirt, button-down collar, and scruffy blue jeans—the architect's dress code of that era. Above the waist, a businessman. Below the waist, casual and independent and arty.

Next, his wife stepped out of the Jeep. Architects, having an eye for structure, always marry great-looking women. She glanced around the job site, caught my eye and held it. She smiled at me.

The Architect had a goatee and a worried frown. He strode over to our new fence and drew a sharp breath that whistled with stress. He said, "This isn't what I want."

"Did we get it wrong?" I asked.

The Architect cocked an eyebrow at me. I was being told, *Shut up, carpenter*. He took another sharp intake of breath, another whistle of stress. "I'm making a field adjustment," he said. He told us to knock out every fourth 2×10 and reinstall it with a piano hinge so it could open like a vent.

It would break up the mass and provide an interesting, quirky detail. "Nice," I said.

Again the Architect cocked an eyebrow at me: *I don't need your approval*, it said.

Over his shoulder I saw that once again his wife was staring at me. No longer smiling, she was biting her lip, looking concerned for my job security.

I learned later that he was a well-known, up-and-coming architect with an eccentric style. He considered a floor plan to be like a rough outline, with multiple adjustments made in the field. His detractors—and building inspectors—accused him of making it up as he went along.

New architecture grads—in this case Jim and Pierce—would apprentice themselves to the Architect just for the experience.

I quickly caught on that the man never smiled or showed any emotion except irritation, which was constant, accompanied by sharp, whistling intakes of stress. The way I could gauge his mood was to see how it was reflected by his wife. She, in turn, always seemed to be watching me.

After the Architect moved on, Pierce proudly showed us an antique tool he'd bought at a flea market. He'd haggled it down to twenty bucks.

This was his first chance to try it out. Looking like a weird cross between a pry bar and a riding crop, it was called a slide-hammer nail puller. You place the jaws over a nail head, then slide the handle up and down to get a grip on the nail. Then you pry.

Pierce tried it on a few nails. After five minutes and several failures, he actually removed a 16-penny nail. "There's a learning curve," Pierce said. "Have at it." He tossed the antique to Jim, then drove off to a hardware store to buy some piano hinges.

Jim studied the slide-hammer skeptically, then passed it to me and brought out his crow's foot nail puller. I examined Pierce's tool and could see that the jaws were chipped so they couldn't get a good grip on the nail head. It might've been a wonderful tool at one time. Now it was crap.

I brought out my own crow's foot. By the time Pierce returned, we'd removed all the nails from all the vent boards.

"How'd you like it?" Pierce asked.

"Nice tool," Jim said.

Pierce beamed.

There were fourteen boards to be hung on piano hinges. Each bright-brass Stanley hinge was six feet long with screw holes every two inches on each side of the hinge. For this little task, Jim and I would need to drive 980 bright-brass screws. Slot-head screws.

I don't know when cordless drill/screwdrivers first went on the market, but nobody had them in 1976. Most screws were slot-head, and mostly you drove screws by hand.

Pierce, as it happened, had another flea market bargain: an old Yankee screwdriver that operated by a push-pull spiraling, ratcheting action. Jim tried it. For the Yankee to work, the screw couldn't offer much resistance. The slot had to be deep enough to keep the blade from sliding out. With these rasty boards, the tool jammed and the blade slid out.

Besides Jim and myself, there was one other carpenter on the job, and he was the real thing: a German master carpenter named—I kid you not—Adolf. No mustache.

Adolf could hang a door in six minutes flat. Jim and I were in awe of him.

Adolf wandered out on a break just in time to see Jim struggling with the Yankee driver. Adolf studied the tool. "*Scheisse,*" he said. He held out one cupped hand. "Give me your hammer." Borrowing Jim's Vaughan framing hammer, Adolf looked around to see if anybody was watching, then whacked a screw. One whack, one installed screw. No predrilling, no twisting. Just *whack*.

It held tight like a ring nail, but you could back it out with a screwdriver.

"No foss, no moss," Adolf said. Then he wandered away.

Together, Jim and I whacked 980 screws in less than an hour.

After my first day on the construction crew I had a painful sunburn. Less than a week ago I'd completed my final graveyard shift as a computer operator. I was like a miner emerging from three years underground.

In the next few weeks I did the grunt-work that a rookie was expected to do. There were bricks and lumber to be hauled, small batches of concrete to be mixed, dirt to be shoveled. There were impossibly heavy 4×8-foot sheets of Plexiglas to be carried to the central atrium, then lifted to the roof or tilted up to the side, caulked, and held in place.

Muscles started rippling over my body. My sunburn peeled; then I turned bronze. I sweated buckets. I lost ten pounds.

Every chance I could, I watched Adolf. He was my silent teacher. Unfortunately I started badly with him: Pierce gave me the assignment of chipping some concrete from the surface of the driveway. A delivery had been sloppy. I was to clean up the hardened droppings, which looked like concrete turds. Pierce said, "You can just bang with a hammer and it will break off from the surface. The bond is weak. Just don't use your good hammer. Here." He handed me a big old hammer that had pock marks on the hickory handle and rust on the top. "I found this lying around. Use it."

Pierce was right. With a couple of blows, the hammer would break the bond and remove a turd. I was thinking about coprolites, which are fossilized dinosaur droppings. I'd bought one once from a rather strange store and given it as a birthday present to my brother, Ed, who could appreciate such things. Suddenly I was shaken by Adolf's voice shouting: "What are you doing with my hammer!"

"It's yours? Pierce gave it to me. He said it was some old hammer he found lying around."

"Give me."

I handed Adolf the hammer. Indignantly he pointed to the letters engraved in the head: Stiletto. "This is the *best* hammer," Adolf said. "Pierce is *Arschkriecher*. You want to be a good carpenter? Don't listen to Pierce."

"I don't want to listen to Pierce. Whatever you called him, it sounds about right."

"Good."

"Could I listen to you?"

Adolf smiled, surprised. "*Ja*," he said. "Follow me."

"I have to finish chipping."

"Forget Pierce. Follow me. No foss, no moss."

Adolf was hanging more doors today. He had a rolling, home-made box on wheels containing chisels, screwdrivers, routing jigs, hole saws, drill bits, a Bosch drill, and a Bosch router. I'd never seen anybody work so fast—or so precisely. He'd say, "Hold the door," or "Hand me the three-quarter chisel," and I'd do as told. I felt like a nurse assisting an orthopedic surgeon.

When Adolf hung a door, he'd use one screw on each side of the hinge and leave off some of the trim. "Finish," he'd say. "No foss, no moss." And he'd roll on to the next. I'd install the remaining trim and make sure there were six screws in each hinge—no fuss, no mess. Then I'd dash to catch up. I had to work fast.

I soaked up skills at a rapid clip, along with a few German swear words. My favorite was *schnoodle noodle* which meant, as best I could gather, "dick snot."

Another day, Adolf was given the assignment of building a fireplace mantel. The Architect had bought several massive slabs of black walnut, rough cut, with the bark still attached. He gave Adolf free rein to design and construct a mantel.

Adolf worked alone on this project, though I watched whenever I could. He spent three days cutting, planing, sanding, working, and reworking the wood until he was satisfied.

At last the Architect stopped by and studied the finished mantel.

Accompanying the Architect were his wife, his father, and his mother. They'd been around before. The house, when completed, would be occupied by the father and mother. The Architect saw the project as an opportunity to showcase his somewhat eccentric style. The father, a dapper little man with a white beard, was coming to see the project as yet another example of his son's overactive ego.

I was coming to see that the apple didn't fall far from the tree.

The Architect's mother, meanwhile, mostly frowned and nodded. She was in the early stages of dementia.

"The mantel is wonderful," the Architect said. He pointed at one slit in the face of the top where the old walnut had split. "All we have to do is fill that crack, and it's done."

Adolf jumped to attention. "There is no crack," he said.

"It's right there," the Architect said, pointing.

Adolf studied the slit. *"There is no crack!"* he shouted.

We all could see it. Adolf wasn't to blame. Long ago, the drying walnut had developed a small check.

Adolf was shaking his head. "There. Is. No. Crack."

The father said, "Whatever you call that thing, a little epoxy will fix it," and he hustled off to the garage. There was a chest freezer out there filled with dozens of canisters the size of yogurt containers, each canister a different component of epoxy. The father, I was told, was one of the world's leading experts on epoxies. More than once on the job I'd already heard, "Nothing a little epoxy won't fix," which would be followed by a trip to the freezer.

The father produced a dark gray mix that was a close match to the color of the walnut. "I'll dab it in," the father said, turning to Adolf, "then when it's dry you can sand it down." The father smiled. "You're the only person I would trust with that task."

Adolf nodded solemnly.

The next day, after the sanding, even knowing where it had been, I couldn't find it. There was no crack.

The weather cooled and my energy surged. I was working outdoors for a week, while a subcontractor installed a hardwood floor, maple with inlays of mahogany, most of it removed from old bowling alleys. To the Architect's credit—and he was ahead of his time—he incorporated used lumber whenever possible, even when he had to pay more to recondition it than it would cost to buy new lumber.

Another newcomer had joined the crew: Kenneth. As with me, Kenneth started the job pale, blinking as if he'd stepped out of a cave. He was on the pudgy side and wore big black eyeglasses. We were working together laying a brick patio while clouds of fine sawdust from the floor sanders billowed out the open windows of the house.

It took only a minute to see that Kenneth was careful and methodical in the positioning of bricks while I had a rougher hand. I quickly ceded the job of placement to Kenneth, while I kept him supplied with bricks and sand.

"Have you done this before, Kenneth?" I asked.

"No. I just got out of the Air Force. Now I'm collecting unemployment."

"And getting paid at a job."

"Yep. Unemployment is my Polish Guggenheim. I start school next week."

"What school?" Since he was joking about Guggenheim grants, I assumed he was an artist.

"It's in San Francisco," Kenneth said.

"San Francisco State?"

"No." Kenneth sighed. He set down the brick he was holding and wiped sweat from his eyes. "The College of Mortuary Science."

"Wow!"

"Yeah. I get that a lot."

"You like it?"

"Yes, actually. You could say I really dig it." He smiled. "I found out in the Air Force that I didn't mind handling dead bodies, so that's what I did for three years."

"You know, I just finished three years of graveyard shift, but it was nothing like what you did."

"People make fun of me, but it's an art, you know. Not just a science. Morticians make good money. I'll do it for a few years, save up the bread and open a recording studio. That's what I really want to do."

"You could record the Grateful Dead."

I heard laughter. The Architect's wife.

The Architect's wife had settled herself nearby, leaning against a tree, arms folded, watching us. It unnerved me how often she seemed to be following me around at a distance. Often she was smiling at me, though, so it wasn't particularly threatening.

She approached me. She'd turned serious. "What do you really do?"

"What do you mean?"

"You're not a carpenter."

"I'm *that* bad?"

"You're a beginner. And that's okay." She was squinting at me. "What are you, really?"

I didn't know it yet, but I would be getting this question a lot. Somehow I just don't present what people expect in a carpenter. I have middle-class manners, a large vocabulary, a face that seems to belong at a desk. "I'm a writer," I said.

"Oh, no."

"You don't believe me?"

She seemed angry. "Writers are drunk and depressed. They work in universities. Or they get grants. Either way they're sucking on a teat and they hate it."

I was speechless.

"Did I shock you?" she asked.

"You seem to know all about it."

"My ex-husband is a writer." She furrowed her brow. "If you gave him a hammer, he'd write a poem on the handle. After five drinks." She looked me up and down. "Better what you do. Be a carpenter. Or—" she glanced at Kenneth, "a mortician. It's so much better."

Pierce was calling me. I began a new assignment: digging ditches, laying drainpipe from the downspouts for a graywater system. Another new skill to learn.

After that conversation, the Architect's wife seemed to lose interest in me. Given how she felt about writers, I wondered how she felt about architects who frown all the time and draw in their breath with sharp whistles of stress.

As for my life over the next thirty-five years, I forgot about the advice of the Architect's wife. I can't even say I agree with her. If I were offered a grant, I'd probably grab it. But I've never applied for one.

Here's how my career played out: Construction work. Physical labor. No university. No grant.

And no teat.

All of a sudden, Winston, father of the Architect, along with his senile wife and their Chicana maid, started moving into the unfinished house. Chaos ensued. The kitchen had no sink; bathrooms were incomplete. The floors had been sanded but not yet sealed. The sealing was supposed to begin on that day Winston decided to move in. It was postponed.

We all worked in our stocking feet.

A king-size bed was moved into the master bedroom, with newspapers placed under its legs so it wouldn't mar the unfinished floor. A color television was set on some boxes in the den so the Architect's mother could watch KQED, whatever was on, from her wheelchair. She watched The MacNeil/Lehrer Report, Sesame Street, fundraising appeals.

The maid, who looked like a sixteen-year-old with big brown eyes and long fingernails painted blue, would hover near the mother picking up crumbs as they fell on the bare floor or brushing sawdust as it settled over the TV screen.

The walls of several rooms were covered with hardwood planks— not 4×8 sheets of ersatz paneling but real honest-to-gosh lumber, different species interwoven for different rooms, selected and arranged by Adolf, the master German carpenter. I had the job of sanding. I rented a Makita half-sheet flat sander, a heavy machine that made a pleasing *vrummmmm* as it ground its way up and down the walls.

Gorgeous wood. I loved the mood of it, smoothed to a soft glow. Adolf had selected and placed each board to blend into splendid patterns of grain just waiting for a touch of oil. The walls would be magnificent.

After a few hours, the six-pound weight of the Makita combined with the vibration of the motor left my arms and shoulders aching. As I took a break, allowing blood to recirculate to my fingertips, the Architect and Pierce stepped into the room to inspect my work. The Architect never spoke directly to me. There was an annoyingly strict hierarchy.

The Architect ran his palm over a section I had sanded. "Okay," he said, frowning. "We can stain it now."

"Oh no!" I said. "Please don't stain it. Use a natural finish."

Immediately I knew I'd committed a grievous sin. I'd violated the structure of command, and, worse yet, I'd disagreed with the design decision of a hotshot architect. Me, a five-dollar-an-hour laborer.

The Architect nodded his head toward me, speaking to Pierce. "Take care of this," he said. Then he walked out.

I didn't even have a name. I was "this." The hotheaded rookie. I believed in purity of wood. I've mellowed since then, but that's how I felt at the time. Passionately.

Pierce said, "I'm supposed to fire you now."

"Sorry," I said. "My fault."

"What do you have against stain?"

"Stain is for cheap wood. Stain is to hide things. Stain is for mediocrity. This is fantastic wood. Oil will bring it out. Let it glow."

"What makes you an expert on stain?"

"I'm not. I'm just opinionated about wood grain."

"You've done a lot of woodwork?"

"Some. I built some furniture. Just a hobby."

"Unstained furniture?"

"You bet."

Pierce folded his arms across his chest. "Stain is also for color. Color sets a mood. This house isn't a museum. It's meant to be a functioning home with a color scheme and an overall design. It's not all about grain."

"You're right. I'm sorry."

"Just lay low for a while. Find something to do outside."

"I'm not fired?"

"Not quite yet."

I put on my boots, went out to the yard, and busied myself drilling holes and installing bolts for a trellis that was to be constructed out of redwood that had been rescued from the wreckage of an old warehouse. Salvaged! As much as I wanted to dislike the Architect—and his personality sucked—I admired many of his choices.

Jim, my fellow rookie, was given the job of completing the sanding. I don't know what conversations took place in my absence, but at the end of the day, dipping rags into a can, Jim began swiping the walls with linseed oil. No stain.

The garage was packed with furniture and boxes and incredible souvenirs from Winston's career as a chemist and civil engineer. There were carved figurines from Africa, ornamental stone from India, vases from China, an immense metal platter with intricate etchings. The collection was probably worth a fortune.

Winston strode about the house like a king, ordering workers to drop what they were doing and vacate the room, contradicting the schedule and plans of his son the Architect, plans that had never been firm to begin with.

A truckload of gravel was dumped in the driveway. It became my job to shovel the gravel into a wheelbarrow, roll it to the back yard, and dump it into a pit for the graywater system.

After a couple of hours of my shoveling and wheelbarrowing, dapper, white-bearded Winston wandered out and stared at the pit. "Stop," he said.

I was about to dump another load. I stopped.

"What is this rock?" Winston said.

"Gravel," I said.

"I specified pea gravel. This is not pea gravel. Pea gravel is round. Pea gravel will always have drainage. This is crushed rock."

"Pierce said it was drain rock."

"*Pierce!*" Winston shouted.

Pierce came over. Winston explained that this rock was not pea gravel.

"Yes, it is," Pierce said. "When you order pea gravel around here, this is what they deliver. I'll show you the receipt."

Winston's voice was cold fury. "I've supervised the building of dams in Africa. I built levees in India. Don't tell me about rock. This is not pea gravel."

To my amazement, Pierce said, "Yes, it is."

"Don't tell me—"

"It serves the same purpose."

Winston closed his eyes. His shoulders and neck were taut—and then suddenly drooped. He opened his eyes and stared at Pierce with utter contempt. Then he walked away.

What use is it to be king when you are surrounded by insufferable fools?

I still had a wheelbarrow full of gravel. "What should I do?" I asked Pierce.

"Carry on," Pierce said.

The kitchen was designed with an island cabinet in the center that could be accessed from all four sides. A plumber—in his stocking feet, of course—installed a triple-basin sink in the island and then informed the Architect that there would have to be a vent of inch-and-a-half pipe running from the island to the vaulted ceiling twelve feet overhead.

The Architect argued and the plumber argued back, each waving code books at the other. Finally the Architect accepted the fact that the open sight-lines of the kitchen would have to be interrupted by a twelve-foot, boxed-in plumbing vent.

A window-washer named Don was roaming the house—also in stocking feet—with a bucket of foamy liquid and a long-handled squeegee. He set down the bucket for a moment to observe the kitchen vent argument, and when he picked it up he'd left a dirty, soapy ring in the unfinished floor.

Anybody could have seen it coming. If not the window-washer, somebody else would have spilled something, dropped something, scraped something.

The sealing of the floor had never happened. Production had simply moved on. The Architect—or Pierce—or Winston—*somebody* should have demanded that all work stop until the floors were sealed.

A construction crew functions like a temporary family. Ours had become dysfunctional.

The Architect blew up. First a vent in the kitchen, then a ring on his floor. His mother was becoming visibly more senile by the day, his father crabbier and more authoritarian. His crew was an incompetent collection of hippies and surfers and a goddamn mortician; his foreman was a snot from Yale. He ordered everybody to get the hell out.

Outside, I asked Pierce, "Are we all fired?"

"I don't think so," Pierce said.

I was coming to like Pierce. He was arrogant, especially in areas where he was ignorant, such as pea gravel. But, based mostly on intuition, he'd hired Jim and Kenneth and me, three rookies who needed to start somewhere, and he'd protected us as best he could.

Pierce told everybody to return tomorrow. Everybody except the window-washer, who Pierce ordered to get his dirty blue van out of here and not to expect one cent from his half day of work.

The next morning when I showed up at 8 a.m. there were two police cars in the driveway. The garage door was wide open. Somebody had stolen Winston's lifetime collection of art from around the world. In addition, the thief—or thieves—had stolen a case of jewelry and a restored 1930s vintage jukebox. Nothing else. They seemed to know exactly what they were looking for and where to find it.

A neighbor said she'd seen a blue van backed up in the driveway sometime during the night.

Pierce said the job was over. We'd all get paid in a day or so. He'd mail everybody a check.

And he did.

The check hardly mattered. For five weeks as a rookie I'd seen the creative stew of muscle and skill and personality—and I was part of it—and I loved it. I could do this for a lifetime.

Four days after the job ended, my first child was born.

There was so much to learn.

Cold Out There

Monday, March 14, 1977

I knock on the door of a run-down little dump on the scruffy edge of Redwood City. I drove forty-five minutes to get here. She sounded dotty on the phone.

"Who are you?" she asks through the screen. An older woman, unkempt. A bit of drool at the corner of her lips.

I introduce myself. Then I say, "You wanted to replace your kitchen counter."

"Did I?"

"On the phone. You called me. You told me to come at nine o'clock, and it's nine o'clock."

"I said that? Nine o'clock in the *morning*? So you're a carpenter?"

"Yes, ma'am."

"Do you cheat?"

"What?"

"I know *all* about that." She spits on the screen, accidentally (perhaps). "My husband was a carpenter before he left, and believe me, I know. He wanted a younger redhead, but he ended up with a woman as old as I am, so I guess it's colder than it looks out there."

"Would you like me to come in and take a look at the kitchen counter?"

"Not today." She thinks a moment, chewing her lips. "Not your fault."

"Good day, ma'am."

As I'm walking back to my truck, I hear a door slam.

Cheap Labor

Monday, February 28, 1977

I learned how to thread pipe from a scientist named Edgar.

I'd posted an ad saying I'd do plumbing, carpentry, and electrical jobs for seven dollars an hour (at the time, real plumbers were charging thirty and up). I was working by trial and error, charging cheap rates for the trials and nothing for the errors. It was my personal vocational training school with dollars instead of letters for a grading system.

I learned fast.

The first lesson: Cheap labor is hired by cheap people.

Edgar was one of those cheapskates. I don't know what kind of science he was engaged in, only that upon hiring me he said we couldn't start until next week because, "I've got a lot of experiments going." He was in the middle of converting a garage into two bedrooms and a bath. The job was taking longer than he expected because, he explained, "I keep losing carpenters."

A week later I began. Edgar and I worked side by side. With cold chisels we chipped away stucco at the base of the garage in preparation for jacking up the foundation. Until now I had never chipped stucco nor jacked a foundation. I'd only been in business for six months, plunging blindly into areas I knew nothing about. Now I was getting on-the-job training from a man who, I later realized, knew not-so-much himself. (Chipping the stucco, for example, a two-day job by hand, would have taken thirty minutes with a rented demolition hammer.)

Edgar was a small man, bald, with a New Jersey accent. Late in that first day, his wife Rhoda came home with two small children. Rhoda was a pediatrician with a New Jersey accent. She asked Edgar about a piece of wood that a previous carpenter had cut wrong. Edgar said, "He paid for it."

I began to understand why Edgar kept "losing" carpenters. And why was Edgar, a highly educated scientist with a wife who was a pediatrician, both employed full time at presumably good-paying jobs, taking a day off to chip stucco?

Rhoda and Edgar had an edgy conversation about how he should stop work so he could eat dinner with his children. He said he was already behind schedule. Rhoda, rolling her eyes, said she was *very* aware that he was behind schedule. Then she turned to me. "What do you think of a man who won't take time to eat dinner with his children?"

Caught in crossfire, asked to choose sides, I did the best I could: "I would be quite happy to call it a day."

Edgar said his goal was to finish the chipping today. Rhoda returned to the house, muttering to herself.

Edgar and his vanishing carpenters had already framed the walls inside the garage. In my ignorance—and to further my education—I asked, "Why didn't you raise the garage before doing the framing inside?"

"Because the motherassfucking inspector rejected the framing. He said the motherassfucking ceiling wasn't high enough. He wanted more motherassfucking headroom. I showed him the plans that his own motherassfucking building department had approved. He said just because the motherassfucking plans were approved didn't mean I could break the motherassfucking building code."

Edgar's wife reappeared. Sternly she said, "Eddie, that's enough. The kids can hear you. Come inside *right now*. You're grounded for the evening."

With a sheepish look, Edgar followed her inside without a glance at me, not a word. I was a tool, set aside at the end of the day.

Wednesday, March 2, 1977

Edgar had collected a half dozen car jacks of dubious power and reliability. The plan was to raise the garage using one jack at each corner and one at the center of each of the two longer walls. Each jack would push on a 2×4 nailed as a ledger to the interior side of the wall. As the 2×4 was lifted, it would in turn raise the wall to which it was attached.

I had several qualms about this plan. The car jacks seemed puny compared to the mass of the garage. The 2×4s seemed equally puny as a way to transfer the load of each wall to the jack. The nails connecting the 2×4s to the walls would have to remain straight under tremendous stress—the same 16-penny nails that bend if you hit them slightly off center with a hammer. But my biggest qualm was that the 2×4s were attached to the interior of the walls, so to jack them I'd have to be standing *inside* the garage.

A few months earlier I'd bought a hard hat at a garage sale for twenty-five cents. So far I'd never worn it. Today I did. If twenty tons of concrete and lumber and roofing asphalt were going to collapse on top of me, at least I would be wearing my yellow plastic hard hat.

Edgar stood outside the garage and told me to start jacking. Being an idiot, I obeyed. Crouching at the sound of every creak, I moved from jack to jack, raising each one a sixteenth of an inch at a time. It took me four passes to raise them one-fourth of an inch. The only result was to embed the head of each jack one-fourth of an inch into the soft wood of the 2×4s.

Impatient, Edgar marched into the garage and pumped one of the jacks up by a full inch. The wall groaned. You could hear cracks popping open in the stucco outside and then the pitter-pat of little chunks of plastered concrete striking the ground.

We both ran outside. The stress of lifting one corner so abruptly and unevenly had turned the exterior into a spider web of fractures. Still groaning, the wall settled back down to its original starting position, minus several nuggets of stucco.

Returning inside, I saw that the nails holding the 2×4 ledger were bending, and the 2×4 was separating from the wall. The jack, meanwhile, had folded like a drinking straw. It was ruined. The good news was that we had somehow managed to avoid toppling the entire building onto its side. Another bright spot: nothing had caved in on top of us.

Something snapped in me. "You can't do it like this," I said. "You have to use a four by six. You have to bolt it to the frame. You have to rent some stronger jacks. You have to raise them in increments of one-sixteenth of an inch—as I was trying to do."

Bear in mind that I had never jacked up a building before, nor had I seen it done, nor had I read anything about it. Some things are simply obvious.

Equally obvious was the fact that Edgar had no idea what he was doing. A curious reversal took place. I'd spoken with such authority—fury, actually—that Edgar assumed I was the expert, whereas before I'd assumed he was. The yellow hard hat also seemed to invest me with power.

"All right," Edgar said. Then he thought for a moment. "Don't say anything about this to my wife, okay?"

I'm sure that when his wife asked him about the cause of all those cracks in the stucco, he blamed it on me. No matter. Over the next two days I did exactly what I'd proposed. Two wonderful days. Edgar went back to running his experiments, whatever they were, and left me alone.

I found inexplicable pleasure in lifting that building. Who knew? Elevating houses may have been my calling. I fell instantly in love with that lowly tool, the bottle jack.

I don't wear the hard hat much anymore. It's gathered several years of dust on a shelf in my basement workshop. But it stands for something basic, something good.

To lift a building, to fix the foundation, and then to bring it back down is gritty work, totally without glamour. Take joy wherever you find it. When I lower jacks nowadays, when an old structure settles onto familiar and comfortable support, renewed and strengthened, I hear it moan with pleasure.

It's a lesson I learned while doing cheap labor.

March 1977

Having underestimated my skill at jacking up buildings, Edgar next made the mistake of assuming I knew all about electrical wiring. He bought a couple boxes of Romex and a bag full of electrical boxes, and he told me to wire the two bedrooms, the utility room, the workshop, the one bath. Then he left me alone.

I thought I knew wiring. I'd done it before, but never on this scale and never in freshly framed, bare stud walls where all your work is naked and visible.

The building inspector stepped in, took one look, and laughed. "This won't pass," he said.

"What's wrong?" I asked.

"Neatness counts," he said.

"It won't show," I said. "The Sheetrock will cover everything."

"Doesn't matter. If it's sloppy, it's a dead giveaway."

He then inspected every box, every staple. To his surprise he found that I had secured the Romex within twelve inches of each box and every four feet in straight runs, though he shook his head and muttered, "I shouldn't be looking at staples. You know why I have to? Because you didn't flatten the Romex into neat and tidy runs. It's twisted. Yeah, I know the electricity runs through it just the same, but it just reeks of cheap work."

In the end he signed it off. I'd marked myself as cheap labor, but I'd passed. Never again would I run sloppy wires, even though it doesn't matter to the electricity and it doesn't show to the outside world and clients like Edgar would never know the difference. It matters to the *electrician*. It's the mark of good workmanship, of professionalism, of pride. Neatness counts.

April 1977

In April I began plumbing for Edgar. He'd "lost" his previous plumber, so I was picking up in the middle of somebody else's plan. It was a bad plan.

The drainpipes had been installed, but there were no vents except for one main stack, which was unfinished. The rules for plumbing vents are somewhat arcane. Cheap labor that I was, I was no expert. I simply accepted the plan of the lost plumber and continued the main vent up through the roof. The assembly was easy: cast iron with no-hub joints.

The water pipes, again half installed by the lost plumber, were galvanized steel. Again I was no expert, but I knew that nobody recommended steel pipes anymore. I asked Edgar why he wasn't using copper, and he replied, "Galvanized is cheaper."

It might have been cheaper (at least in 1977) but it would corrode and eventually fail. Copper tubing would last forever—or at least for a human lifespan. Steel pipe would require more time—and more labor expense—to install. By providing cheap labor, I made it cost effective for Edgar to make a bad choice. And it was only cost effective in the short run. In the long run, twenty years later he—or, more likely, some subsequent owner—would have to replace all those pipes, which would mean tearing open ceilings and walls.

I'd been sweating copper pipes since high school. I don't even remember learning how—it just seemed like something I always knew. But I'd never cut threads into steel pipe.

Edgar had a threading tool—a cheap one, of course, hand operated. He taught me the basics, and I set to work.

Threading pipe is muscle work, whole-body work, shoulder and arm braced by your back and legs, a tight grip with the hand. I found it sensual: the musty scent of the cutting oil, the crackle of the blades as they gripped and gouged, the emerging grooves, the thin steel waste curling, dropping like silver hairs. I was set up outdoors, straining in the warm sunlight, strong, sweating, finding deep pleasure. I tried to describe it once to a friend who was a psychology student. She said it sounded like the perfect sexual metaphor. I couldn't buy that, though, unless you find it erotic to cut grooves into the head of a penis.

Metaphor, schmetaphor. I loved threading pipe. There's joy in the work of the body.

Monday, May 23, 1977

I dealt with the plumbing when Edgar was away at his lab. I also dealt with repairing the stucco—more outside work, more sunshine. Troweling the sloppy, sandy mix into stucco wire wasn't a newfound pleasure as some of the other tasks had proved to be, but it was another skill acquired. Late in the afternoon Rhoda would come home with the two kids and complain to me about the schedule slipping further and further behind—and about her husband seeming farther and farther away from his own kids. I came to dread the sight of her. She felt safe nagging me as a substitute for Edgar.

When Edgar was around, he wanted me to help him with carpentry—some additional framing, installing a window, hanging some doors. He seemed to enjoy banging nails. Maybe, like me, he needed more in his life than brain work; he needed the satisfaction of working with his hands. He even cracked a joke once—the only one in the four months we worked together—something about substituting a Polish nail for a Finnish one. I didn't get it until he explained: a *finish* nail.

One door that I hung by myself turned into a botch. Edgar became upset and said he would dock me an hour's pay.

One of the "lost" carpenters dropped by when Edgar wasn't around. He asked if I'd seen a metal pry bar. As it happened, I had. It was in Edgar's tool closet.

"Unbelievable," the carpenter said. He grabbed the pry bar. "It's mine. I left it here by mistake. I didn't miss it until now. He never called me, never asked if I wanted it back. He just put it in his closet. He was gonna keep it. What's he paying you?"

"Seven dollars an hour."

The carpenter laughed. "Oh, my God! And does he dock your pay if you make a mistake?"

"Yes."

"That's *hilarious*." The carpenter was guffawing. "Here's a word of advice. When you quit—and you *will* quit—don't tell him until after he's paid. He still owes me forty bucks."

The job dragged on. Edgar would tell me not to come for a week while he had many experiments to run. He didn't want me doing too much unless he could keep a watchful eye on me. He couldn't trust anybody.

I was happy to stay away. I had other jobs to do, for which I'd increased my rates. I knew a rate increase wouldn't fly with Edgar.

One Monday in May the building inspector came for a plumbing inspection. He rejected everything. The drain system, planned and installed by the lost plumber, was undersized and used an S-trap where it was illegal. The vent system was unworkable. It needed a separate vent for the sink, another for the shower—another legacy of bad planning by the lost plumber. The water system was puzzling—"Why for the love of God did you use steel pipe?"—but legal except that the house needed a main shutoff valve. Edgar in his cheapness had never installed one, requiring me to traipse thirty feet across the lawn to the underground street valve and thirty feet back every time I needed to shut off the water.

When the inspector departed, Edgar was dejected. His wife would be home soon, and I didn't want to be there.

I said, "You owe me for twenty-seven hours last week and today."

Silently, Edgar wrote out a check. Handing it to me, our eyes met, and we both knew I wasn't coming back. He didn't say I was fired; I didn't say that I quit. We both knew it was over. None of the shortcomings of the plumbing were my fault; I had simply inherited them. But I would be blamed.

I went straight to Edgar's bank and cashed the check before he could commit any hanky-panky. Only as I cashed it did I realize he'd paid me for twenty-six hours. He'd docked me one hour. When I'd told him he owed me for twenty-seven, I'd already docked myself down from twenty-eight.

Edgar owed me seven dollars. He still does. I never went back.

After the bank I stopped at a house where I'd checked out a yard sale over the weekend. A man had been offering 200 square feet of tongue-and-groove knotty pine for fifty dollars. Now, this Monday, I was in luck. The man was there, and so was the knotty pine, unsold.

We haggled. The man said he'd rather burn the wood than sell it for the five dollars I offered. Immediately, his wife said she'd toss gasoline on it herself this evening if he didn't get rid of it.

I bought the whole truckload for seven-fifty. On a whim, without haggling, I also bought an old plumb-bob for twenty-five cents.

I could be as frugal as Edgar. I only hope I'm more sensible.

I drove home loaded with pine. In one hand I cradled the plumb-bob. It felt so solid, so simple, so *honest*. In some sense I was cradling my diploma. With my instincts plus a few tools, I would find what's plumb and true.

I was a graduate of cheap labor.

French Lessons

Monday, July 25, 1977

Gabrielle has a small house in a struggling neighborhood of Redwood City. There are diplomas on the walls and French signs on the doors: *Cuisine, Chambre à coucher, Penderie.* A teacher.

I begin by repairing a leaky tub faucet in the *Salle de bain.* Gabrielle stands in the doorway, chatting, inquiring about my schedule, so I explain that ever since my first child was born my wife and I split childcare, each of us working part time so at least one of us can always be home. That's why I'm working at 8 p.m.

"If my husband had done half the child-raising, I wouldn't be divorced today," Gabrielle tells me. She's cute, slightly plump, with little gold earrings in the shape of teardrops.

Debra, Gabrielle's soulful-eyed five-year-old daughter, comes into the bathroom and without a word hands me three chocolate eggs.

"You sure you want to do that?" Gabrielle asks.

Debra nods silently.

"Thank you, Debra," I say.

Quietly Debra glides out of the bathroom.

"Mon dieu," Gabrielle says. "She's been saving those since Easter."

"What did I do?"

"I don't know, but Debra has very good taste in men." Gabrielle stands over the tub where I'm tightening the faucet handle. She pushes hair around on her head, fluffing. "Are you finished?"

"Just about."

"Ah! No!" There's a tinkling sound, and one of her earrings bounces around the walls of the tub and then shoots straight down the drain. *"Merde!* Can you get that?"

"It's in the trap. I'd have to go under the house."

"Would you please? Can you stay longer? It was a gift. Of course I'll pay for your time."

As I gather tools and a flashlight, Debra comes into the room and silently starts stuffing little coffee candies into my shirt pocket.

"Thank you, Debra."

Without a word, she walks out.

"Bedtime, Debra," Gabrielle calls. Then to me she says, "You won't make a lot of noise? I need to settle down, put Debra to bed, have a glass of wine. *Un verre de vin.*"

"A little clunking, maybe. I shouldn't need any power tools."

"C'est assez bon. That's good enough."

"Are you tutoring me?"

She smiles. *"Pas encore."*

"What?"

"No."

A tight crawlspace. A rusty steel trap. I have to hunch my body like a worm, return to my truck for Liquid Wrench, hunch in again. It takes over an hour to recover the golden teardrop in a mass of gooey soap and hair.

When I return to the house—quietly, so as not to waken Debra—I find Gabrielle on her bed sipping red wine, wearing a flimsy gown.

I duck quickly out of the room. Softly, from the hallway I say, "I'll, uh, leave the earring on the table with my bill."

I stand at the table, writing an invoice. I'm smeared with dirt, carrying the penetrating odor of sewage.

"Would you like some wine? *Par hazard?"* Gabrielle has come out of the bedroom wrapped in a white, fluffy robe. With one hand she holds the flaps tightly closed at the neck. With the other hand she holds up a glass.

"I shouldn't have wine," I say. "I'm dirty. I have a long drive."

She fidgets, studying her toes, her bare feet. Nervously, softly, she says, "I could wash you."

Our eyes meet and hold. After a few moments she says, "I'm sorry." She lowers her eyes. *"Je suis désolée."*

"I'm honored," I say. *"Merci.* Really."

Now here's a strange fact: back in Maryland when I was at Walter Johnson High School, 1964, my French teacher had a crush on me. It sounds like a school boy's fantasy, but it was actually awkward and embarrassing. She was attractive enough, but even with my inexperience I could tell there was something off-center about her. She asked to see me after class. She offered me a ride. There was a French movie she wanted to see. Did I like *crêpes?*

No. No. And no. Nothing happened. Given my unformed social skills and complete lack of interest, I handled it badly. I already had a girlfriend my own age. The only benefit for me was that I got straight As in a class for which I had no talent.

Anyway, by the time I meet Gabrielle, July of 1977, maybe I have more social skills. I have a nine-month-old child at home. I'm still getting used to this fathering business. One thing I know: when you cheat on your wife, you cheat on your child.

Another thing I know: sometimes attraction seems random and weird.

Gabrielle whispers, *"C'est moi qui vous remercie."*

"What?"

"Thank you, sir. *Je vous remercie de tout coeur.* Next time something breaks, can I call you again? I'm sure Debra would like to see you."

I work for Gabrielle off and on for a couple more years. We never speak of that evening again. Whenever I visit, little Debra quietly gives me candies flavored with cocoa, raspberry, or cherry.

Late one afternoon as I'm replacing some light fixtures, I see Gabrielle rushing about and overhear her asking eight-year-old Debra if this sweater goes with this skirt. Debra seems to be the final authority on how her mother should dress for a date. Or Gabrielle in her wisdom is giving her daughter some power in a fraught situation. I'm still there when a gentle, friendly man appears at the front door. "Hi, Debra," he says. "How's it going?"

Debra shyly, wordlessly hands him a chocolate truffle.

Gabrielle stops hiring me.

I see Gabrielle one more time, years later, when we happen to meet in the coffee line at Peet's. Gabrielle and her husband—the same gentle, friendly man—have moved to Los Gatos. Debra is studying engineering at Stanford. In the wallet photo Debra looks serious and shy—and deeply attractive.

"She took Spanish in high school," Gabrielle says. "German in college. Never French. How's that for rebellion?"

The barista takes my order.

Two minutes later, I'm in my truck, driving away with a cup of strong French roast. I suddenly feel like an idiot. I wish, back at the coffee counter, I'd grabbed a bag of chocolate-covered espresso beans and handed them to Gabrielle. I wish I'd said, "Give these to your daughter, *s'il vous plaît."*

I could have repaid a debt. But after all these years I'm still slow on social skills, and I've forgotten all my French.

"Nice to see you, Gabrielle," was all I could say.

"Au revoir," she said.

Marmalade

Tuesday, January 17, 1978

Miss Randal is a delightfully batty old lady who hires me for a day of "chores." In an upscale town, Palo Alto, she lives in a downscale house shaded by sycamore trees. The white wood siding needs paint. In fact, as I look closer, most of the house is rotten and infested with termites.

She sees me studying the soft post on her porch. "It's a game of chicken," she says. "Who will cave in first? The roof? Or my body?" She giggles girlishly. "I was born in this house. My father had just finished building it when I came along. This house and I are practically twins. And now we both have bad plumbing."

Inside the house the furnishings are sparse and threadbare. A sofa tilts at an angle, missing one leg. She points at it and says, "Can you do something?"

"I can slip a board under that corner so it doesn't rock. You'd need a professional restorer to match the leg."

"I should throw the whole thing away. But then where would I sit?"

"It's an antique. You could sell it."

"I bought it brand new." She laughs. "Does that make me an antique? I was interviewed by the *Palo Alto Times*. I was here, seventeen years old for the nineteen-oh-six earthquake. Stanford fell apart. People died. San Francisco burned. This house was just fine. And so was I. See? We're twins. When one of us goes, so will the other."

Miss Randal follows me, chattering constantly, as I repair two faucets and a toilet. She asks if I can repair a clothes line. I use a dowel and epoxy while she explains that she never bought one of "those drying machines." She cleans her clothes in the bathtub with a washboard from Montgomery Ward.

She picked the oranges from the tree in her back yard and won the blue ribbon for marmalade at the Santa Clara County Fair. "All those farmer wives—and I beat 'em!" Palo Alto used to be a fine town but now it's not. She wishes she could live some place in the Sierra where people don't steal. "I should've married," she says. "I had my chance. You have children?"

"Yes. One."

"So how do you feel about your house?"

"I'm just renting. And my place is even worse than—uh, I mean, my place is just a tiny cabin. I have to sweep the termite wings off the table every morning."

"So it will collapse," Miss Randal says. "But your life won't."

"Would you let me replace the post on the porch? So the roof won't crush you?"

"How much would it cost?"

"Fifty dollars."

"How much will I owe you for today?"

"Fifty dollars."

"I'm sorry. I can't. Maybe next year."

At the end of the day I come home to my tiny rental termite cabin. My one-year-old son is having a bubble bath. My wife is sitting on a bathmat next to the tub. Puffs of bubbles are caught in her hair.

She looks up. "I'm pregnant."

I sit on the toilet. "Okay," I say. We'd sort of suspected.

With one finger she's idly peeling shriveled caulk at the edge of the tub. From the wall, dirty black water oozes through the crack. Pointing at some Mason jars on my lap, she asks, "What's that?"

"Marmalade. My day's pay." I explain that I haggled Miss Randal down from fifty dollars to three jars of marmalade. "Tomorrow I'm going back to fix her porch. For that she'll pay me fifty dollars."

My wife is smiling. "I always knew you had a great future in business."

"Let's build a house somewhere," I say. "And live in it forever."

"Okay," she says.

Do You Believe in Miracles?

Friday, February 22, 1980

A tree falls, shutting off electrical power for my section of town. I've been waiting for just such an opportunity.

My family and I have been living—sort of camping out—in the shell of a house that is under construction. It's time to move incoming electrical power lines from a temporary power pole to the new permanent service entrance of the house. For various tawdry reasons (saving money, avoiding bureaucracy, beating the Man), I want to move the wires myself.

Bootleg wiring is sort of a tradition in this town. And today, with the power out, I get my chance.

I climb a ladder and attach rope to the three incoming wires and then disconnect them from the temporary weatherhead. Next, standing on the roof, I pull the rope and the wires to the new permanent weatherhead. I'm twenty feet above the ground. Using split-bolt connectors, I attach two of the wires. It's more difficult than I expected. Split-bolts aren't the ideal connectors for this situation. You need three hands to do this job: one to hold the wires, one to hold the split-bolt, one to tighten the nut.

How much time has passed? I really should have clocked it. Outages can last for minutes or for days. What if the power is restored while I'm connecting the final wire? First a jolt, then I'll fall twenty feet. I'm wearing an old pair of gloves—leather, damp, fingers partly shredded. Basically useless.

The sun is setting, casting the last dusty shafts of light through wood smoke among the trunks of the redwoods. I'm kneeling on wet shingles. Inside the house, my wife is lighting lanterns while my kids play with the dog.

My hands are shaking.

PG&E linemen connect live wires all the time. They have the knowledge, the tools, the experience, the safety equipment. With damp, worn-out gloves, kneeling on wet shingles, I'm electricity bait. How much time is left? I could climb down the ladder, bring up a plastic sheet to kneel on, drive a half hour to a store for better gloves—or I could just bleeping do it. Attach the wire and be done with it.

One difference between young people and old people is that young people don't believe they can die. On this February 22, 1980, I'm a young man, thirty-two years old.

I just bleeping do it. I hold the two ends of wire plus the metal split-bolt connector in my fist while tightening the nut with a metal wrench.

Twist, twist, twist.

Got it.

As I'm wrapping black 3M electrical tape around the final split bolt, I hear a radio. Lights go on in the house next door.

I beat it by five seconds.

By five seconds a stupid young fool avoided a pathetic death.

Now my entire body is shivering. Cautiously, humbly, I finish wrapping the connection with tape.

Indoors, after dinner, the 1980 Winter Olympics are on television. Tonight, the USA ice hockey team is playing the USSR. The Soviets, of course, are expected to win. They always have; they always will.

Cuddled on the sofa, the entire family—dog, kids, wife, and a not-so-young man—watch the thrilling hockey game that comes to be known as the Miracle on Ice, in which a bunch of USA kids beat a tough and seasoned Soviet team.

In one man's life it was the lesser of two miracles that day.

The Legal System

June 1980

I'm a little nervous about working for Judge Luther. As a superior court judge he's undoubtedly aware of the California handyman law, which prohibits unlicensed contractors from performing jobs that cost more than $300. I'm not licensed yet, and he wants me to build a closet at a cost of $750. With no building permit.

His Honor puts me at ease by explaining that judges aren't paid very much, far less than the attorneys who appear before them, and furthermore, he says, "I don't want any building inspectors snooping around this house."

Actually, nobody gets a permit for an interior closet. But the judge doesn't seem to know this.

Inexperienced, I learned several lessons on that closet, such as that good paint won't hide bad wood, that building drawers takes twice as long as you could possibly imagine, that it takes forever to paint louvered doors, and that good spackle can hide a lot of sins. If I were to build that same closet today, it would look better and take half the time. And I'd charge twice as much. Judge Luther got exactly what he wanted: plain and simple construction at a low price.

December 1983

I'm still not licensed. Judge Luther wants me to convert his backyard garage into a living unit for his teenage stepson because, he says, "We need him out of the house."

I inform the judge that he can't convert the garage unless he builds another one to replace it—that's the law in Palo Alto.

"No new garage," says the judge.

It's a concrete floor. I'll build a wooden floor above it to provide space for the plumbing pipes. With the elevated floor, the ceiling will be lower than minimal—the teen will not be able to jump up and down. The sewer drain will stretch over thirty feet to reach the main house drain, with a drop of only two inches along the way, giving the pipe a slope of one-sixteenth of an inch per foot of run. One-quarter inch per foot is normal, so this will be far less than adequate for a long sewer run and will be subject to occasional blockage. The drain will run above ground, which is not allowed, though it can be hidden beneath his backyard deck.

To save money I'll use ABS pipe, which is prohibited in Palo Alto. In fact the whole job is flagrantly illegal. Nothing will be up to code. Fortunately, it will be hidden in the back yard.

"Fine," says the judge. "Homicide is not up to code either, even if I give the body a decent burial in the back yard. And that's what will happen if that kid doesn't move out of this house."

"You need good relations with your neighbors," I say. "They could turn you in."

"I haven't sent any of them to jail," he says.

Building an illegal living unit for a superior court judge, things could go very wrong for both of us. You need mutual trust. Your contract is a handshake, and you need to honor that handshake.

It's a pleasant job—with an extra frisson of danger when the building inspectors are on patrol. I smile and wave at all the neighbors and make sure to park in the judge's driveway and don't play any music or start work too early. One day the judge tells me to stay home because a house on the block will be under scrutiny.

No problem. A day off.

There's one glitch in my design when it turns out that you'd have to step over the toilet to enter the shower. Oops. Fixed. Then there's the tarantula that lurks in the leaves outside and bites me on the finger. Survived.

I practice and improve all my skills—rough plumbing and finish plumbing, rough electrical and finish electrical, rough carpentry and finish carpentry, window installation, stucco patching, roof repair, drywall—challenges, good experience.

Everything comes out fine. No red tags, no homicide. New living unit.

Judge Luther has a brass plaque over his desk that says:

> To live outside the law you must be honest.
> —Bob Dylan

Pocketful of Sawdust

December 1982

Back in 1982 the Reagan Recession was crushing me. Construction was scarce. Supporting three kids including an infant while trying to complete—and heat—the house in which we lived, desperate for money, I took a carpentry/cabinet job beyond my experience level. For a week before it began I slept badly, imagining all the ways I could screw it up.

The frigid evening before I was to begin, I loaded my radial arm saw plus ten sheets of birch plywood and twelve sheets of Wilsonart laminate, and I drove to a house on the Stanford campus where I was to work. The client had a Nobel Prize and an intimidating bearing. He had been, in fact, an advisor to Ronald Reagan—on economics, no less. Needing the gig, I kept my mouth shut about politics.

I'd brought my son Jesse, who was all of six years old but wanted to help. In the truck, after "If We Make It through December," I let Jesse select the music. At the time his favorite song was about having a shotgun rifle and a four-wheel drive. A country boy can survive.

Jesse knew I had a .22 rifle and a two-wheel drive. Close enough. If we were starving, I could shoot a squirrel. (I never did.)

Jesse was a willing worker, small, but strong for his size. We dragged the unwieldy radial arm saw from the bed of the truck, using the tailgate as a fulcrum, tilting, lifting the machine upright to set the table legs on the driveway. Our lungs puffed clouds in the frosty air. The Nobel Prize–winner came out in his bathrobe and said, "Can I help?" Next out the door came his daughter, a chubby, cheerful college student wearing bunny slippers. Together we lifted the heavy saw and awkwardly shuffled it into the heat of the garage.

Right then, I knew it all would end well. Carrying plywood, each of us taking a corner, leaning sheets against the wall of the garage, something wonderful was happening.

As I closed the tailgate of the truck, I thanked them for the help.

"Hot chocolate?" the daughter asked.

At a hardware store on the way home, cashless, I used my credit card to buy a dado blade and a laminate-trimming router bit. I'd never cut a dado before, never installed laminate. I was scared, but I was ready.

Back in the truck, wipers slapping, again I let Jesse select the music. He went for "Crazy Little Thing Called Love." Warm air blew from the vents. A wind was rising, shaking the trees as we headed to our half-built house in the mountains.

The next morning after sound sleep I woke tingly with anticipation on a foggy, drippy day. At the Nobel laureate's house I cut my first dado and cautiously, with contact cement, laid the first sheet of laminate, trimmed with the router. Success. Then another.

It's good to start scared. It makes you cautious. Then gradually you ease into it. There's a flow—the dado wafting blizzards of sawdust, the sharp fumes of contact cement, the whine of the router—a rhythm of wood and tool, of hand and eye, muscle and mind. Like a dance.

The laureate's son, home for the holidays from the University of Chicago, sneaked out to the garage to smoke marijuana while I worked.

A black limousine pulled into the driveway so a courier could deliver an envelope from the president. The economist read the one sheet of paper and disdainfully flipped it onto a rosewood table where, later, I read it: a condescending, badly reasoned letter written by some Treasury Department underling. Apparently the laureate had dared to publicly disagree with the president about how to push the economic levers of the planet.

At the end of the day, the laureate wrote me a check, first payment, and signed it with a flourish.

On the way home I stopped at the La Honda grocery. At the deli counter, reaching into my pocket, my fingers pulled out one dime—and a shower of powdery wood shavings. Grinning from behind the counter, Bob, the grocer, handed me a whisk broom and a dustpan—and then a slice of salami.

> Carpenter, carpenter, what do you say?
> Cut wood all day,
> bring home the pay:
> a pocketful of sawdust.

Tomorrow I'd cash that check. Also tomorrow—and all the way up to the deadline of Christmas—I'd rise before the sun and work into the night heaving heavy boards, glasses wet with sweat, porcupine fingers bristling splinters. With pleasure. With something like joy.

Julie: Mud and Books

February 1979 to June 16, 2001

I started working for Julie in 1979. She had a big old house in disrepair. My first job involved repairing a leaky water line in her front yard, digging sloppy dirt on a cold day in February.

Water restored, one finger bandaged after I clobbered it with a wrench, coated with muck, I stood in Julie's warm kitchen as we talked for an hour about literature and the modern American novel. She thought it was cool that I could work with my hands and my head, that I could be raising children and building my own house and getting published and even getting reviewed in *The New York Times* (scathingly).

"You're living the ideal romantic life," she said. "With mud and books."

Her son, watching television, was less impressed. "How much money do you make?" he asked.

I didn't answer. But he could guess.

Julie was a single mother in upscale Palo Alto, working full time for low wages as a passionate advocate for troubled children. She was smart, charitable, practical.

For the next two or three years Julie would call me to repair her gutters, garage, light switches, whatever broke down. She'd always ask about my writing and what I was working on next.

One time my hammering caused a large, framed mirror to jump off the wall in a different room. I didn't even know it had happened until Julie showed me.

"We have a problem," she said.

The three-by-four-foot mirror had cracked across the middle in two places but hadn't shattered.

"Looks like I owe you a mirror," I said. And it would cost a day's pay.

Julie looked relieved. If I hadn't taken responsibility, I don't think she would have asked me to replace it. She wasn't assertive that way, though she was extremely assertive about the rights of children in the foster-care system. In her personal world she was gentle, almost shy.

I took that cracked mirror home and mounted it in the newly built, still unfinished bedroom closet in my own house. That would be 1980. If I subsequently had seven years of bad luck, I wasn't aware of it.

Another time I built some drawers to fit under her bed. When I returned the next day, Julie blurted, "I'm really upset about the drawers not fitting right."

I must have looked at her strangely because she next said, "I had an architect visiting here last night, and he told me to say that."

She had a right to say it, even if it was out of character. Sometimes when you build something, you get so close to it that you fail to step back and see the big picture. And in the big picture the drawers were uneven. I fixed them.

I couldn't help but wonder how her teenage son felt about an architect visiting Julie's bedroom last night.

I do know that a few days later, when I was working alone in the house, her teenage son came home with another boy and a girl. The big word among them was "I got really bummed last night." *Bummed* meant stoned or drunk or wasted.

The girl told the boys she'd "partied" last night until 4 a.m. Then I heard her get on the phone and lie for an hour, telling her parents she'd fallen asleep in the Varsity Theater. By phone, they grounded her. She left. With her gone, the boys graded her various body parts.

I cleaned up and departed and didn't see Julie for about twenty years.

I was installing low-voltage lighting at an estate in Atherton. The owner, a wealthy man whose name you would recognize, pulled me off the task to help set up temporary paper-globe lighting in the backyard trees for a party that evening. The event planners had underestimated how big the job would be.

I was still on a ladder among the cherry trees when the first guests arrived.

"Is that you?" said a familiar voice. It was Julie, dressed to the nines, looking twenty years older but none the worse for it. She had long, lovely silver hair. Accompanying her was a dapper man in a tuxedo.

I wasn't muddy that day, but I was wearing a tool belt and cutoff shorts. "Hey, how ya doing?" I said.

Julie peered at me with concern and perhaps a touch of pity. "Are you *still* contracting?"

I guess my life no longer seemed so romantic. Here was the high-school-reunion moment: Where did he go wrong? Such promise, unfulfilled.

Her face softened. "We should talk," Julie said.

But we couldn't. I had more lights to string, and then my tool belt and cutoffs would need to disappear from this affair. The caterers were already wheeling out tables of food, sensational wines.

I'll never know whether Julie wanted to congratulate me for my integrity or scold me for failing to live up to my potential. Either way, she'd be wrong. Maybe she just wanted to discuss the current state of American literature.

She seemed happy.

I wanted to ask what became of her son. And then I could have told her that the mirror still hangs in my closet, where every morning I catch a glimpse of myself. Still cracked.

The Road Not Taken

Clawfoot Bathtub

July 1979

In a wrecking yard in San Jose I find treasure: a clawfoot tub almost six feet long. Love at first sight. From what old house did it come? What old man's weary bones did it soak?

I'm building my new home. I have a bad back. I'm a bath junkie. I listen to music, read books, even write novels while I heat my spine in warm water. I must have that tub.

The junkyard helps load it into the back of my pickup. At home there's nobody to help me unload, so for several days I drive around the peninsula in a bath-truck, bringing smiles to passersby. If I had a little bell like the ice cream man, I could rent time in my portable spa.

Eventually a friend helps me bring it into the house.

It becomes—second to the kitchen—a focal point of home life. There is something insanely appealing about a clawfoot tub. This one can hold a half dozen kids. Visiting children—and the occasional adult—often end up in the bubbles with a flotilla of toys. My favorite is a wind-up submarine. Also a tooting tugboat.

For six years the tub sits on the unfinished rough-wood subfloor next to the old brick chimney that cuts through our bathroom. Instead of tiled walls, surrounding the tub on three sides is prime-painted drywall. We're too busy raising kids and finishing other parts of the house. It's a miracle the gypsum survives all that splashing.

Monday, May 11, 1987

Finally, the time comes to finish the bathroom. Our kids are older, no longer into the group-bath scene. A clawfoot makes for a lousy shower. Three of the feet are broken, replaced by 4×4 blocks. The porcelain is stained, chipped—always was, but somehow it never bothered us while the rest of the room was so raw.

My third and youngest child is about to graduate from Nursery Blue, the same preschool my other children attended.

On May 11, 1987, once again the old tub rides in the back of my pickup. At Nursery Blue twenty children climb over it for water games, sand games, puppet shows, whatever the kids can imagine.

Some people bequeath a legacy to a school. Sometimes a wing or an entire building is built in their honor. I leave a bathtub.

September 2010

My grandson enters the warm and exciting world of Nursery Blue. To my delight the tub is still there, now filled with dirt and planted with petunias. I'd penciled a poem on the side. Along the years, somebody painted over what I wrote, but I still remember:

Grandfather Tub

I give this old claw-footed bathtub
to the citizens of Nursery Blue
and hope that someday when I
am unfashionable, rusty, chipped,
I too can be recycled
for the joy of young children.

Indeed, twenty-four years after the writing I pick up my grandson from school two days a week. I am recycled.

Assessment

Tuesday, January 13, 1981

The biggest job I ever tackled was when I built my own house. My wife and I bought a solid little 600-square-foot cabin on a quarter acre in La Honda. We wrapped an addition around the cabin, creating a house of 2,000 square feet, and I'm proud of it.

We had the final inspection; we're signed off. Today the tax assessor comes out to take a look. Let's call him Earl.

When Earl knocks on my door, he says, "Before I assess your house, come on out to my car for a minute. I want to show you something."

There's nothing slick about Earl. He wears a loosened tie, no jacket, sleeves rolled up. At the car he pulls out a tax assessment list for La Honda. He points to some entries. "See this lot? One acre, kinda hilly but you could build a nice house there. The assessment is forty thousand dollars. Then here, look at this. I rated this one myself. Also one acre, almost level, horse property, lots of sunshine, great view, fit for a king, and the assessment last year was for ten thousand." Earl shakes his head. "A bit of variation, wouldn't you say?"

"Yep," I say.

"Okay, let's take a look at your house."

He walks through the interior talking about how he could give us a break on one thing or another, like counting that unfinished half bathroom as a storage closet, and then he says, "Come on back to the car."

He gets into the driver's seat. Reaching across, he opens the passenger door, then brushes some hamburger wrappers onto the floor. "Come on in," he says.

I sit inside.

"Close the door," he says.

I close the door.

"Well?" he says.

It's pretty clear that this is the moment when I'm supposed to hand him a bribe. Or is this a trap? I'd always heard that government in California was clean, not like Chicago. I've never heard a word about scandal in San Mateo County. But here he is. Here I am.

"Uh, thanks for looking at my house," I say, and I get out of the car. Earl drives away.

In the mail I receive my new tax assessment, and it is definitely on the high side.

Thirty years later, it still rankles me. I don't mind paying my fair share, and yet . . . If I'd slipped him a few twenties, how many thousands of dollars would I have saved over the years? And how many of my neighbors took advantage of what he was offering?

The Road Not Taken

Friday, August 27, 1982

The client paid cash. The job, illegal. No permit; no records. I'd been happy to oblige.

Now I stop for gas. In my wallet, a nest of one-hundred-dollar bills. Thirty of them.

Across the street, a sign:

FREEWAY ENTRANCE

US 101

NORTH

I hold the gas nozzle, thinking, *North*.

At least once in your married, child-raising life, who hasn't had the thought?

The old truck has new brakes. Good tires. A tank full of fuel.

In three days, maybe four, I can be in Alaska alone with a truck full of tools. Pipeline work. No questions asked. Cool mountains, clean rivers. Free, strong, and . . . thirty-four. Or is it -five?

Inside the minimart I pay for the gas, glance at the wide glass doors of the cooler next to the register. Rose asked me to pick up some strawberry yogurt on the way home from work. And—what was it? Oh, yeah. Laundry soap.

A White Rabbit

August 1982

New neighbors. A U-Haul truck pulls up to the cabin across the street. I go over to say hello.

A man is unloading furniture. He tells me his wife and daughter will be living here because "they're having trouble adjusting to the city." The man will be staying in San Francisco and visiting when he can.

His wife, Madrina, is a deliciously beautiful woman with dark, crazy eyes. She is racing exuberantly in and out of the house, playing with a not-so-little girl who is wearing diapers. Neither the beautiful Madrina nor the girl in diapers makes eye contact with me. The girl's name is Chloe.

"I hope you'll, uh, keep an eye on the place," the man says, and I take him to mean more than just the maintenance.

In front of the cabin they place a wire cage containing a white rabbit, the tamest member of the household.

A few days later I get a call from the man. He says the toilet is overflowing in Madrina's cabin.

Wedged in the toilet bowl I find a paperback copy of a novel by Richard Adams—about a rabbit civilization—called *Watership Down*.

When I come out of the bathroom, Madrina is sitting in a chair with her shirt pulled up, breasts bared. Chloe is standing on the floor, nursing. The girl's diaper has fallen to her ankles. Chloe must be about four years old.

"Your children should come over and play with Chloe sometime," Madrina says.

Somehow that play date never happens.

Another day I'm unloading my truck when I hear cries from the forest. Subconsciously I think it's the sound of kids playing. After about fifteen minutes the sound penetrates some filter in my brain—or maybe the quality of the sound changes—and it registers as a soft singsong: "Help me help me help me help me."

I run up the hill. On a hot day I'm wearing shorts and sandals, climbing through blackberry brambles and poison oak. First I find Chloe. She's calling, "Mommy! Mommy!" Her bare feet are full of thorns. Higher up the hill I see Madrina, naked, rolling in leaves.

I lift Chloe and carry her down the hill. In my arms she says, "Mommy ran away because I was crying all day." Oh, shit—she thinks it's her fault.

A neighbor woman takes the child. I return up the hill.

Madrina is crouched in the hollow of a redwood tree. Stupidly—but what words would be right?—I say, "Madrina, how can I help you?"

She seizes my hand—her face possessed by demons—and presses my fist to her belly, knuckles squeezing into heat, grit, firmness of flesh. Her sweat sizzles.

For a moment I'm paralyzed.

She has dimpled thighs, dark electric hair, dazed eyes. Utterly woman, utterly wild.

The La Honda Volunteer Fire Brigade arrives. Then the sheriff. Then two sheriff's rescue cars. A fireman takes Madrina's arm, wraps her body in a blanket, stuffs her into the cab of a fire truck the color of blood.

The back of my fingers tingle as if sparks had flown from that hot, sandy belly.

Flashing lights go suddenly dark. The radio sputters farewell.

Neighbors disperse. Soon street and forest are silent. We will never see Madrina or Chloe again.

A couple days later there's a white rabbit hopping in my yard. Chloe's bunny, loose. Jesse, my five-year-old son, lures it with a carrot. He accompanies me as I carry the rabbit across the street.

We place the bunny in its cage. The cabin is empty and silent.

A few days later, rabbit and cage are gone.

Brotherhood of the Sidewalk

Saturday, January 22, 1983

I'm replacing the water heater in my brother's garage. Because of the rain, I back my truck into his little driveway, blocking the sidewalk, so I have easy access to tools and supplies.

My brother, Ed, lives in Albany, which is a lively, funky, low-rent town just north of Berkeley.

As I work, a woman outside starts ranting to her companion in a self-righteous voice about how "some people think they can park anywhere."

Her voice cuts through the drumming of rain. "Some people think they're the center of the world."

The voice is shrill, deadly, rising in pitch: "Some people think they own the whole sidewalk."

Irritated, without thinking I call out, "For two bits you can have it!"

She barks indignantly, "What? *What* did you say?"

Oh, shit. I've yelled at an old lady in Albany. I'm pretty sure that's against the code around here. Albany is a psychic extension of Berzerkeley, where rioting is a regular weekend sport. I imagine a picket line, university students throwing rocks, a mob of old ladies banging on my truck with umbrellas, police lobbing tear gas.

Ed is at my side. He shouts, *"For two bits you can have it!"* Our eyes meet in spontaneous solidarity. I love him so much at that moment.

The woman says to her companion, "Did you hear that?"

"Well, I never!"

"Who do they think they are?"

"We should *report* them!"

And so on. But as they speak, they move on. What remains is the flash of brotherhood.

Nobody riots. Nobody returns. The weather's too nasty.

When I finish, as always, we argue about whether he should pay me anything. The argument ends when Ed violently stuffs some twenty dollar bills in my pocket. He's my big brother; he always wins.

"You shouldn't have blocked the sidewalk," he says.

"I know," I say.

El Niño

Monday, March 7, 1983

It has rained for twenty of the last twenty-four days. The road is treacherous with mudslides and drop-offs. In the truck, after work, I'm driving the kids home from school, telling them that next weekend we will meet a cousin from France and take her on a ferry ride to Sausalito. My daughter, age four, touches my arm and with a serious, concerned-for-my-welfare look on her face says, "Daddy, fairies aren't real."

We stop at the post office in "downtown" La Honda. As I step out of the truck, a powerful gust of pelting raindrops nearly blows me off my feet. The door slams open. Across the street the redwood trees above the church bend like giants bowing in prayer. The rush of wind through branches sounds like a low-flying Blue Angel jet. There is a *Crack!*—a sound so forceful I feel it pass through my body. Instinctively I duck. No tree in sight is falling. My daughter says, "Daddy, I'm scared."

I say, "Me too."

"Why did you duck?"

"I thought a tree was falling."

After a moment of thought she asks, "How would ducking help?"

Another half mile to the house. As the kids and I pile out of the truck, my neighbor George comes running down the road. Without a word he grabs me in a bear hug and clings to me, shaking with sobs. We are not close, George and I, certainly not hugging close, but we are neighborly. George teaches math at Foothill College.

"George, what happened?"

"My house," George says, letting go.

A fir tree has crushed the house, splitting the top floor in half.

"Anybody hurt?"

"No. It got Inga's too."

We're still getting pebbled by rain. I usher the kids indoors. The power is out.

Together George and I walk up the road. Inga has just built a brand new cabin. It's smashed. I installed the plumbing just a week ago. Inga's not home.

The tree was uphill from Inga and George. Inga had hired a cutter to trim the lower branches. She'd wanted more light. With only its top branches the fir had looked like a lollipop. Now that it had no lower branches to spread the load, the gust of wind had bent the top to the breaking point while the bottom remained straight. The *Crack* I had heard from a half mile away was the trunk, three feet in diameter of healthy, strong Douglas fir, snapping above head-level and leaving a spar. The unbelievably heavy top of the tree—about a hundred feet of it—apparently had sailed, striking Inga's cabin, slicing it like a hatchet through a cupcake, and then landing farther downhill on top of George's house.

The spar smells of sap and fresh, bleeding fir, as if someone had just mopped the road with Pine-Sol. As George and I stand there staring at two wasted houses, another rush of wind builds to a climax as before our eyes a hundred tall redwoods wave like rippling stalks of red wheat. Redwoods, in spite of their size, can flex—for centuries. The Douglas fir is a stiffer tree, stronger but less yielding. Fir trees go down all the time.

Inga's cabin is a total loss. George's house is half demolished—the upper floor is gone while, incredibly, the lower floor is untouched. The roof must have slowed the fall of the tree, and then the joists stopped it. I open and close doors, marveling to George that the frame of the first floor must be perfectly straight or else the doors would be binding. The contractor built it tight.

George is not listening. He bolts out of his house and throws up in the driveway.

George's phone is out but mine is working. He calls his wife at work, telling her not to come home. "There is no home," he says. He's going back over the hill to get a room in a motel. He doesn't even want to return to the house for clothes or a toothbrush. He's gone.

I don't think I'll ever see him again.

A branch fell on my own roof and stabbed right through it like a dagger. I don't dare go up there in the wind and the wet. I shut off Inga's gas and water. She still hasn't come home; somebody says she's in New Mexico buying sheepskins—she makes jackets and sells them at flea markets.

My wife arrives home after a scary drive, big branches in the road, asphalt slick with mud. We light lanterns and build a fire for warmth. She feeds the kids, cooking on a camp stove. I place buckets, catching drips. Then we move downstairs, taking a lesson from George's house. Downstairs, a roof and then joists might protect us.

We consider spending the night somewhere else. I refuse. Some instinct, possibly a bad one endangering my family, will not let me abandon this house that I built, where less than one year ago my third child was born, where we plan to live out our lives. This is home.

Most of the night the wind blows through the redwoods, a pulsating roar like surf in a storm. Branches rip and fly. Downstairs we all sleep together in one room, a bobbing sea of blankets: three kids, one dog, my wife, myself, and a flickering candle. In the middle of the night there is a thunderstorm. With each clap of thunder I imagine the snap of a Douglas fir. For most of the time I lie awake, on guard — as if I could somehow take the blow, protect my family from a crashing tree.

By dawn the power returns. The candle lasted the night. Rain stops; wind ceases. The refrigerator hums, catching up.

So will I.

One Pressed Flower

Wednesday, July 27, 1983

First thing in the morning my six-year-old son sets the toaster on fire.

I pour baking soda into the slots.

Holding the toaster upside down over the kitchen sink, I shake out crumbs, ashes—and a scorched pink-rubber pencil eraser.

"Jesse, why did you put an eraser in the toaster?"

He shrugs.

It's an omen for the day, though I don't yet know it.

Yesterday, on the phone, Janice told me that her cabin is on a private road and the directions are "sort of complicated," so today she'll meet me in downtown Pescadero in front of Duarte's Tavern. "I'll be driving an Alfa Romeo with the top down. I have white hair. You'll recognize me. I sort of stand out."

Yes, she does.

Janice is lovely, an albino in dark sunglasses, bright hair blowing like a sexual semaphore in the wind. The cabin is indeed a long way from town but wouldn't have been difficult to find on my own. I suspect she met me in town because she wanted to check me out. Safety. Privacy.

We pass a sheep ranch.

> Clustered in the shade of a live oak tree:
> dirty ragged balls of yarn.
> And two tail-wagging yarnlets.

In 1983 Pescadero is in the process of being discovered by city people who are buying up local acreage and constructing classy weekend getaways. Janice's spot is a hilltop surrounded by acres of golden meadow with a view of the ocean. Serene, lovely, isolated.

At the cabin I meet Janice's partner, Kate, yang to her yin, a dark beauty who sulks on a sofa by a corner window. She's reading a book, sipping lemonade, frowning, sighing.

I'm installing a fiberglass whirlpool two-person tub that Janice and Kate bought on their own. As it turns out, the tub doesn't quite fit in the roughed-out space. I inherited the problem; I didn't cause it. I have to notch the ledger board, sizing by trial and error. Then the drain doesn't fit. The mixing T is the wrong size. And the directions that came with the tub are utterly useless.

Working so far out in the country, you don't run to the hardware store when you encounter a problem. You improvise. Adapt. I'm used to country work and pretty good at it. I've brought a truckload of plumbing parts.

Just me on a hilltop with two beautiful women—there is a weird vibe. They don't act one bit friendly toward me. Occasionally they exchange glances. Janice has no expression; Kate scowls. Maybe it all means nothing.

It takes five hours. When I present the bill to Janice, Kate for the first time bestirs herself from the corner and says, "I feel totally ripped off."

"Why?" I'm stunned.

"We were supposed to leave here three hours ago."

"There were problems. I had to—"

"I saw you reading the directions."

"Of course I read the directions. Don't you think that's a good idea?"

"You should know already. You're supposed to be a plumber."

"I *am* a plumber. But there are thousands of different—"

"Simms could have installed it in half the time."

Simms is a Pescadero plumber. "No, he couldn't. Even if he didn't have to read the directions, he would have had the same problems. And if he's so good, why didn't you call him?"

"He's so expensive."

"So I did the job for less money and maybe took a few minutes longer."

"I feel totally ripped off."

Janice is fingering the bill. With a glance at Kate, she says to me, "We'll talk about this."

I leave in a state of shock. And utterly depressed. Sometimes you see trouble coming. Not this time. I did a darn good job.

Anybody who deals with the public knows that most people are fine, a few are difficult, and every once in a while, without warning, somebody will clobber you right between the eyes. It's that one rare customer who makes you want to quit. Kate has done that to me.

That night an old friend from college calls. She's working at Hewlett Packard and has quickly ascended to dizzying heights. I tell her about my day. She says, "You're too smart to be putting up with that crap. You're a writer. We need technical writers all the time. Come in for an interview." Then she quotes an hourly wage that is fifty percent more than I'm earning as a plumber. For writing! Incredible.

So a day later I'm in a glass cubicle being interviewed by a man with a sign on his desk: MANAGER OF THE ~~MONTH~~ ~~WEEK~~ DAY

He explains that he is the third manager of the section this week. He says the great thing about Hewlett Packard is the dynamism and adaptability of the culture here, that unlike most corporations it's flexible, and growing so fast they can hardly keep up. Then he asks about my experience in technical writing.

"Well, I read operating manuals."

"I mean, have you *done* any?"

"No."

"What about your training? Any classes in technical writing?"

"Uh, actually, no."

"What's your experience with computers?"

"I worked as a computer operator in college and for several years after that."

"When was your last computer job?"

"Seven years ago."

"A lot has changed."

"I'm flexible. Dynamic. Adaptable."

"Why'd you quit?"

"I wanted to write novels. It just didn't mix with a computer job."

"But you think it would mix now?"

"Yes."

As my friend told me to do, I leave two of my novels as samples of my writing. One of them is *The Naked Computer,* a somewhat psychotic novel I wrote just out of college, published—wretchedly—by a small press in San Francisco. I don't know what I'm thinking, offering it as a work sample. The title, I guess. The other book is *Famous Potatoes,* the seemingly autobiographical story of an alienated young man who works occasionally as a computer operator and is a total fuck-up. Not the best resume.

I never hear back from the manager-of-the-day, nor from anybody at Hewlett Packard. I'm sure he took the novels as a compilation of my life. And gave it a bad review.

Meanwhile, more jobs come in: carpentry, plumbing, electrical. I slog along. I appreciate the physical immediacy of manual labor. It's a kind of therapy.

You can't predict a pencil eraser in the toaster. You just deal with it. You put out the fire.

After two weeks, Janice mails a check folded into a note card with a photo of an elephant seal. Full payment. A better review. There is no written note, only one pressed flower.

Since the House Is On Fire,
Let Us Warm Ourselves

Friday, December 9, 1983

My daughter, Ruth, age five, sleeps in the top bunk. This morning when I wake her she sits up, looking puzzled. She leans over the side railing and vomits all over the lower bed, which, fortunately, my son has just vacated.

Cheerfully she says, "Well, Daddy, you never know what will happen next, do you?"

She's fine. So fine that she goes to school while I work on a bathroom that I'm building in a garage (without a permit, for a Superior Court judge). The judge greets me saying, "Could I make an observation?" Leading me to the garage, he points out that the shower unit I installed yesterday can only be entered by stepping over the toilet.

Oops. So I spend half the day rotating the shower. While cutting copper pipe I gash my index finger.

Checking an electrical connection outside, shoving some leaves aside, suddenly I'm eyeball to eyeballs with a tarantula. Hairy. The size of a golf ball. It's injured. One leg appears to be broken. I did that. I'm so sorry.

On the way home, making a stop at Orchard Supply Hardware, I'm lightheaded, feeling as though I'm constantly falling. I guess the finger's infected where I gashed it on the pipe. Standing in the checkout line, I almost faint but somehow stifle it by telling myself not to make an ass of myself. That is, more of an ass.

Back home, stepping inside, the house is full of dark diesel smoke. In the basement, flames are erupting out the sides of the old oil furnace. I hear my wife, Rose, arriving with the kids and tell them to wait outside, not to panic but please just—*please*—stay outside. Running downstairs, I point the fire extinguisher, wondering if it still works after three years of hanging on the wall—and it does. Foam, foam, everywhere foam. Only then does it occur to me to shut off the electrical switch that powers the oil pump.

The temperature's going down to twenty-five degrees tonight. The house smells like a truck stop. Could've been a disaster if I hadn't come home just then.

We open windows and go to the local restaurant for a spaghetti dinner, the cheapest meal. We never eat out, can't afford it. To the kids it's a treat, a special occasion.

Back home we close the windows and turn on two electric space heaters. The kids all bed down in the living room in front of the fireplace, which the dog thinks is a wonderful idea. My wife and I prefer the comfort of a mattress, so we heap a mound of blankets on the bed. Only now, snuggling near midnight, do we have time to talk, to tell each other about our day. Rose thinks the tarantula bit me. "But," she says, "it probably won't kill you."

May the little beast thrive somehow, seven-legged, sheltered again under its pile of leaves. A female tarantula can live for thirty years.

We awaken to sunbeams streaming in the window through a slight haze of lingering smoke and the scent of burnt oil. In the bathroom there's ice in the bottom of the water glass. We still have a house. We have our lives. It will be a day of cleanup, hot chocolate, warm jackets; but the sunshine feels cheerful, and, really, you never know what will happen next, do you?

Sunsets

October 1984

Mrs. K asked me to do an unusual project: convert a sauna into an in-law unit. Her husband was CEO of a Very Large Bank. She looked to be about fifty years old. Mr. K, who was proud of her looks, said she was seventy-two (which irritated her). (And I hadn't asked.) They lived on a hilltop with a breathtaking view over the Santa Cruz Mountains to the Pacific Ocean.

"Oh! Would you *look* at that *sky!*" she said.

"It will cost three-thousand, six-hundred-fifty dollars," I said, "but if you step over here I'll show you how we can eliminate . . ."

"Oh! But just *look* at that *sky!*"

> She has white hair to my brown,
> bright eyes to my lids hanging down.

I was trying to give an estimate; her eyes were on the sky. Her husband and I were annoyed that she wasn't paying attention. As I drove home, I started cursing myself for not joining her, not pausing to appreciate the splendor on display.

> I will never live that long.
> She knows a better song.
> To close one more deal
> to pay one more debt,
> I miss
> one more sunset.

Sometimes, though, you need to keep your eye on the job.

A few years later—after I converted the sauna, after several more projects—I saw their names in the newspaper. It was a car accident near Monterey. Their beloved old Mercury flew off the highway and into a drainage ditch next to an artichoke farm. Two field workers beat out the flames and ran from the cops, though it didn't matter. She and her husband were already dead. Instantly. The police speculated that the setting sun was in the driver's eyes, blinding her. I think I know what really happened.

"Oh! Would you *look* at that *sky!*"

What's My Crime?

What's My Crime?

Friday, April 8, 1983

Once a week I meet Sonny at a cafe in Los Altos. We sit at the counter talking shop. He's become a specialist at hanging doors, and today he offers me a job as his assistant. I say I don't feel qualified and, anyway, I have all the work I need right now.

"I'll do it," says a voice. It's a man sitting two stools away stirring a cup of cold coffee. "You need a carpenter? My name's Gary." He begins telling Sonny that he's a chemical engineer with a bad health history. Just out of the hospital and might have to go back, so nobody will hire him, but he'll work for peanuts and he knows what to do if Sonny will just loan him seventy-five dollars for a bus to Seattle where his tools are in storage.

Silently the waitress is shaking her head.

Sonny turns him down.

Then Gary sets to work on me, saying he'll do anything. By now I judge he's either an alcoholic or a nut. Gently I turn him down.

Gary smiles, shakes his head, understanding that I understand.

Gary has been glancing out the window toward a Ford station wagon, where a woman and two children are staring back at him. The woman looks wild like an alpine stream, splashy and rocky and cold as snowmelt. The kids are freckly, dirty, hollow-cheeked. Hungry.

Suddenly Gary jerks to his feet and dashes to the men's room.

The waitress follows him with her eyes, then turns to Sonny and me. "He's throwing up in there," she says. "It's true, most of what he said. He's sick. He's out of the hospital. Napa."

She pauses to let the word Napa sink in. Napa is a state-run psychiatric hospital.

"It's true he was a chemical engineer," the waitress continues. "But he kind of forgot to mention that he served time in San Quentin. That was before he met her." She glances at the woman in the Ford. "And got them." Glancing at the kids.

"And if I gave him bus fare?" Sonny asks.

"You'd be out seventy-five dollars," the waitress says. "And that's okay as long as you know where it's going. He's worked a couple of churches. Bus fare for a funeral in Vancouver. The money doesn't go far. I've seen him taking old milk from the dumpster out back. For the kids. I just happened to throw away a can of peanut butter and a perfectly good loaf of bread. For them. But . . . jeez."

I ask, "How do you know all this?"

"Police. They sit here and talk. It's not against the law to live in a car like that, but some people are saying it's child abuse, milk from a dumpster."

"Couldn't they get help?"

"People try. Hey, I tried. Some people can't take help. Help has . . . conditions." She shakes her head. "I don't like it, but I've got to say . . ." She winces, as if it hurts. "It's something like love. What they've got. It's almost cute."

In a glance, Sonny and I come to silent agreement: we'll buy Gary a "bus ticket." The waitress reads our faces and says, "I'll kick in twenty-five."

We don't get the chance.

Returning from the rest room, Gary sees two police cars parked outside, one on each side of the station wagon. A policeman is talking through the window to the woman inside.

Gary rushes to the door of the cafe and is met by an officer who puts him in handcuffs.

"What's my crime?" Gary says. "What's my crime?"

A week later, as usual, Sonny and I meet at the same cafe. The station wagon is parked nearby, stuffed with sleeping bags and clothing and filth but no people.

There's a different waitress at the counter. "Where's Gary?" Sonny asks.

"Who?" says the waitress.

Next week, the car is gone.

The Jogging Bandit

Wednesday, April 20, 1983

His name was Bob Bullitt. He liked to jog in rich neighborhoods. He volunteered at the La Honda school, coaching kids to run long distance.

He called me one day. He lived in a crummy little shack behind the La Honda grocery store. "I need an estimate for wiring a kiln," he said, meeting me at the front door, blocking entry with his body. He showed me the kiln in the back yard—220 volt. Above his roof I could see the weatherhead for the electrical service entrance, but no panel box.

I said, "I need to see your circuit breaker box."

"It's fuses. Old stuff."

"Okay. I need to look at your fuse box."

"It's inside." He doesn't move. "Maybe some other time," he says.

Caged in the yard are two rabbits, fifty pigeons. Uncaged, one cat. Nutcase, I thought.

About a month later, he was arrested. They called him the Jogging Bandit. His house was the Louvre of La Honda. No visitors, no guests. Within mildewed walls, under a leaky roof, he ate off gold plates. With Queen Anne silver. On rare oriental rugs.

He never burgled La Honda. It wouldn't be neighborly. Besides, nobody in La Honda had what Bob was seeking: the good life of old money.

He wore gloves and could vanish like a quark. He didn't steal stereos. He took art. Antiques. And a cat.

The cat did him in: an abyssinian worth two grand, hanging around the grocery eating scraps, scratching fleas. Some flatlander on the way to the beach stopped for potato chips and recognized a valuable feline. When the cops arrived, Bob ran like a fox among the redwoods. They hunted him down.

He was convicted of twenty-one counts of burglary and was suspected of ripping off about five hundred homes along his old jogging route in Atherton, Woodside, Portola Valley, Stanford.

The loot was worth two and a half million dollars.

He couldn't sell it. He would've done better stealing televisions. But Bob was not the first to suffer in the pursuit of art.

A year after Bob was caught, I'm called to snake a sink drain in another run-down La Honda shack. Molly Bullitt, a pretty woman, dark-haired, with girl-next-door freckles, lets me in. The name should have tipped me off, but I don't recognize her until I see a gold plate on the plastic table.

"Is that—?"

"Please don't tell," she says, smiling shyly. Behind her, two kids are clutching teddy bears. "It's the only one. It's all I've got."

She's living on food stamps. Even if she wants to sell the plate she can't. It's the same problem Bob had. She's probably safe here. Who would turn her in? La Honda is, at heart, an outlaw town.

We chat. "He didn't jog," she says. "That isn't how he did it. They were looking for a jogger, which is why he got away so many times."

But of course! You can't jog with an oriental rug in your arms. A framed Monet. A kiln.

"Then how did he do it?"

She smiles again, shy and secretive. No answer.

I give her a break on the labor charge. Licking her fingers, counting out bills, she pays cash.

The Bill

Monday, April 2, 1984

For seven and a half hours Mr. Lunder follows me around through the five apartments he owns in Mountain View. He says, "I had a handyman before you who charged half as much."

"So why isn't he your handyman now?"

"It got sticky," Mr. Lunder says.

I don't say so, but his previous handyman did shoddy work—and I'm fixing it.

I'm happy to have owners watch me work, ask questions, chat, as long as it's of a friendly nature or out of a genuine curiosity to learn what I'm doing. Mr. Lunder is neither friendly nor curious. He's standing over me, checking his watch and frowning. I'm beginning to see why it got sticky.

Among other chores, I patch a foot-size hole in a wall. Mr. Lunder says his previous handyman could have had that wall patch mirror-smooth in one pass. I say you can't do that. You have to let it dry, then come back and finish it—and his handyman would have done that too.

In the morning, before I came to this job, I called Mr. Lunder. Because space in my truck was tight that day with a cabinet I was delivering, I asked if I needed to bring my plumbing tools. *No*, he said. Now he asks me to replace a sink drain. "Can't," I say. "I didn't bring my plumbing tools. You told me I wouldn't need them."

"No, I didn't."

I install a timer for a recirculating hot water pump. Mr. Lunder only wants the water to recirculate when people are likely to use it. This man is cheap, which is okay, but irrational, which isn't. The price of the timer and the labor to install it will cost more than he will ever save on utility bills. And saving money is the only motivation—he couldn't care less about the environment.

When I finish with the recirculating pump, the thermostat quits working. I try to test it, but Mr. Lunder is fussing, distracting me: "What happened? Did you break it? Don't you know how to put it together? Can't you do anything?"

"Please be quiet so I can think."

When Mr. Lunder talks, he doesn't meet my eyes. He's short, so he's talking to my chest or else looking away toward a wall. He says, "Have you ever worked on a recirculating pump before?"

"Yes. Once or twice."

"Did you break those ones, too?"

"I didn't break this. Please be quiet so I can think."

"I'd better call a real plumber."

The man has me thoroughly rattled. I give up. "I'll have to get a new one," I say.

"You'll pay for it," Mr. Lunder says.

"I didn't break that thermostat. But I'll go out right now and get a new one. Let's see how much it costs. Then we can talk about it."

"Just leave," Mr. Lunder says. "Don't come back. This whole job is a botch."

"What did I botch?"

"The wall. The thermostat. You didn't even bring your plumbing tools."

"I'm not charging you for plumbing. I didn't *do* any plumbing. But I *will* charge you for the work I've done."

"I don't think I can pay you."

"Why not?"

"It's a rip-off. I'll have to call my mother about this."

At this moment, I realize I'm dealing with a sick man. Sick in the head. Which doesn't give me one bit of sympathy toward him. He is one irritating little fart. I write out a bill. I raise my voice as I say, "I'd like you to pay me *right now*."

Mr. Lunder flinches at the raised voice. Interesting. He says, "I have to call my mother. I don't think she'd approve paying a crook."

I raise my voice another notch. "Mr. Lunder, I am not in the business of ripping people off. I've been doing this for eight years now. I can give you a list of references as long as your arm. I have a waiting list. I have to turn away jobs."

"Don't shout at me. I have a heart condition. Don't get me excited."

I raise my voice another notch. "You're questioning my honesty. My integrity. Your previous handyman probably installed that thermostat *wrong* and it would've stopped working no matter *who* touched it next." I'm so angry I'm shaking.

Mr. Lunder backs off a bit. He looks fearful. "This bill is unprofessional," he says. "You wrote it in pencil."

"Got a pen? I'll write a new one."

"You should have a pen. You should be more professional. I'm not paying you for the time we spent talking."

"I already wrote the bill. This talk is free."

"We spent time talking before the job."

"Of *course* we did. You had to show me what you wanted me to do."

"I shouldn't have to pay for talking."

"God *damn* you annoy me!"

"Now you're shouting. I'll pay you half. This is hurting my heart. I'll pay you half just to get rid of you."

He's right—I'm shouting. He's also right that it was unprofessional not to bring my plumbing tools. And the time spent talking would normally be negotiable but not with this man. Not now. I continue shouting: *"Call your mother! Tell her I'm taking you to court!"*

"Keep my mother out of this."

"I'll take your mother to court!"

Mr. Lunder is clutching his heart.

I feel cruel. I don't care. "PAY ME NOW OR I'LL KEEP SHOUTING!" This isn't me, I'm thinking. But it is.

Still he hesitates.

"I'll knock off fifty dollars. Okay? Now please pay the fucking bill."

"Sixty."

"JESUS CHRIST!"

"Fifty-five."

One Mississippi. Two Mississippi . . . Ten Mississippi. "All right."

With shaking fingers, Mr. Lunder writes a check.

I drive straight to his bank and cash it. As the cashier counts out the money at the teller window, my own fingers are trembling.

A few weeks later, examining a similar thermostat, I realize that I had reversed the wires in Mr. Lunder's device. If he'd just left me alone for a minute, I would have figured it out.

There is no redeeming way to end this story. Physical work isn't just physical. There are personalities involved. Personal chemistry. The wrong mix can explode.

To my credit, I was never tempted to lay a hand on him. And yet I almost killed that man. Death by shouting.

Jerry the Tile Man

May 1986

Jerry lived by the creek down the hill from me. He scuffed out a living doing odd jobs. He was a short man with eyeglasses, rough speech, somewhat older than me.

I hired Jerry to rototill the hillside below my house. This would be about 1980. He did the job over several hot days—hard work for cheap pay. We talked a bit. Though his speech was unschooled, there was something respectful in his manner, the way he'd adjust his glasses, cock his head to the side, and squint up at you as he spoke. He didn't curse. He was good with machines, if coaxing and maintaining that old rototiller was any indication.

In those subtle ways you can't quite explain, you sensed that you could trust this guy, that there was a history to him—and a future—of more than odd jobs. Maybe his life had taken a detour. Maybe the world had chosen him for random bad luck. Jerry was guided by a moral core and would find his way back.

Around town Jerry and I would see each other from time to time, exchange a few words, pass on.

One evening I brought my kids to the La Honda school so they could roller skate on the flat parking lot. At the same time, an Alcoholics Anonymous meeting was taking place in the school multipurpose room. When the AA meeting ended, among the people walking out was Jerry.

Another time at the school Jerry was among a group at an adult literacy class. I thought of the time I'd shown Jerry a newspaper clipping and he'd said he didn't have his reading glasses.

All this time, Jerry was fixing up the old wreck of a house he'd bought down by the creek. He gave me a tour of what he'd done. This was an honor, as Jerry didn't like having visitors. The place was magnificent, a work of love, a museum of self-taught craftsmanship. Among his treasures was a bathroom of wonderful tiles. I asked if he liked tile work. *Yes.* I offered him a job at my house.

Jerry, I discovered, was a natural designer. He talked me into adding an alcove between the studs, which would add difficulty to the project but didn't seem to worry him. He suggested adding a corner soap dish he'd found at a flea market. He was a perfectionist. He laid a solid base and then meticulously, artistically set the tile. A natural craftsman. Some people are born to it.

I recommended Jerry to some clients of mine.

At one job I removed a toilet for a wealthy stockbroker and his wife. Jerry would retile the floor, and then I would install a new water closet. Jerry asked if he could haul the old crapper away, offering some cockamamie story: "I want to break it up and spread it on my driveway." Of course it was fine with the stockbroker.

Later I asked Jerry, "Did you really break up that toilet?" It was a one-piece lo-boy model, once considered the Mercedes of toilets around here.

"Of course not," Jerry said. "I just didn't want them to realize what it was worth."

He had no idea what world these people lived in, how trivial small sums of money would be to them, how they would never engage in something as demeaning as the sale of a twenty-year-old toilet.

I called Jerry back to my house for another tile project, this one a fireplace. He asked if my clients were happy. I told him my clients loved his work and he should be charging what he was worth. He was billing fifteen dollars an hour when the going rate was thirty to forty dollars.

While he set tile around my fireplace, Jerry told me a bit about his life. He grew up near San Francisco. He and his wife were high-school sweethearts. Jerry took over his father's liquor store. One day three men held up the store. They made everybody lie on the floor. Jerry thought he was going to die. The men ran out. Jerry ran out after them with a pistol and fired six shots. He hit one guy in the shoulder, who was arrested when he went to the hospital. Jerry was in trouble for shooting a fleeing man. And Jerry decided he'd had enough. He got out of the business and moved to La Honda. It was the beginning of a bad period, he said. Then cocking his head with a squinty half-smile he said, "Lately I think it's the beginning of a better one."

I'd given him a break just when he needed it. I hired him, recommended him to clients, got him started on a path that used his talent. Mostly, of course, he did it himself. Rehab jobs aren't always of houses, and the best are the ones you do yourself.

At the end of the fireplace job, he gave me a bill. The labor charge was at thirty-five dollars an hour. I had to laugh.

Jerry was back.

Knob and Tube

Friday, May 9, 1986

Lyle, the homeowner, a manager at Lockheed, keeps me waiting a half-hour and then arrives without apology. A bad sign. He shows me the job: install two low-voltage lights to spotlight the Steinway piano in his large living room. His wife will be giving a recital here.

Easily done. The only surprise is knob-and-tube wiring in a house that was built in the 1960s. Not a problem, just unexpected. Knob and tube started phasing out in the 1930s. When properly installed it's safe, but it's more costly and more trouble, offers no advantages, and has several disadvantages, including a relative incapacity for expansion as the electrical needs of the house increase. Lyle bought the house already built, so it wasn't his decision. But for the original builder, why knob and tube? Why would somebody choose a method that's more expensive and less adaptable? Nostalgia? For wiring?

It's as if the house has a birth defect hidden in its core, relatively benign: a central nervous system that can function adequately as long as no sophisticated demands are placed on it, an inability to grow and adapt.

When I finish, Lyle is pleased. The lighting is dramatic and effective. As I'm about to put away the ladder, Lyle points at three faint fingerprints that I left on the ceiling.

"Sorry," I say. "I'll get that."

"I'll do it. Hold the ladder."

With a moist sponge, Lyle climbs the ladder. He rubs. The fingerprints smear. He rubs harder, the smudge deepens. He's rubbing the stain into the flat paint. It's a blue sponge. Maybe some of the blue is joining the paint. Maybe the sponge was greasy already.

He's taken barely notable fingerprints and created a big mess.

"Here, you fix it," Lyle says, handing me the sponge.

With paper towels and some spray cleaner I try for salvage, but Lyle has already embedded a stain and removed half the paint.

"I want you to repaint my ceiling," Lyle says.

"What?"

"Those were *your* prints. This is all *your* fault."

"You did the rubbing, Lyle."

"*You're* the expert here! If you saw I was doing it wrong it was *your* job to stop me."

"Oh, come on, Lyle."

He's now shouting. He actually stomps his foot. *"YOU'RE THE ELECTRICIAN. NOT LEAVING FINGERPRINTS IS RULE NUMBER ONE! YOU KNOW THAT!"*

He hasn't paid. If I walk away, I'm kissing off $235. That's his point of power. My point of power is that I'm a grown-up. Lyle is suddenly an out-of-control four-year-old.

Two years ago, I let Mr. Lunder get under my skin. I've learned a few lessons since then.

I speak calmly, soothingly. "Lyle, for an electrician rule number one is 'Don't get electrocuted.' Number two is 'Don't cause a fire.' Number three is 'Make it work properly.'" I smile; he glares. I continue: "Yes, part of my job is to leave a clean site, but it's down around rule number fifty-six." Again I smile. He softens. "That doesn't excuse me, but let's acknowledge that I fulfilled the first fifty-five rules."

Lyle is calming down. His eyes were darting about. I think he knew he was losing control, and it frightened him. I have a four-year-old at home right now, my third time down this path. A kid will test the limits—throw a tantrum—but ultimately be reassured when the limits hold.

At this point I think there's no recourse but to repaint. Fortunately the ceiling is divided by faux wooden beams, so with a good color match it should only be necessary to repaint one two-foot-wide section. As soothingly as possible, I explain this to Lyle. We can share the responsibility. I offer a compromise: if he will take a paint chip to the store and get a color match, I will come back another day and do the painting. There should be plenty of time before his wife's recital.

As I'm speaking, it occurs to me that Lyle's pent-up anxiety about this recital has just been released in full fury at me. Unwittingly, I've served a purpose. I've released his tension.

Lyle agrees to the compromise.

I'm pretty sure the new paint won't look like a perfect match even if the color is right. It will be cleaner, fresher. I've deliberately structured this compromise so that Lyle is responsible for the color, not me. And given his sponging ability, I am responsible for applying the paint, not him.

We proceed as planned. A few days later I paint the section of ceiling between the beams. As I expected, the fresh panel looks slightly glossier, even with flat paint. Lyle doesn't notice. It's his color. In his knob-and-tube mind, he's incapable of making a mistake.

Two hours setting up, painting, cleaning up. Which is two hours of psychotherapy, unbillable. But I get my $235. Sheesh.

A few months later, Lyle calls. "The recital was magnificent," he says. "Now could you come over and install some new outlets in my kitchen?"

I love children. But I won't work for them. "I'm really busy right now, Lyle. I'll call you when I have time."

Somehow, I never find the time.

Unit #2

Monday, June 9, 1986

The manager shows me what needs to be done: decking, handrail, painting. Nodding her head toward one particular door, the manager says, "Stay away from number two."

"Why?"

"Just stay away."

It's a condo complex in Palo Alto. A row of second-floor units hangs over first-floor parking like a motel, a cheap look in an expensive neighborhood.

A sagging handrail: I tighten it. Loose decking: I screw it down, working in front of all the units, but skipping number two.

A teenage girl with tight pants, haughty eyes, red claws for fingers—looking cheap, like the building—bursts out of door number two onto the balcony. She's conducting a high-decibel, arm-waving, teary phone fight with her mother—outdoors, for better publicity. "How could you? How *could* you?" The subject seems to be her graduation present.

I move to the parking area where I'm to paint red diagonals for a no-parking zone. I've never done this before, but how hard can it be?

Traffic lines, I discover, require thick application of paint. Needing another quart, lacking cones, I set a cardboard box in front of the partially red-lined parking space and go to the hardware store.

Ten minutes later, I'm back.

Crap. Some son of a bitch has moved the cardboard box and parked on my red lines. A sharply dressed young man comes out of condo number two, looks right through me, gets in his BMW and drives away. On the asphalt his tires print dashed lines of red leading to the street.

With paint thinner and a rag, I clean the tire marks up to the edge of the street. The dash marks continue, fading toward downtown Palo Alto.

After completing the diagonals, I pile more boxes in front of the parking space. On the cardboard I paint:

> DANGER
> TOXIC RED PAINT
> DESTROYS TIRES

All done. Clean the brushes. Lock the toolboxes. Start the motor. Aw, cripes. A limo—long, cold, black—is blocking the driveway to the entire complex.

I honk. Lean on the horn. Let me out of here.

A young man comes out of unit number two. He makes no apology or eye contact of any kind. A driver holds open the door. Wheels smoking, the limo speeds away.

The manager is right.

Just stay away from unit number two.

Diary of a Small Contractor

The Zen of Aluminum Windows

Tuesday, September 16, 1986

I shut off the engine. Suddenly there is silence except for the crackling of the motor as it cools. I'm scared.

Good. Fear inspires my best work.

I'm scared because there are hundreds of ways to goof up a job and only one way (or, at most, a few) to do it right.

My first task is in "the cottage," which is the original house built on this land in the 1930s. Now the cottage is used as a rental.

Two old wood windows are rotting. The tenant has stuffed newspapers into the holes. There's that musty, dusty smell like an old leather-bound book, partly powder.

It takes ten minutes to tear out the windows. They probably took hours to install plumb and tight. Makes me queasy. How easy it is to destroy a work of carpentry.

I'm no longer fearful. Like stage fright, it disappears as soon as you begin.

Gingerly, expecting the worst, with crowbar and screwdriver I pry the outside trim. Here's a surprise: the wood doesn't split. It's virgin redwood, tight-grained, bone dry. Wonderful wood. Fifty years on this house and not a trace of rot, even though the nails within it have nearly rusted out. More durable than steel, this wood.

The lumber probably came from a 600-year-old institution of a tree growing on this same mountain, felled in the desperation of the Great Depression. This vertical grain—clear heart—would be much too valuable to use as window framing today. Back then they used redwood for everything. It was cheap and convenient.

So should the new windows be cheap and convenient? It's up to the owners.

Mr. Barley is a retired professional. He has three Irish setters and wears a silver whistle on a lanyard around his neck. When he blows it, bedlam breaks loose as three dogs run to him and dance about, eager for a command.

Mrs. Barley is an elegant but easy-going woman, a gracious hostess with an East Coast accent. She seems to make all the decisions when it comes to questions of taste.

Choice of windows is the usual triangle: cost versus quality versus aesthetics. Plain aluminum: ugly and cheap. Bronzed aluminum: better-looking, twice the price. Thermopane glass: better insulation, twice the price. Wood windows: beautiful, three times the price.

Mrs. Barley sorts it out: If it were for her own house, she'd go for wood thermopanes. Since the cottage is a rental, wood is out of the question. Since the rest of the cabin is uninsulated, thermopane would not make a great difference. (Also unspoken, but present, is her apparent indifference to the comfort of the renters.) But she chooses bronzed because it looks better. Aesthetics, in this case, are worth doubling the price.

My next task is to install a screen door. I rip off the plastic and cardboard packaging, which says, "All hardware included."

There is no hardware.

There is supposed to be a closer, a handle, and a package of screws. From this mountain, the store where I bought the door is a thirty-minute drive.

I have screws. My truck is a miniature hardware store exactly because of situations like this. I can scavenge the handle from the old screen door. But there is no closer. For that, I will have to return on another day.

My next task is in the main house, which was built of adobe bricks in the 1950s on the side of a mountain overlooking the southern San Francisco Bay. A lovely spot. I can see over the smog of San Jose to Mount Hamilton, with a tiny white dot on its peak, the Lick Observatory, thirty miles away.

A ceiling has water damage. Mr. Barley says that the roof leaked but now is fixed. The damage is over a bed that is too heavy to move, so I cover it with a drop cloth. On the floor surrounding the massive master bed are three round dog beds. I slide them under the drop cloth. I place a sheet of plywood over the drop cloth to spread my weight over the mattress, and I stand on it, a bouncy platform. There's something strangely intimate and at the same time callous about using somebody's marriage bed as a scaffold.

Cutting out the damaged section of ceiling, I have two surprises: first, the drywall is five-eighths of an inch thick, whereas I brought half-inch drywall to replace it, and, second, the damage is directly beneath a bathtub drain.

I'll bet that the damage was caused by the tub, not the roof. I go upstairs and run water in the tub. I come downstairs and shine my flashlight into the hole. No water. I go back upstairs and run the shower. I come back downstairs and examine the hole. No water. I go upstairs and hold my hand over the shower nozzle so it splashes against the wall. Downstairs: water is dripping.

It takes several trips up and down the stairs for me to pinpoint the source of the leak—the shower valve. My knees are getting tired. On each trip my eye catches on a book lying on the staircase about a pet owl "the size of a beer can with the personality of a bank president."

I explain the problem to Mrs. Barley. Plumbing problems are never pleasant, always unexpected, usually expensive. When the news is bad, blame the messenger. Which is why plumbers tend to be defensive people. Fortunately Mrs. Barley has already weathered many home-owning crises, and this is a small one. "So can you fix it?" she says.

"Yes," I say. And I do. I seal the escutcheons with Macklanburg-Duncan caulk that states on the tube: "Guaranteed for 50 years!" Total bullshit. The stuff was only invented a few years ago. Who knows how long it will last? And what if it fails after, say, forty-seven years? Can I tell, by looking at a forty-seven-year-old bead of caulk, what company manufactured it? Do I bring in the original tube and cash register receipt, which of course I've been saving for forty-seven years? Will Macklanburg-Duncan still exist? Will mankind? If I'm still alive, I'll be eighty-six years old.

To repair the ceiling, needing extra thickness of drywall, I cope by using shims and extra joint compound as filler. Why did they use five-eighths-inch drywall in the first place? Extra fire protection? Highly unusual in a bedroom ceiling. The adobe brick walls are already fireproof on the exterior. Maybe the house was intended as a fireproof bunker.

Or—built in the 1950s when I was doing duck-and-cover drills in grade school—an above-ground bomb shelter. But it sure doesn't feel like one.

I love this house. The space is generous. The view, stunning. The furniture, comfy and worn. The walls are covered with weavings—macramé—and photos of Irish setters. There are dog scratches on the doors and floor. The fixtures, though old, are of high quality. Books overflow from shelves. The rooms are arranged for human interaction. The television, in a corner of the bedroom, appears to be an afterthought. There are magazines piled on top of it. I don't even see a stereo. Every room smells slightly doggy in a nice way.

It's been a good day's work. Nine hours. Satisfying. Useful. Somewhat hard on the knees.

I'll be back.

After the Barleys, I drop from the wealthy hills of Woodside to a strip of neighborhood more like Appalachia. It's an unincorporated area in a hollow at the foot of the mountain. This house belongs to a man named Rufus on a street called Rufus Lane. He says there's no relationship.

I'm here to make an estimate.

Unlike the Barley's adobe house or its well-built cottage companion, here I see wood siding split and chipped, loose boards, a sagging fence overgrown by roses, and a general sense of the temporary nature of poorly built shelter. Inside, an old woman, Mrs. Rufus, is boiling potatoes.

Mr. Rufus shows me a fence and says, "She wants it fixed." Then two double-hung wood windows: "She wants to replace them." Apparently *she* decides what must be done. But it is his job to talk to tradesmen. He says, "What kind of window do you recommend?"

"Aluminum," I say without a moment's hesitation.

"Coffee?" He offers me a chair.

"No, thanks," I say. "I stiffen up if I sit down after a day's work." In a hard chair, I mean.

He nods. "Me, too," he says. He's thirty years older than me.

Listen to me. I'm thirty-nine and I sound like an old man.

"I'll call you with an estimate," I say. Already we trust each other, a gut feeling.

"All right. I have to go to work now," Mr. Rufus says.

He's beyond retirement age and he works an evening shift. I can't resist asking, "What kind of work do you do?" He looks rough-edged, like a longshoreman or a truck driver.

Mr. Rufus shrugs, his hands palm-upward. He lifts his eyebrows as if the answer is a surprise even to himself and says with some puzzlement in his voice: "I'm an accountant."

Ancient calendars decorate the walls. The Salvation Army would reject the furniture. On the floor is a magazine, *Field and Stream*. Mrs. Rufus, in a calico apron and soft slippers, is humming, boiling potatoes. The kitchen is warm and steamy. It feels like a home.

Thursday, September 18

I spend a couple hours at my desk figuring some estimates for people and order Mr. Rufus's windows, which are an odd size. In other words, expensive, even for the most basic aluminum model. He asked for thermopane, which costs twice as much. Can he afford it? I call Mr. Rufus, quote a price. "Okay," he says. "Let's do it."

Friday, September 19

I'm rebuilding a deck at the Barley house. My instructions are vague. Mrs. Barley has told me: "Replace anything that needs replacing," and also, "Do something about the railing."

It's going to be a physical day. I love working on decks. I love the muscle work, the big results, the fact that you're outdoors in a scenic spot, because people don't want decks in ugly places. This one is fifteen feet above the ground on a hillside with a view across the valley, thirty miles.

The railing wobbles. Whoever built this nailed the posts. A few bolts will firm it up.

Half the decking surface is cracked, weak. No question: I tear it out. Underneath, the joists are soft in spots but mostly sound.

What do the Barleys want? A twenty-year repair? Or a five? For twenty years, I'd have to tear the whole substructure out and replace it. For five, I need only replace one rotten post. The Barleys aren't here today, so I decide to go for a ten-year repair: replace two posts and one joist, and treat the other joists with Copper Green. Tomorrow, if the Barleys wish, I can do more.

The delicate part of the operation comes in replacing one of the posts, a sixteen-foot 4×4 that's surrounded by poison oak. Armed with a shovel, I attack. I clear an area large enough for me to stand plus space for a temporary brace. I have to maneuver a sixteen-foot piece of lumber in a four-foot clearing. One false move and I'll suffer for a week.

My shoes touch a branch. My Levis brush against a leaf. Is that contact too much? I'll know tomorrow.

Back home I gingerly remove shoes and all my clothes and drop them in the wash. I rub my legs and arms with something called Tecnu, which is supposed to prevent reactions to poison oak. Then I take a shower, a long one, washing everything thoroughly, remembering my boyhood back in Maryland when my neighbor was burning a pile of leaves including poison ivy. Just an ignorant little kid, I stood in the sweet-smelling smoke. Within hours I broke out from my hair to my ankles. My clothes had absorbed the toxin. Every inch of my body itched, except the feet. *Every inch*. Inside my nostrils. Inside my ears. And, yes, down there.

Wash, wash. The steam wafts.

Later, in fact all night long, my arms and legs tingle—pins and needles—where I rubbed them with Tecnu. It feels like I'm being eaten by ants. A warning from my skin: don't ever use that stuff again.

Today I balanced on joists fifteen feet above the ground painting toxic Copper Green. I climbed ladders. I juggled heavy lumber. I used lethal tools: power saw, power drill. The only harm comes from a little bottle of cleanser I bought at the drug store.

But at least I don't itch.

Tuesday, September 23

The wind is clinging to the mountainside today. It thrashes the branches over my head and throws a few hard raindrops into my face. I'm back at the Barley estate. Deck repair, an outdoor job. I'm wearing a shirt, sweatshirt, denim jacket, and nylon vest. And I'm still shivering. I can see under the ceiling of clouds to the valley below, where the sun shines and cars are glittering pinpoints. It's always a different world, these mountains. That's why I live in them. And why most people don't.

Mr. Barley approves of my plan: I'm laying twenty-year decking on a ten-year foundation. Go figure. Maybe Mr. Barley knows something about his own body's life expectancy. Maybe a doctor just performed a five-year repair.

Removing the old planks, I find termite damage in one of the joists. The softness leads back to where the board joins the house and beyond— they got into a floor sill. Then it stops. Digging with a screwdriver, I find no live termites. They came, they ate, they left. Why?

I cut off the bad section of joist, replace it, and add metal flashing between the deck and the cabin, which is how it should have been built in the first place. The metal flashing will stop any new generation of termites from entering.

There is also a rotten step. No termites, just fungus. Usually a rotten tread means worse damage beneath it. Not here. So I simply replace the top board and coat the stringer with Copper Green. Good for ten years. Not that I'm making any guarantees, mind you.

Now the railings. My instructions are to "do something" about them. I drill holes, add bolts and shims to the posts. Much better. Ten more years. But again, no warranty. I'm not stupid.

Between the posts are vertical redwood 1×4s toe-nailed into the decking. A poor design. A running child could blast into a 1×4, knock it out, and drop fifteen feet.

Most days I'd consult with my clients and make sure they approved before I changed anything. Today I'm too cold to be prudent, and, anyway, Mrs. Barley isn't home and Mr. Barley is hard of hearing. They said, "Do something."

Here's my something: I cut the rails shorter and add an outside horizontal 2×4. It looks better, works better, and I'm getting out of this wind.

Thursday, September 25

Raccoons have been knocking over the Barleys' garbage cans.

My assignment: stop those 'coons.

I build a fortress for the cans out of boards that I salvaged during the deck repair. I'd like to see them knock *this* over: 2×6 redwood walls, 16-penny nails into 4×4 Douglas fir posts.

And yet I know that after a few winters of rain the wood will soften and split, fungus will grow, and the raccoons will return. All victories are temporary. In the end, nature prevails.

I present Mr. Barley with a bill for the week's work. Three Irish setters bounce around us. Then—the magic moment—Mr. Barley writes a check and casually hands it to me. This simple act always fascinates me: the transfer of wealth. So casual. So vital. A rich man of immense power, a tradesman with none. What if he refused? What would I do?

Tuesday, October 14

I took a big risk with Mr. Rufus of Rufus Lane. I ordered two windows without asking for an advance payment. If he changes his mind, I'll have to eat the cost. My mistake.

Fortunately he doesn't change his mind, and my sense of his character is that he'd pay even if he did. Today I dismantle his two old wooden windows and replace them with new thermopane aluminum windows. The aluminum is uglier than the old wood, but the thermopane will be warmer than the old single glass. As a bonus, the new windows will open and close, whereas the old ones were warped, stuck shut.

Mrs. Rufus, as usual, is boiling potatoes.

The day is warm and sunny. The finished job looks neat and tidy. With a look of serious concentration, pressing his tongue between his lips, Mr. Rufus writes me a check.

Mrs. Rufus offers me a glass of sparkling mineral water and pours one for herself. It seems to be the only bottled drink they keep in the house.

Mr. Rufus climbs into a twenty-year-old Plymouth and sets off to his job as a night-shift accountant.

I really like these folks. Mr. Rufus lives in a dump in a bad neighborhood; his health looks sketchy; his furniture is wretched. I'm guessing he's an alcoholic who's seen the bottom and is coming back up. He and his homespun wife are as cheerful as can be.

When I was starting out in this business, I would have shunned aluminum windows. Now I've suggested them—and installed them—for Mr. and Mrs. Rufus. I used to hate drywall, too. I thought everything had to be high-quality wood, carefully crafted. What a callow prig I was.

Here's to growing up. Here's to the Rufuses of the world. Here's to cheerfully picking among the crap that life throws at you.

Head First

Wednesday, September 17, 1986

The rain breaks. I climb a ladder and then crawl hand-and-knee up the roof to install step flashing around the chimney, an awkward task. I should use roof jacks for safety, but this will only take a few minutes. The roof has a 1:1 rise-to-run ratio, which is carpenter-talk for a 45-degree pitch. It's slick with damp lichen under an overhanging oak. I'm balanced on my butt, leaning forward, half wrapped around the chimney, with my hip lodged against the brick to hold me in place while I chisel mortar for the flashing—when something slips. Me. I'm sliding.

Sliding face-first on my belly down the wet shingles and leaves.

Sliding headlong toward the edge of the roof and a ten-foot fall and—did I mention?—head first.

Sliding like a toboggan, leading with my noggin.

This is the moment when your entire life is supposed to pass before your eyes. Somehow it doesn't. With my arms outstretched, a hammer and cold chisel still clutched in my fists, I manage to grab the rain gutter with a spare finger—my pinkie—and come to a stop with my face in the dark water of the trough.

As I lift my head, soggy leaves cling to my cheeks. A clump of moss is stuck in one nostril. Water tasting of decay—teeming, no doubt, with amoeba and all those busy protozoa—drips from my lips and over my chin. Before my eyes there's a ten-foot drop to the hard deck below.

My feet are uphill behind me. A sharp point of sheet metal—a section of step flashing—is poking into my ribs. Screws and nails and tools are spilling out of my upside-down tool belt, clattering over the shingles, plopping into the rain gutter to mix with all the microscopic critters.

There's a cut on my elbow. Might need a stitch. Might be a portal to my body for all the tiny gutter-dwellers.

Through it all I never drop the hammer and chisel. Fear of losing tools, perhaps. It's true that I'm irrationally fond of that hammer—the hickory handle has almost worn to the shape of my hand—but this cold chisel is just a hunk of metal.

I climb down, wash the elbow, and apply antiseptic. Slap on two Band-Aids, making an X.

Then up the ladder to the chimney, the step flashing. No time for stitches. Gotta get right back on the horse that throws you—with a little more caution this time.

We All Need a Bit of Nursery

Friday, September 26, 1986

It's a modest house, a new client. She's pale-skinned and very pregnant. Her husband is black-skinned and very large—like left-tackle large.

She hands me a Post-It list of problems. On the bottom of the notepaper, preprinted, it says, "Sex maniacs leave notes."

On the wall is a framed drawing of a little boy and a little girl (cute, both white) examining their respective genitals in utter innocence.

The whole vibe is a wee bit strange. The husband sits at a computer, tapping keys. The wife follows me around asking anxious questions about what I'm doing: Does the faucet contain toxic chemicals? Why did I replace the old chrome sink trap with a plastic trap?

I expect her to go into labor at any moment.

I drill a hole through the back wall of the bungalow and extend a water line from the kitchen. I attach a hose bib, turn the main valve back on, and test the hose. Out comes steaming hot water.

The woman asks, "Won't that scald the plants?"

Embarrassing. Humiliating.

I replumb to a cold-water pipe and end up charging one hour's labor for a three-hour job.

Oh, well. I've had worse days. Much worse.

Moving on, I arrive at school a half-hour early to pick up my kids. The older kids would be bothered if I showed up in their third- and fifth-grade classrooms, so I go to Nursery Blue where Will, age four, is folding paper boats and trying them out in a tub of water. I sit on a sofa next to the uncaged rabbit, Bunny Blue, who sniffs me thoughtfully and then closes his eyes. I wonder how I smell to him—soldering paste, maybe, mixed with chips of copper. To me, Bunny Blue smells like slightly damp wool. His fur is soft, gray.

Will glances at me, then continues folding and floating paper boats.

I fall asleep. I dream of water pipes, bursting.

When I awake, Bunny Blue is cuddled against my hip. It's time to go. Will doesn't want to leave. He's still folding and launching his flotilla.

Nursery Blue is a safe, warm spot in the world. Will is my third and last child to pass through here. I'll miss preschool—for myself as much as the kids. We all need a bit of nursery toward the end of a day.

Crawlspace

Friday, October 3, 1986

I have just wriggled on my belly through raw mud and spider webs. There's a smell of clay, like a pottery studio, only not so clean. Now I'm lying on my back with a reciprocating saw in my hands. I'm about to cut a pipe, which will then squirt water into my face and onto my clothes and make a puddle in the dirt that surrounds me. The question on my mind is, *What am I doing here?*

I don't enjoy crawlspace work. I'm thirty-nine years old. I have a bad back. I have a college degree.

What in hell am I doing here?

Of course I'm here because I promised to help Sonny install his new kitchen sink just as he helped me install two pairs of french doors in my house. We trade labor. He knows doors; I know plumbing. We're friends. I wasn't best man at his wedding, but I was the guy who hired a stripper for his bachelor party.

When Sonny was a hippie carpenter, I was a hippie computer operator. He loved his work; I hated mine. I hired Sonny to help me fix up an old house I'd bought in San Francisco. He told me I should quit my job and do what he was doing. He had complete confidence in himself and in me. One day I did quit. My wife happened to be eight months pregnant at the time, but I quit my steady job operating computers and set out on my own as a handyman.

I quickly had an utter disaster: a one-day shower repair turned into a three-day marathon of faulty soldering and squirting pipes. Sonny came to my rescue.

Ten years later I still have occasional disasters, but I no longer call on Sonny to help. He's settled into a specialty, installing and weather-stripping doors. I've become a generalist, a licensed general contractor. And you can't be a general contractor unless you're willing to hump it in a few crawlspaces. Or hire somebody else to hump it.

My niche is the small job, details the big contractors don't want to bother with. Adding an electrical outlet for somebody's new computer. Installing a sink. Repairing a deck. My competition is not other contractors but unlicensed handymen who charge less and therefore end up working for the people who have less money. Which is why I quit being a handyman myself. If I have to wiggle on my belly through somebody's cobwebs, I'd rather they were a rich person's cobwebs.

Sonny is not rich. When Sonny bought this house (cheap, by California standards), my first question was, "How in the world did you qualify for a mortgage loan?"

"I lied like shit," he said.

At my own house in La Honda Sonny replaced two sets of doors that leaked cold air into my rooms and rain-water onto my floors—doors that I had installed myself—and now the air and rain stay outside. He gave up two and a half workdays to do it, and if necessary I will spend two and a half days in this goddamn crawlspace to pay him back.

In my perverted way I love poking around people's houses. A construction voyeur. I don't peek into the medicine cabinet or violate private space. I snoop around the attic where the electrician took blatant shortcuts (probably on a suffocatingly hot day, when I would probably do the same), and I stop to admire the handiwork of some previous tradesman in the crawlspace who took the time to properly insulate each hot-water pipe when he knew nobody would ever see the difference if he left a few gaps—I notice, and I salute his dogged values.

I find beer bottles, candy wrappers, and I wonder: Did somebody linger in this dusty purgatory and goof off? Who could be that desperate?

I witness the work of fungus, and sometimes I bear the bad news of termites.

A house is alive. It breathes. It expands and contracts. It ages. Sometimes it falls sick, and then I'm a doctor of houses. I probe intimate cavities to learn the home's history. I study the bones, the nerves, the flesh of an old house where generations of remodels have built upon themselves—I note the compromise, the painful choice, or the brilliant solution. In new houses I learn the latest techniques, some good, some dismal.

A house reflects the values of the people within. The structure tells a story: tragedy, comedy, or heartwarming family drama as day-to-day life slowly, inexorably leaves an imprint over the attic, on the walls, under the sink—or in the crawlspace.

Anyway, that's what I'm doing here. It's all Sonny's fault, and I'm grateful for it as I cut Sonny's pipe and the first stream of water arcs upward and falls like warm rain onto my safety glasses.

Gunther's Vent

Tuesday, September 23, 1986

Gunther looks like an old hippie. Or an old prophet. He's white-haired, bearded, gaunt. In his basement is a photo of him as a young man—smiling, short-haired, in a business suit.

"I hired a yahoo," he says. "Now I need you to fix his mistakes."

The yahoo plumber installed a vent pipe that slopes the wrong way. In addition, Gunther wants me to divert a bathtub drain out of his septic system and into a graywater line. Illegal, of course, but sensible. Gunther has already dug a trench two feet deep and twenty feet long for the graywater.

"Wow," I say. "I'm impressed. That's a lot of digging for a, um . . ."

"For an old fart? I do okay. I've got a good back but bad knees."

"I'm the opposite," I say.

"Like the pioneers," Gunther says. "You know what was the number-one medical problem of the pioneers who came in wagon trains and settled the west? It wasn't Apache arrows or anything like that. When you think about it, it makes sense. Building houses. Making farms."

"So what was the number one medical problem of the pioneers who came on wagon trains and settled the west?"

"Back trouble."

That's typical Gunther. A fountain of odd but interesting information.

I name a day when I can do the job.

"I'll leave the house open," Gunther says. "I'll be having surgery." He's having an eye operation, a retinal transplant.

He's blind in one eye. I hadn't noticed.

Surgery on someone of Gunther's age is never a sure thing. "I hope the surgery goes okay," I say.

"Oh, I'm not worried," Gunther says. "It comes with a lifetime guarantee."

Tuesday, October 7

I'm in Gunther's basement eyeball to eyeball with a dead mouse. It's sprawled on top of the concrete foundation. I don't know what killed it. Gunther is upstairs, not dead, in bed, recovering from eye surgery.

I'm cutting pipes, drilling holes, banging and clanking and feeling guilty about all the noise. Gunther's wife is at work—teaching my daughter, who is in third grade. Neither Gunther nor his wife seems to take this surgery seriously, though I do.

I, too, am doing minor surgery on his house, though there is nothing delicate about this operation of cutting and installing two-inch-diameter pipe, correcting the errors of the yahoo plumber—minor errors, ones Gunther could have lived with. Gunther doesn't seem to tolerate minor imperfections in plumbing, though you'd never guess it from the slapdash style of the house. Or maybe he can't tolerate being reminded of the yahoo, who must have been arrogantly ignorant. Gunther is a retired schoolteacher, an affable and generous man.

Today's yahoo error is a vent pipe that dips in such a way as to hold water like a sink trap, which defeats the purpose of venting. And what is the purpose of venting? To equalize pressure, the same way you can improve the pourability of a can of tomato juice by poking a second hole—a vent—in the top of the can. Vents also allow sewer gases, which are both poisonous and explosive—methane, for example—to go out through the roof of your house instead of bubbling out in your bathroom sink. Vents are not a glamour item, but you need them.

My other task for Gunther today is to divert two bathtub drains into the graywater line for which Gunther has dug a trench.

While I'm working, one of the neighbors, an oldish woman, comes down to the basement and says, "I'm Karla Kartoffel. *Kartoffel*. That's German for *potato*. I'm wondering if you could look at a drain in my house that isn't working right."

Later, I go to Karla's house, which her husband built in 1952. He's dead. Karla has religious quotations on her walls. She can't look at me when she speaks. She gazes off at a ninety-degree angle, squinting, pursing her lips as if she's reading from a teleprompter located too far away.

All Karla's drainpipes are buried under a concrete slab. There's no way to change the pipes now. "You'll have to accept the fact that once a year or so you have to call a rooter service to clean them out." I point out the plumbing vent protruding through her roof under an oak tree. "Put a screen over your vent so it doesn't fill up with leaves. They're plugging your drain and could cause gases to build up. I'd do it myself but I didn't bring a ladder."

This seems to be vent day.

I charge her nothing for the advice though I've spent a half-hour here. I'm too easy sometimes.

Karla Kartoffel's house, like the houses of many old people, is a house that is gradually shutting down. She lives alone in one end of it.

Gunther's house is more fully active, though the basement is full of old file cabinets and the smell of fermentation.

Gunther tells me that the doctor instructed him to call if he experienced "really severe pain" after the anesthesia wore off at home. Gunther awoke at 4 a.m. in pain and wondered, *What is the dividing line?* When does it become "really severe"? He vomited. Is vomiting severe? He was sweating. Gunther decided that sweating meant severity, so he called the doctor at 6 a.m. His wife drove him to the doctor's office at 7 a.m.

By the time I finish, Gunther is up and about. Just twenty-four hours after surgery, he's inspecting my new pipes, praising modern drugs and medical techniques. He's been blind in one eye for twenty years. When his eye patch is removed, theoretically, hopefully, he will see.

We test his graywater pipes. They leak—a slow drip. I tell Gunther that I can fix them but that the soap in his wastewater will eventually plug the leaks if he does nothing. Soap is a wonderful sealant.

Gunther will let the soap do the work. Apparently he'll tolerate imperfections in my plumbing but not the yahoo's.

Gunther invites me to have dinner with him. His wife has a meeting at school. He's lonely, though he doesn't say so, and maybe a little scared, though he'd never admit it, and—I think I detect—a little ticked off at his wife for leaving him alone all day and all evening. Women, take note: when a man says he doesn't need help, he means (a) he really thinks he doesn't need help, and (b) he'd appreciate a little chicken soup.

I stay for dinner. My job, after all, is home repair. I talk about how much my daughter enjoys third grade, how she blossoms under the teaching of Gunther's wife.

Omelet, prepared by a one-eyed man. Salad, prepared by a plumber. Nothing glamorous, but something he needs. Conversation. Venting. Equalizing the pressure.

Mucking with Clients

Wednesday, September 24, 1986

Some houses are so poorly built that I hate working in them. They depress me. Houses like this one, Michael's house. It has no foundation. The roof is rotten. The ceilings buckle; the floor tilts. There's the stink of decay. And the plumbing is a nightmare.

Unfortunately, I am Michael's plumber.

Clogged drain: clean it. Broken toilet: fix it. Faucet: replace it. Dishwasher: hook it up.

I start at 9 a.m., finish at 3:30, and leave a bill for five hours' labor, plus parts. Trying to head off an argument. People never believe plumbing can take as long as it does, and I get tired of justifying myself. Most plumbers can tell you: it's not the mucking in sewage that's so unpleasant, it's the mucking with clients.

Back home I shower, wash my hair, shave, cut my toenails—trying to remove all traces of sewage sludge from my body. It seems to penetrate skin the way oil penetrates wood. My clothes I drop in the washer.

At last I'm ready to begin my own bathroom.

The first step is always the most frightening: cut a hole in the floor. Once cut there's no turning back.

As luck would have it, I have to cut through a floor joist, leaving the floor dangerously weak—directly under where I want to place a 300-pound bathtub to be filled with 400 pounds of water and 150 pounds of human.

Normally you'd solve this problem by cross-bracing with a perpendicular joist, but in this case there's a cast-iron drainpipe in the way, so I need a more creative solution.

Study. Measure. Think. Trade off. Finally I come up with a plan involving minibraces and a sheet of 1⅛-inch plywood under the tub.

I don't have 1⅛-inch plywood on hand. I cut and install the minibraces, and I repair some gaps where flooring was never laid properly. Then I call it a day. Four hours of work.

When my wife comes home, all she sees is a hole in the floor. "*That's* a day's work?"

"Four hours. I was at Michael's until three-thirty."

"Four *hours*? One hole in the floor?"

"And a lot of planning."

She laughs. She's familiar with how my simple projects can expand. "You want a hamburger?"

"Please."

"It'll take about four hours."

Somehow, though, it's ready in fifteen minutes.

Afterward, It's Still There

Wednesday, October 8, 1986

The porch is rotten. Rusty doorbell button. A dog barks. The person opening the door has an undefined body: shirt, blue jeans, short hair—what gender?

"Hello," I say. "The owner asked me to look at two small decks. She said they needed rebuilding."

"Oh, yeah." The voice of a young woman. So, okay. Female. "The one you're standing on. And another. Out back."

She leads me through the living room. She smokes. The air stinks. Massive stereo equipment, stacks of tapes. A ratty chair. Rock posters on the walls. A bookshelf sagging with college texts. A fine old oak floor covered with scratches and stains, ruined.

The back porch has termites. No concrete pad. Wood in contact with earth. I take measurements, then return through the stale air of the kitchen and living room to measure the front porch, where somebody built a nice pattern into the handrail, though now it wobbles.

The young woman is lifting weights in the living room, taking breaks to puff on a brown cigarette. Half the books are in German. Rock music is blasting from the stereo. In one corner there's a playpen full of toys. There's no other sign of a child.

The house is a crime. Absentee landlord. Careless renters. At a nearby pay phone I call Carol, the owner, and tell her that the two porches are well on their way to becoming two piles of termite turd.

Carol asks, "When can you fix them?"

"I'm booked up for a couple months, but I've got the rest of today. I could juggle tomorrow, free it up. Two days would do it."

Carol laughs. "Somebody told me, if you want to get a job done, call a busy man. You sound like my guy."

Her reasoning seems flawed, but I'll take it. Cash flow, needed.

As I lift off the boards, dismantling the back porch, I start to wonder how far the termites have spread. I'd better inspect the house to find out where, if ever, the destruction ends.

In the crawlspace I see evidence of termites and evidence of repair. No active infestation. The foundation, however, is crumbling away. There's a smell of cement powder. Good grief. As if termites ate the concrete. The grade beam is turning to dust. I can pull it off with my fingers—by the handful—collapsing like a sandcastle. There is practically *nothing* holding the house up. If the earthquake chooses this moment to strike, I'm a goner.

Back outside, the almost genderless young woman is straddling a motorcycle. I ask her to leave the door unlocked for me.

"What for?" she says as she pulls on a helmet.

"So I can use the bathroom. The telephone."

She laughs. "No way," she says.

Renters. Bah. There's a shadowy man who comes and goes in a van and never speaks to me. Another woman, living in the garage, orders me to move my extension cord so it won't crush her plants. "They may not look like much to you," she says, "but they mean a lot to me."

Actually, I'd admired her plants, especially an oddly shaped purple flower. I'd intentionally placed my extension cord so as not to hurt the plants, but somebody moved it, perhaps the shadowy man.

I tear the porches out and leave them in a pile in the yard. Mix and pour two concrete landings. When I leave, both the front and back doors are three feet above the ground. I could build a temporary step, but I don't. Take that, motorcycle mama.

At night I call the owner and tell her that before I build porches over the exposed foundation, I should do something to brace it.

To my surprise she agrees: "Let's do it right." I didn't expect such an attitude because nothing in that house is right. She must have recently bought it. Maybe she doesn't know what a wreck it is.

"What you really need is to jack up the house and build a whole new foundation. It'll cost big bucks, though."

"Will you do it?"

"You'll need a different contractor. I only do small jobs. Since the house is in Palo Alto, the permit will be a nightmare. It'll take months. I can place some piers. That'll remove the time pressure."

"Do what you can."

Thursday, October 9

I pull out the old concrete. By hand. Amazing. Whoever mixed this stuff must've used the wrong proportions. Too little Portland cement. Impure water. Something.

I mix a fresh batch of Quikrete in a wheelbarrow and pour it. Then I shove two pier blocks into the puddles of concrete and wedge wood between the piers and the sill. One corner of the house has already sunk an inch, and I don't try to jack it up. At least it won't sink farther.

Next I rebuild the front porch. It goes up fast.

Two Stanford students are practicing football plays in the street.

The motorcycle mama, who wouldn't unlock the house for me yesterday, today gives me a black cherry seltzer to drink. On the wall by the telephone is a photo of her and another woman and a baby, all three naked, smiling, in a bathtub. Definitely not genderless. I feel like a voyeur.

> Two mothers bathing
> with one baby. All look up
> smiling at the man.

My hands are eroding. The fingers crack and peel. Copper Green, dry Quikrete, they do a job on your skin. My thumb has a big, tender bruise from a misguided hammer. A nail scratched one knuckle; rebar scraped one wrist. You can't always wear gloves. Now I rub my hands with jojoba oil while contemplating the completed front porch. It's simple but solid. Honest, plain, strong. It'll outlast the house.

And that's one of the reasons I like this kind of work: afterward, it's still there.

Friday, October 10

This is my third day on a two-day job. I had to postpone and reschedule; some clients are sore.

Today I'm under time pressure because I have to pick up my son at five o'clock. On the back porch I cut one board badly but use it anyway, leaving a half-inch gap where there should be a tight butt joint. I bet nobody notices. To me, though, it makes all my good work look bad. Half-inch gap. Gotta move on.

I load up the truck with leftover lumber and concrete plus the debris of two porches, with the wheelbarrow on top. Then I pick up Jesse, my son, age ten as of today.

With Jesse beside me in the front seat, there's probably a one-ton load in this half-ton pickup. The truck sways from too much weight. After four miles on Page Mill Road, greasy, smelly smoke starts rising from below the gearshift knob. It fills the cab.

I open the hood. A cloud erupts, escapes. It seems to be coming from underneath the engine instead of the radiator. No, now it's coming from the rear sparkplug. How can steam be coming from a sparkplug?

I fix houses, not engines. I know enough to use a rag as I open the radiator, but no steam rushes out. It's empty. Bone dry.

Two hundred feet away is a large brick house that looks very rich and very private and very not-to-be-messed-with, but, bless them, they have a hose faucet right by the road, so Jesse and I, without asking

145

permission, form a bucket brigade with a Coke bottle and a thermos, filling them over and over until we've topped off the radiator.

No water is dripping out. Hoses tight.

What happened? How'd I lose it?

I wince, thinking of the miscut board, the half-inch gap.

We fill the Coke bottle and thermos again, just in case. I drive on. A few miles later the engine is overheating. I'm now at the foot of the mountain. I stop, empty our spare water into the radiator. I teach Jesse how to open the radiator cap.

> Smoke billowing from
> beneath my little truck on
> a road leading home.

At the top of the mountain we're overheating again. There's a gas station. Jesse opens the hood for me. I try to show him how to set the bar to hold the hood open.

"I *know*," he says, and sets it for me. So far he's known a lifetime of car trouble. It's normal for him.

We re-water, then coast seven miles downhill with the engine off, and arrive home with the radiator still cool, still full.

Back home, my wife has left notes all over the house. A plan has developed: to celebrate Jesse's birthday, my wife and daughter and younger son have hiked to the Sierra Club Hiker's Hut, which sits on a mountain ridge in Pescadero Creek Park, not far from where we live. Jesse and I are to join them there. We'll spend the night. Perfect.

I shower and change. Jesse gathers supplies.

You can only reach the Hiker's Hut by hiking. Jesse and I, wearing backpacks, carrying flashlights, climb through the woods up the side of the ridge, starting in a grove of creek-side old-growth redwoods, then rising through oaks. There's no moon. Through a break in the trees I see bright stars. I say, "There's Cassiopeia."

Jesse walks ahead.

There's a sudden sound—a whoosh, a crash—from the dark woods. I stop, spooked.

Jesse says, "It's a branch falling, Dad."

Things fall apart. Even trees. Half-inch gap.

Jesse hikes fast. I'm getting winded. My backpack gains weight as I ascend. I want to protect Jesse from mountain lions in the forest, or at least from falling branches, but I can't quite keep up with him.

With my son climbing
a mountainside at night
toward stars.

The Hiker's Hut is no hut. It has electricity, a refrigerator, stove, running water, even *hot* water. Well built, nice details. No half-inch gaps.

The rest of the family has eaten, but Jesse and I finish up the spaghetti, garlic bread, and salad. Somehow my wife carried a small cake a mile uphill, only slightly smudged. Candles.

We lie in sleeping bags on the deck overlooking a meadow on the ridge top. Deer settle, making beds in the oat grass. The stars are magnificent. The Milky Way oozes across the bowl of sky from the ocean in the southwest to the distant glow of San Francisco, northeast.

A raccoon is rattling logs in the woodpile.

Ten years ago on this exact day Jesse came into my life and changed everything forever.

Next week, some evening after work, I'll go back and cut a new board, half an inch longer, fill the gap. Make things right.

Banker, Retired

Saturday, October 11, 1986

Mr. K is the retired CEO of a Very Large Bank. He conferred with presidents and had the power to rescue—or bankrupt—entire small nations. His wife rules the house, however. She has good aesthetic sense. She will also break off a business conference to admire a sunset, which drives Mr. K crazy and makes me adore her.

They want floodlights installed in an oak tree. Mrs. K offers me the use of their rickety old ladder. No thanks. I've brought my own. She doesn't want the wires to show or the floods to be visible from the patio, and she wants them to shine there, there, and there.

Hiding wires is a challenge. I run Romex UF cable up channels in the tree bark. I scramble over branches. I hide the floodlights in the crotches of limbs. It's fun, working in a tree. More fun than banking, if you ask me.

Mrs. K also wants me to adjust a sagging door. Mr. K says, "I'll fix it myself."

Mrs. K says, "I don't want to wait for months."

It's a loose hinge. I say, "I can fix it in five minutes."

"Please," Mrs. K says.

Without comment Mr. K watches as I drive long screws.

Next Mr. K asks me to look at a problem with their electric deer fence.

I look at it. "What's the problem?"

"It makes a snapping noise," Mr. K says.

"They're supposed to. That's normal."

Mr. K puts his hand on the deer fence wire.

Snap!

"Oh, yes," he says, trying not to look embarrassed. "It's working."

Deep Woodside

Sunday, October 12, 1986

Woodside, California, is a wealthy town with a semirural vibe. If you want to keep a few horses on a few acres, Woodside's for you. If you're an eccentric billionaire, so much the better. You'll fit right in.

Today I check out a job in *deep* Woodside. Deep, where the estates are so vast you can't even see the houses from the road. Deep, where alpacas romp and Ferraris honk and an army of groundskeepers serve the whims of the trickle-down theory.

I find the address on a mailbox. The gate is open. I drive along a paved path around a curve, but still I can see no house. I'm in the pickup, with its rusty lumber rack and dented fender. If this isn't the right driveway, I could get shot.

Another bend and there it is: a huge Spanish tile and stucco house with seven cars in front, a tennis court with floodlights, and noisy banging inside, which turns out to be a crew of moonlighting plumbers replacing all the old galvanized pipes with copper. They've torn jagged holes in the walls next to elegant lamps and comfy leather furniture.

Rayette Wilson is the hyperactive owner. She's brown-haired, freckled, thirtyish, but awkward like a gangly teenager. She "just had" a baby that turns out to be a toddler. In a whirlwind tour she shows me the room that used to belong to her elder daughter, a room the size of a small house. Rayette moved the elder daughter to a smaller room merely the size of a presidential suite. To keep the elder girl from becoming resentful, Rayette is converting an adjoining porch into an enclosed space that will be part of her room. The daughter's closet is twice as big as the bedroom I grew up in.

My job is to install some lights, switches, and outlets and to repair some outdoor lights that her previous electrician had installed.

All during the tour, a dapper little man with a mustache has been quietly following us, hands folded behind his back. At last he speaks: "Perhaps, Rayette, you should mention what happened to the last electrician."

"Oh, he died," says Rayette. "He was my electrician for five years and really inexpensive, too, but he moved to Oregon where the cost of living was lower and set up his own business. He was working on a Sunday, which he usually didn't do. His wife and child went for a walk to see how he was doing and found him dead of a cracked skull at the bottom of a six-foot ladder. All alone."

149

I ask, "Was there a live wire?"

"No. Nobody could figure why he fell. The police suspected homicide but there were no suspects. No motives. Everybody liked him."

"So. I'm next."

"Do you still want the job?"

"Sure." I explain my rates—time and materials—and tell them I'll start tomorrow.

The dapper little man listens quietly.

As I leave, he follows me out to the truck. As I'm getting in he speaks for only the second time: "You like cars?"

"I don't make a hobby of them."

"I collect cars. I have six classics in that garage under the tennis courts. I have a 1929 Mercedes Benz, a 1939 Mercedes Benz, a Cobra, a . . . Would you like to see them some time?"

"Oh, yes." He obviously wants me to.

Obviously, these cars are his whole life. Obviously, this is Rayette's husband. He's sixtyish, twice her age. Does he work? Is he simply born rich? Is he sane?

"I'll show them to you some day," he says, and he walks to the house with his hands folded behind his back.

Monday, October 13

Rayette Wilson and her house in deep Woodside seem more normal today. Plumbers are gluing pipes outside. Rayette's husband, the quiet, dapper little man, goes off "to work." I notice a doormat that says *Dr. Wilson*. A Spanish-speaking maid named Carmen is washing laundry, dressed in skimpy clothes, jiggly.

The house has a bizarre floor plan as if layer upon layer has been added. The plumbers have cut more holes in walls and shoved more furniture aside.

Rayette works on paint preparation in the elder daughter's cavernous closet, sanding. I love it that she's doing the prep herself in an old spattered shirt, with chips in her hair. She must come from less opulent roots. Maybe she started as Dr. Wilson's receptionist.

Meanwhile, little Brittany toddles in and out among paint buckets, my wiring supplies, the workers outside, the house, and the grounds in general. Everybody seems to be expected to keep an eye on her, including me. At one point I follow her out to the patio. There's no fence in sight, just a meadow and some trees. A man is rototilling.

Brittany heads straight for the rototiller. Just as I'm about to grab her, the man shuts off the machine and holds out his arms. Brittany laughs, leaps to his embrace, and smiles as he lifts and swings her around.

"I'm Clark," the young man says to me. "I'm the caretaker here." He has a burly body but short height, with soft, curly hair down to his shoulders, an earring in one ear. The body of a strongman, the hair of a librarian. "I'll play with her," he says. "You can go back to work."

I install three downlights, crawling through a complicated attic strewn with obstacles—rafters and sheathing that form slanted walls, the ghosts of previous roofs, previous remodels. Some of the heat ducts up there appear to be wrapped with asbestos. What am I exposing myself to?

After I install the downlights, Rayette is disappointed by the results. She'd wanted more brightness. She selected the fixtures herself. Thank goodness.

I hear Clark talking to a plumber outside. Clark says he tried out for the 49ers. They told him if he were three inches taller, they'd take him.

The plumber asks, "You ever try wrestling?"

Clark says, "Yeah, I tried it one year. I was all-conference champion. But I wanted to concentrate on football."

He doesn't have a bragging tone. He's simply stating the facts.

I touch no live wires and fall off no ladders.

Tuesday, October 14

Rayette Wilson is not home when I arrive, but the plumbers are plumbing, and Clark the caretaker is digging a trench. Brittany is toddling. Carmen, the jiggly maid, gives up on working and simply follows Brittany.

I install some wires on the porch, which is now an addition to the elder daughter's bedroom. I tell Clark I'm going back up to the attic.

"Don't you just love it up there?" he says sarcastically.

"There are a lot of obstacles," I say.

"My trouble is I'm big," Clark says. He talks of his body the way athletes do—as a tool that can do some tasks and not others. "Your trouble is you're long."

Later he asks me if I'd like him to shut off the power. He says, "I don't want to come back here and discover you've got a new hairdo."

I ask him why he's trenching the yard. He describes all the work he's doing: trenching for sprinkler pipes, building retaining walls, repairing plaster that the plumbers (and now I) have knocked out—and keeping an eye on Brittany. "I love that little girl," he says.

"What's the older daughter like? I haven't met her."

Clark snorts. "Lucky you," he says.

Clark has the speech and the bearing of somebody who could do better than digging ditches (which of course is what people say about me). He seems so fond of this place. Come to think of it, Brittany looks a lot like Clark.

Rayette breezes in with a station wagon full of insulation. Clark rolls his eyes—another job for him.

Rayette shows me where some circuit breakers are located in the garage—behind the Cobra, Dr. Wilson's sleek, black prize. A powerful car for the quiet little man.

"Don't hit the Cobra as you're walking by," Rayette says cheerfully. "My husband would kill you."

Suddenly I think of the previous electrician. I want to ask, *Did he hit the Cobra?*

Rayette says she has to go to work. Prying, I ask, "Where do you work?

"At my husband's office. We have a clinic in San Mateo. One of our doctors quit. I have to interview a new man today."

In what seems a well-oiled routine, Clark distracts Brittany so she doesn't catch sight of Rayette driving away. "It always makes her cry," Clark explains to me later. "She asked me to keep her out of sight."

"That's amazing self-awareness for a two-year-old, to ask that."

"No, no. Not Brittany. Rayette always cries. Rayette asked me to keep Brittany out of sight."

The clinic—a chain of them—is the family business. And this is the family compound. Hyper Rayette, her dapper, older husband, little ringleted Brittany, Clark the ringleted powerful caretaker, Carmen the sexy maid, even the never-at-home elder daughter who leaves bras and uncapped perfumy bottles of shampoo on the carpet—all seem part of a vibrant, busy clan, a separate world in the privacy of deep Woodside.

If I wanted to be a more popular writer, I'd reveal the trashy scandals and dirty deeds behind the pleasant facade of these wealthy enclaves. I know a few. Maybe I've hinted at one or two right here. But I don't pick fights with billionaires (because they'll win), and, anyway, most of Woodside consists of families with quirks and personalities just like yours or mine. The only difference is money.

I spend two and a half hours walking back and forth between the circuit breakers and a pod of outdoor lights. I'm trying to find a short. I probably walk six miles wearing a tool belt. Chalk-marked on the soil in the yard is the outline of a swimming pool.

I find the problem—caused by shoddy work of the previous (dead) electrician. I repair it. And I don't hit the Cobra.

Rayette returns in time to write me a check. "We'll keep you on call," she says. "There's always something."

Half-Assed Bath

Wednesday, October 15, 1986

I have not been looking forward to this day. Strike one: I'm working for Bella the moaner, Bella the groaner, Bella the habitual victim. Strike two: it's crawlspace work. Strike three: I'm charging a discounted rate.

I have a "friendly rate" that I charge to old friends and a few hardship cases. Bella is not a friend, but her son Carl is in my daughter's third-grade class—though he's not her friend. Not even close. Carl has no friends. He's the angry kid with the permanent scowl. Nobody likes him, including me. But somehow he touches me. It's for him that I'm charging Bella the friendly rate. That plus the fact that she's a long-time customer and also a hardship case.

Bella lives in the Fifth Avenue area of Redwood City, a neighborhood of small houses on small lots. Many of the residents are Hispanic. They keep tidy yards.

Bella is white. Her yard looks like the city dump.

Bella shows me two closets. She says, "Tear out the wall between the two closets, put a shower at that end, a sink at this end, and figure out where a toilet can fit."

That's the plan. It's the opposite of architecture. It's . . . audacity. A desperation remodel to be done without a permit. The sink will have to extend over the toilet, it's that tight. The connection to the main drain will be essentially flat, so the pipe will probably clog from time to time. Bella knows all this, but she wants it done. She has two kids and no breathing room. Everywhere I step there are broken toys and unwashed laundry. The house is chaos.

I hate doing cheesy work, but I feel sorry for her. I'll use cheapo fixtures and bare-bones plumbing.

I expected a one-day job, and she gives me four or five days' worth of work. I explain to Bella that I'm solidly booked up. I could start today but I'm not sure when I can come back.

Bella says, "Start. *Please.*"

This day I tear out the wall, shop for supplies, cut holes in the floor, begin to install vents and drains of ABS plastic. ABS is illegal in this county but far less costly. In the crawl space, as I glue black pipe, I am accompanied by a cat who paws dirt, squatting, fastidious, yellow eyes gleaming at the edge of the flashlight beam. I am less fastidious than the cat but wear a crawl suit, a one-piece top-and-bottom combination that I bought at a garage sale along with a classy three-piece suit. The woman who sold it charged more for the beat-up old crawl suit than the good-as-new three-piece. From her husband. Who died. She said she had a lot of fond memories associated with the work clothes, none with the dress-ups.

A ten-hour day, at the end of which Bella has the skeleton of a bathroom and I am filthy, bone-weary—and paid in cash. Crisp hundred-dollar bills, fresh from the bank. Bella understands the underground economy and what she's getting for her money—her ex-husband was a contractor. She tells me about him after I emerge from under the house, smelling like cat pee.

"He's Korean. He worked very hard but he was too desperate about getting jobs. He underbid on a remodel in Pacifica. Thirty thousand dollars for thirty-three-hundred square feet. Naturally he got the job. Right away he knew he'd blown it. After the tear-out he couldn't afford the dump fee, so he filled our yard with construction debris. That's why it looks like a dump. It *is* a dump. I was pregnant. He was living on Pepsi to save money. He worked twenty-four hours a day. He was going crazy. He was a victim of child abuse from his father, which his mother accepted.

"The fire department red-tagged the yard. He said, 'You called them, didn't you?' I said, 'Yes,' knowing at that moment the marriage was over. We fought, he split. That was two years ago. The fire department came around again last week. They hate my yard. Well, so do I. I'm going to rent a truck from Rent-A-Wreck and haul everything to the dump. It'll take twenty trips. My little boy, Jimmy, has never seen his father. I can't toilet train him until you finish the bathroom. He's scared of the old toilet. So we hope you can hurry. All of us."

Tuesday, November 4

I'm back. Again the crawlspace, among cats. Then I slap up some drywall and install a flimsy plastic shower unit. The ABS pipe won't fit into the shower drain. I start pounding it with a wrench. The drain breaks. Piece of crap. I'm behind schedule, of course. Poor Bella. Her house is a shambles, waiting for this room to be built. Well, her house is *always* a shambles but worse right now.

I quit early.

I'm sorry, but her crawlspace just wears me out. I'm exhausted. Shaky. Forgot my lunch, too. Left it home on the kitchen counter. All I had to eat since breakfast was a glass of milk from Bella's refrigerator.

On the way home I stop at a gas station and buy a bag of potato chips. Change my clothes, then meet my in-laws at a fancy restaurant. An architect, two attorneys, and me, smelling faintly of cat pee. They order wine. Just water for me, thanks, no ice. I'd order beer, but I know they'd disapprove. It's a class thing.

Wednesday, November 5

Carl and Jimmy sit on the sofa watching television, violent cartoons. When I ask where Bella is, Carl ignores me. Jimmy shrugs. Maybe I'm supposed to watch them while I work. Why aren't they at school?

Bella is gone all day.

Jimmy is sweet. Carl is the angry one, his lips pressed together, his eyes in a permanent frown. I try to be friendly, but I don't know how to reach him.

"Carl," I say, "I have two boys, and one is your age."

Carl glares at me.

"My son plays soccer. Do you play soccer, Carl?"

No answer.

I say, "You know what happened to me yesterday? A bird flew up to me and rested on my finger."

No response.

"Hey, Carl. Do you like pizza?"

A quick nod of the head. He keeps his eyes on me, glowering. Something is brewing. Suddenly Carl speaks: "When I'm a father, I'm gonna go off and leave my kids too." He pauses for a moment, thinking. "But I'll come back."

Wow. I'm thinking this is good, maybe, that he can say that. Let it out.

Then he shuts down, silent, scowling at the TV set.

Bella returns home in the late afternoon. "Sorry," she says—to me, not the kids. "Work emergency." She's a commercial artist. "Were they okay? I told them not to bother you."

"Carl is amazingly articulate."

"Yes, when he chooses."

I wish I could give more than what I'm doing. These kids deserve better than a half-assed job.

Tuesday, November 25

With fixtures installed but details remaining, I am halted when Bella returns and we discover a misunderstanding over money. She thought I was working for a fixed price of $1,500; I thought I'd made an estimate of $1,800. The bill so far is $1,979. She pays me $1,500, will owe me the rest.

Bella's from Utah. Mormon family. Bella's an atheist, but her folks don't know. She expects money for Christmas to pay me off.

I don't even have to explain to her that I won't come back to finish the details until she has the money. At least now Jimmy can try a new and friendly toilet.

Wednesday, February 26, 1987

At last I return to finish the details.

The yard has been cleared and raked. There's a sense of relief in the air, or at least in my mind — relief in the emptiness enclosed by the picket fence.

Nobody is home. Clothes and toys still cover the floor.

Bella has left an envelope of cash on the toilet seat. I hope Jimmy's using that thing.

I extend the vent through the roof, tighten the sink trap and hang a towel rack.

Before I leave, I stand at my truck and look back. From the outside it's a tidy little house. A few blades of grass somehow survived under all that demolition debris. Already new sprouts are popping from the earth, new growth.

Stealing Ansel Adams

Wednesday, October 22, 1986

It's a medical office building near the Stanford Hospital. A silent, carpeted corridor. The sign on the door says *Doctor Van Dyke*.

I tap on the door.

It springs open as if the man had been standing right behind it, hand on doorknob, waiting. "Hi!" he says. "I'm Mike Van Dyke. It's good to meet you."

He shakes my hand. He smiles warmly, genuinely.

I wonder about the handshake. Was my grip too firm? Is my tight grip a sign of excessive machismo masking a subconscious fear of homosexuality?

Mike Van Dyke is a friendly psychiatrist, a heck of a nice guy, and he gives me the creeps. Headshrinkers do that to me.

Mike shares a waiting room with five other shrinks, each of whom is warm and friendly, but I only feel five times more creeped having them around.

I'm hanging six Ansel Adams prints on security hardware that locks the frames onto the walls of the waiting room. These psychiatrists' patients have been stealing the prints. And the magazines. The ashtrays. Even the chairs.

Do they then confess their sins to the shrink?

And are they then forgiven? Told to recite ten Hail Marys? Billed for the loss?

With this new hardware, they will have to rip out gypsum and studs to steal a photograph. Which they just might do.

I like Ansel Adams, but he's so—how can I say this?—he's so admirable. So *safe*. I guess you don't want surprises in a psychiatrist's waiting room.

Each print has to be level—and spaced correctly—and lined up exactly with the other prints. Charging for three hours' labor, I feel like a bandit. All I did was hang six photographs. But it takes that long to get the details right. Meticulous Mr. Adams would approve.

Dr. Mike Van Dyke writes a check, and with it he jots a warm, friendly note: "Good job. Thanks."

Even the note gives me the creeps. And it embarrasses me that I feel this way. The problem is me, not him. We all need warm, friendly psychology from time to time.

Back home my daughter is on edge. She's eight years old. She tells me she had a bad day: "First thing this morning, I fell off the sink."

"What were you doing on the sink?"

"Brushing my hair, of course. Then I came home today and you didn't welcome me."

"I said 'Hello'."

"You didn't say, 'Welcome home.'"

"I've never said 'Welcome home,' in my entire life. What's wrong with 'Hello'?"

"Then you *yelled* at me for taking a cookie."

"I didn't yell. I told you no cookies before dinner. And you took one anyway."

She's shouting: "Then the *dog* licked the cookie and got *dog* germs all over it so I couldn't *eat* it and you made *fish* sticks for dinner and you know I *hate* fish sticks. You're *always* making fish sticks every *night*. I *never* get what I like. Never, *never!*"

"I'm sorry."

"And I didn't do well on my math paper at school and everything is hard with Carrie away."

Ah.

Carrie is my daughter's best friend. Carrie's gone off on a ten-day trip with her parents. My daughter is lost, alone without Carrie. Those two girls love each other, plain and simple.

Channeling Dr. Mike, I say, "I wish Carrie were back right now."

We fall silent. Apart. But together.

After a few minutes, my daughter gives me a hug. Her little hands pat my back. "I know, I know," she says. "I know you don't really make fish sticks every night."

Ansel Adams in Suburbia

Thursday, October 23, 1986

Andrew owns a music store. He must be doing well. On an acre of lovely land in Woodside, his house is cutting-edge 1950s style with big windows, high ceilings, flat roof.

A bachelor who rarely cooks, Andrew has a big kitchen in serious need of an update. For advice he's hired Isabella, my favorite decorator.

I tell Andrew I've worked at another music store, Swain's House of Music, his competitor.

"Don't tell them any of my business secrets," Andrew says.

"Do you have any?" I ask.

"No," Andrew says. "But maybe they think I do."

My job is to install new lights and a new vent fan. When I tell Andrew what it will cost, he chuckles and says, "I may be in the wrong business."

The kitchen—in fact, the whole house—is wired with low-voltage light switches that were considered high tech in the '50s but now seem laughably crude, involving an entire closet filled with clunky equipment that belongs in a museum of archaic electrical gear. "Tear them out," he says.

Besides running a music store, Andrew is a serious photographer. On the wall in the hallway is a series of photos, the kind that turn a naked woman into a black and white abstraction of lines and light. I don't like them. Then there's one that's a straightforward shot of a naked woman awkwardly climbing out of a washing machine. It makes me laugh.

"What's so funny?" Andrew asks.

"I don't know," I say. "It just is."

"That's what everybody says. How about this: it comments on the dual role of the American woman as sex object and domestic laborer."

"Were you thinking that when you created the shot?"

"No. I was just goofing around with a model."

"It's funnier without the commentary."

"That's what everybody says."

I tell Andrew about the Ansel Adams prints I hung—just yesterday—for Dr. Mike Van Dyke. Andrew says, "I used to study with Ansel. But I'm more of an indoor guy."

I cut holes in the ceiling and the roof, install the wires, the ducting— and discover that the vent fan is a piece of shit. I fiddle with it for a couple of hours, trying to make the fan blades turn freely. It's underpowered. The mounting is so poor that the blades tend to chatter. It has no damper, so when it's not in use there will be a back draft into the kitchen. Made by Braun, which should be ashamed to sell this crap.

Isabella selected the fan. A botch of a choice.

Now I'm in the position of somehow making this fan work—and work well—or else I make Isabella look bad. I'm loyal to Isabella.

Friday, October 24

I drive to San Carlos and pick up a roof jack and a cap into which I fabricate my own self-designed, custom-built damper. Back at Andrew's house I install it and beef up the fan mounting with some self-designed, custom-built straps made of sheet metal. Sheesh. A lot of extra work, but now it's solid.

I cut out strips of drywall, run the wires (replacing old knob-and-tube), install the downlights. When I leave for the day, there are holes everywhere as if the house had been attacked by a slasher. I'm falling further and further behind.

Saturday, October 25

I'd hoped to take the day off. Instead I spend eight hours at Andrew's taping and mudding drywall, texturing, sanding, touching up details. I use hot mud, which is quick-drying joint compound that allows two or even three coats in a single day. I'm talking to myself. Drywall is so mindless. I walk out to the truck, singing. A couple of thrushes are hopping among the tree limbs. They have the loveliest song.

I practice bird calls. I must look dotty.

Andrew notices. "There's a bag lady who hangs around outside my store. She makes bird calls like that. You okay?"

"Sorry. Drywalling does this to me."

"Is it toxic?"

"No, just boring. Take a photo of me, naked, climbing out of a five-gallon bucket of joint compound. Leave out the commentary."

Andrew studies me while he rubs his neck. "Hold your hand in the right place, and you'll cover up the commentary."

"I was only joking about the photo."

"So am I." Andrew pulls a roll of bills out of his pocket. "How about if I just pay you?"

Licking his thumb, he peels off twelve one-hundred-dollar bills. Good commentary.

Tuesday, November 15, 1988

A couple of years later Isabella and I return to Andrew's house. Isabella is a mother of three, divorced, a grandmother, still cute and peppy. Behind a facade of blondness, she's one wise woman.

Andrew isn't home. Isabella says our job is to de-bachelorize the decor. After twenty years of living alone, Andrew is preparing for his girlfriend to move in. My job, specifically, is to add some soft lighting.

In the hallway, the photos are already gone.

"Hey, Isabella," I say. "Just wondering. When the girlfriend moves in, who does the laundry?"

Isabella sighs, wistfully. "The girlfriend, of course."

And I'll do the drywall.

Sweat Test

Thursday, November 6, 1986

At 8 a.m. I drive the truck to Peter and Judy's house. Nobody is home. The TV and radio are both on, blaring.

Maybe the noise is for the menagerie of cats. Or maybe to ward off some curse placed upon this house. A curse of loneliness. Because I sense it: something is missing in this family, and no amount of construction can fill it.

I'm here to wire an addition—two bedrooms and a bath.

Around 9 a.m. a tile-setter named Greg arrives and starts laying a base for the shower. Greg is an apprentice with a drug problem. He seems okay today.

At noon a teenage housecleaner named Sheba shows up. Sheba lives in a trailer outside town. Her father is in jail. She likes to wear almost nothing as she vacuums. When she leans over to pick up a trash can, my heart stops. I think it's even harder (literally) for Greg.

After a few hours, Greg is done for the day. So is Sheba. For a long time they talk in the driveway, leaning on their separate junker cars. The body language tells it all. At first Sheba and Greg stand as opposite sides of an upper case letter *V*, arms folded across chests, heads bowed, studying toes that are nearly touching. Later they are a lower case letter *m*, squatting side by side on the curb. Then they drive away, one car following at the bumper of the other, for what I presume will be an episode of *Y*. Or judging by their youth and limberness, it might be an episode of *&*.

I, too, must leave early. Today I pick up Will, my son, from preschool and bring him to Children's Hospital for a couple of medical tests. Will has no apprehension, because my wife and I haven't explained why he needs testing. To Will, as to any four-year-old, the world is full of crazy things that need to be done.

He's calm. I'm not. But I try to appear calm for Will.

The woman giving the tests is not your gushy, reach-out-to-children type. She's not cold either. Simply quiet. Respectful, perhaps, of the serious consequences of what the tests might confirm. She straps an electrode to Will's forearm, sets a timer, and starts giving Will mild electrical shocks.

"It hurts," Will says with surprise, and he wiggles in his chair.

"Oh, really?" she says. She holds his arm firmly and stares at the timer.

"Yes. It hurts."

I try to distract Will by talking about where we'll go after the tests are over: we'll buy a treat at the grocery store. "Would you like a treat?"

"Yes."

"What'll you get?"

"Chewing gum."

"You don't want a cupcake?"

"No." He looks at me. "It hurts."

"Just a couple more minutes," says the woman.

I'm sure he's only getting a mild tingle, but it's still a long two minutes.

For the next test, the technician folds a pad against Will's arm, then covers it with a plastic sheet and seals all the edges with tape. The purpose is to make him sweat. It's called a sweat test. One of the symptoms of cystic fibrosis is salty sweat: the kid tastes salty when you kiss him.

And that's what we're here for. Will's pediatrician doesn't think Will has cystic fibrosis, but because of certain symptoms he wants the tests "simply to remove the possibility."

Cystic fibrosis is characterized by thick secretions of mucus that cause lung infections and difficulty in breathing. The difficulty increases over time. More and more, the child needs time on the respirator. Then full-time on the respirator. Then the child dies.

Treatments have improved. In 1959, median life expectancy of children with cystic fibrosis after diagnosis was six months. In 1986, the moment of these tests, life expectancy is into the teenage years.

Arm sealed, the technician tells us we can go to the waiting room. In thirty minutes she'll remove the pad.

I brought a pile of books. Will selects his current favorite, *Cars and Trucks and Things That Go,* which was written by Richard Scarry, apparently after dropping acid. For thirty minutes Will searches for Goldbug in the truly great drawings while I read the inane text.

The technician quietly removes the pad and collects whatever she needs to collect. We'll get the results next week.

Normally we don't allow gum-chewing at our house. But, as promised, at the grocery store I let Will select a pack of gum. For some reason I go soft and let him select three different packs, three different flavors. Which, as far as Will is concerned, makes this a special day.

Friday, November 7

As I drop Will off at Nursery Blue, both his teachers—Margie and Lowell—seek me out. They look concerned.

"What was this test Will had yesterday?" Margie demands.

"Will said he had to go to Children's Hospital," Lowell adds.

I begin, "It was—"

I can't say it. If I say cystic fibrosis it'll be like dropping a bomb in the Nursery Blue play yard. Or am I simply denying to myself the actual possibility that this beautiful little creature I love might be dying?

I say, "It's so unlikely, I don't even want to say what it was."

Margie frowns. She asks, "How was the test itself? The experience."

They're his teachers. They just want to help. If something is bothering Will, they should be told. "It was mostly boring," I say.

"That's the best kind," says Margie.

So nobody knows about the electrical shocks—except Will and me and a technician who doesn't seem to care.

For the rest of the day, at Peter and Judy's, I run cable and install junction boxes.

Judy is somewhere inside the house while her children are at school. I rarely see her, but I hear the radio playing mainstream pop from various wall speakers scattered throughout the house. Simultaneously with the radio, three televisions in three separate rooms are tuned to a succession of soap operas and talk shows. Judy never sits in front of any of them.

Judy has no garden.

Judy takes no walks.

Judy hates dogs, mushrooms, and owls.

It's late afternoon. Maybe it's because the November sun is sinking so early, or maybe—honestly—I'm just temporarily stupid, but I'm drilling one-handed with a ¾-inch bit.

The bit binds in the hole.

When the spinning bit binds, the body of the powerful Makita drill must spin. My hand, holding the drill body, must spin. The hand twists the forearm. The forearm twists the elbow, which twists the upper arm, which twists the shoulder, where something gives with a *crack!*—and the drill wrenches out of my grip.

I drop to my knees.

Closing my eyes, I see stars.

The whole incident lasts less than half a second, but it's enough time to rotate my shoulder socket much farther than the manufacturer's recommended allowance.

Then, miraculously, the agony disappears. Maybe my body's natural morphine kicks in. I work three more hours.

As I drive home, my shoulder begins to hurt again. At home I ice it. Even with ice the ache grows worse.

Rose, my wife, is baking homemade pizza. She asks, "So now that you've worked at their house, tell me, what does Judy do all day?"

"It involves soft rock and talk TV."

"But what does she *do*?"

"I have no idea."

By bedtime it's almost impossible to take my shirt off. Rose helps. No results yet from the sweat test.

Monday, November 10

All weekend I keep my right arm in a sling. By Monday I can work. I just have to do most things left-handed. It takes concentration.

I don't tell Peter or Judy that I injured myself in their house. Maybe I'm embarrassed. One-handed drilling with a ¾-inch bit was idiotic.

Greg the apprentice tile-setter never returned after making letters with Sheba the housecleaner. Today his father, Jerry, comes to finish the job. He says, "I guess everybody knows my son has a problem."

Carpenters are banging and sawing and shouting. I'm drilling holes for cables (holding with both hands). Judy is in bed all day with a migraine—with soft rock and TV talk.

The lead carpenter is named Oshay. That's his entire name as far as anyone knows. He's a white Okie with high self-esteem. He never shuts up, commenting lovingly on his own work: "It orta fit; it sure orta . . ." (setting a board in place). "Yes, look at that! Tight as a twat, my boy, an' purty as your sister. A perfect fit . . ." Oshay's assistant is a dour Latino named Junior who follows Oshay around saying, "Eet look like sheet, mon."

Oshay spent the weekend in Reno and lost two weeks' pay in one night.

Oshay and Junior set bolts and hang insulation. About every fifteen minutes Oshay interrupts his monologue to ask Junior, "You wanna loan me a hundred? Just until payday?"

Junior says, "Sheet, mon."

"How about twenty?"

"Sheet, mon."

When I'm within range, Oshay chats at me: "You know, I had a vasectomy, and it hurt for a year. The doctor's scalpel slipped. He said I had slippery tubes, maybe everybody does. It scraped me. Felt like a kick in the balls, man. We are blessed by God. You wanna talk about God?"

"No."

"I hear ya. Children are a blessing. But I had to do it. Child support is killin' me. Got a court date on Wednesday. She gonna crush my balls. Don't you wanna talk about God, man?"

"No."

"Christmas is for children. You know Christmas is named for Christ?"

By the end of the morning I could kill him. Which might be what he wants: gambling two weeks' pay just before a deadbeat-dad court hearing is tantamount to some kind of a death wish.

What's amazing is that Junior hasn't already throttled his partner. Maybe I misjudge them. At lunch hour, when Junior could go anywhere, he fetches his lunchbox from Oshay's clunky old Chevy pickup, then sits himself down on a bucket of joint compound right next to Oshay. Junior chews silently, staring out the window at the blowing mist. Oshay tries again to ask for a loan and then talks about how he used to work as a rodeo cowboy, a time in Salinas when a bull ate his boots.

For seven hours I twist wires and wire nuts until my fingers are raw. Every half-hour the radio plays "If Ever You're in My Arms Again," which constitutes working under hardship conditions.

At the end of the day Ed Snow, the building inspector, shows up wearing a bright-brass belt buckle in the shape of a pig. I like Ed—and his self-deprecating belt buckle—even though he informs me that the subpanel I've installed is against code. Nowadays you can't have a subpanel in a closet.

It was Peter's design, but it was my job to know the updated code. Imbecile.

Fortunately I can simply rotate the panel 180 degrees so it opens into the bedroom instead of the closet. It will be an hour's work—if it's okay with Peter to have a subpanel facing into the master bedroom. If not, I'll be starting over.

Judy emerges from her cocoon of pop and soaps holding a wash cloth to her forehead. She asks, "Did I miss anything?" Beside her bed lie piles of celebrity magazines and murder mysteries. Here's the answer to what Judy does all day: absolutely nothing.

I explain the problem with the subpanel, and Judy says, "Oh, Peter won't mind. He'd only worry that it might bother me, and I don't bother about anything. As you can tell from my housekeeping."

She rinses the washcloth with cold water, wrings it, then wraps a few ice cubes within. Again holding washcloth to forehead, she winces and says, "Don't worry about Peter."

I think it's not really a migraine. I think Judy is seriously depressed. Still no word from the hospital.

My daughter, age eight, wants quail eggs and pomegranates packed in her lunch bag. Her best friend gets them, along with roast beef sandwiches. I explain to my daughter that we can't afford roast beef, much less quail eggs. Pomegranates, maybe.

"Daddy, why can't we afford them?"

"Because we don't have enough money."

"When we have enough money, can I have quail eggs?"

"Yes. Absolutely. What did you do in school today?"

"I made up a poem." She's seen me write poetry. Now she shows me a scrawl that looks like Chaucerian English:

> me hed aeks.
> my stomik aeks.
> my thort aeks just the same . . .

At her school they emphasize creativity, not spelling. In modern English her poem would appear as:

> My head aches.
> My stomach aches.
> My throat aches just the same.
> I feel like I will yell.
> My mom tries to make me well.
> My head stops hurting.
> My throat stops hurting
> but my stomach hurts more than ever
> and whoops!
> I throw up.

"So you're sick?" I ask.

"No. This was a long time ago."

It seems like a weird subject for a poem. Is she sending me some kind of a message? Is this her way of worrying about her little brother Will? Impossible—we haven't told her, or anybody, about the sweat test. So I ask, "Are you sure you're okay?"

"Daddy," she explains as if I'm an ignorant rube, "it's what I remember. It's a *story*."

My shoulder, alas, could be another weird poem. The pain is deep, and mine alone. Already I suspect the ache will linger in some form for the rest of my life. Let's write my poem as a wince-inducing comedy, with pratfalls. Which is the spirit of what my daughter wrote. Instinctively she knows it's better to laugh at your fate.

> and whoops!
> I crack my shoulder.

No whoops, though, no laughs in a positive sweat test. There the tale—our lives, this family—would take a dark turn with no good outcome possible.

I make up my mind: I will never tell Judy or Peter what happened to my shoulder. My injury wasn't their fault. Nor should it be part of their story, their home.

Tuesday, November 11

At Peter's I install switches and outlets. This will be my last day for a few weeks, then I'll return.

Oshay and Junior are working their last day as well, cleaning up details. Desperately now, Oshay asks Junior for a loan. Court date tomorrow. Junior says, "I buy your truck."

"That baby's worth five grand," Oshay says.

"That truck is sheet, mon. I give you five hon-dred."

All day, Oshay enumerates the valuable features he's added to the truck. A spotlight. Oversize mirrors. And what about those dancing–go-go girl mud flaps? Junior just shakes his head.

At nightfall they settle at $525. Junior pulls a roll of bills from his back pocket and peels them off. Junior had arrived as a passenger. When they leave, Junior is at the wheel, starting the engine in a cloud of blue smoke that belches from the rusty tailpipe.

Junior adjusts the mirror. Oshay, for once, is silent.

Back home, Rose comes out to the garage as I park. Our house is on a hillside. Will is chasing our new puppy, laughing.

The weather is gorgeous. All week we've had fresh, clear, warm days and nippy, twinkling nights. The redwoods around La Honda are shedding, showering duff—dead needles—at the slightest breeze.

Rose says, "We got the results of the sweat test. Negative. He's fine."

> Little four-year-old
> with muscles of a tractor,
> how you race up hills!

Tuesday, December 23

I clean up some final details at Peter's house, replacing a faulty four-way switch. I'm done! Already finished are the carpenters, Oshay and Junior, the tile-setters, Greg and his father, Jerry—each worker a subplot, gone, but a part of this dwelling where we have embedded our sweat, blood, and pencil marks.

> Last nail driven,
> sawdust swept.

In each house,
many stories.

Sheba is housecleaning today. She's like a serialized saga, new episode every Tuesday. In the past month she's gotten married—not to Greg—her profile suddenly, visibly, a lower case *b*, not necessarily thanks to the groom. That baby must have been cooking for several months already. It's a credit to the effectiveness of birth control that she wasn't knocked up any time in the previous six years. In late December she's wearing a halter and soccer shorts. In three years she'll be old enough to buy alcohol. She says her dad got out of jail and is repairing cars instead of stealing them.

There's a Christmas tree surrounded by brightly wrapped packages. Judy is a Catholic, but mostly she's a Christmas junkie. "When it comes to the holidays, I believe in wretched excess," she says as she hands three gifts to Sheba, one to me.

I write an invoice for Peter. Peter writes a big, fat check.

The pagan festival of light. It must be the passing of the solstice that makes me so happy. That and a hefty check. Tomorrow I'll buy pomegranates—and maybe quail eggs if I can find them. And a pack of gum for Will's Christmas stocking.

Wednesday, June 20, 2012

Building shelter, making children, we construct our cluttered lives.

Will is thirty, in perfect health.

My shoulder gets grouchy in bad weather when the daylight is brief. I never told Peter or Judy of my ill-fated drilling.

They're divorced.

Judy lives alone in the big house in La Honda with dozens of cats. In the years since the addition, the structure has never had an electrical problem. I made sure of that.

A couple of years ago Judy called me to look at remodeling a bathroom in the old part of the house. She had to cancel as the economy collapsed, but not before I explored the project. To understand the plumbing, I ventured into the crawlspace.

Under the house, the beam of my headlamp caught a mass of dusty spider web. There it hung: sawdust. Like the wispy threads of an old legend. The same sawdust, preserved. Suspended by cobwebs beneath holes I had drilled, so painfully, for that job long ago.

Spiders, too, build to last.

The Good Life

Amelia

Monday, February 9, 1987

Amelia is an attractive woman with a muscular body. In her garage she parks six Kawasaki motorcycles and a Chevy van. She races on weekends for fun. I asked Amelia once what the best thing about racing dirt bikes was—the danger? The difficulty? The dirt?

"Winning," she said.

But it's just a hobby. Weekdays she's vice president in charge of sales at a large pharmaceutical company.

Amelia was one of my first clients back in 1977 when I was charging seven dollars an hour. She was a single mother with a run-down house and a five-year-old boy. My hourly rate—and her career—have grown through the years. So has her son, Lyle, now age fifteen.

Today I'm replacing a bedroom door. Amelia explains that she had to kick the door open when Lyle "went into a snit and wouldn't come out."

Amelia makes quick decisions—about opening a door, about shopping, remodeling, relationships. "Let's get rid of that fireplace." Or, "Let's turn that wall into a window."

Over the time I've known Amelia and glimpsed little scenes of her life, one thing hasn't changed: there's always a man around. Moths to her flame.

For a couple years now Amelia has had a boyfriend named Dave. Dave is in his forties, bright of eye and firm of handshake. He has two children who are in the custody of his ex-wife. Dave is the go-getter kind of guy who when playing poker would bet everything on a pretty good hand. Silicon Valley is full of people who don't fear failure, which is why it's such a great incubator for start-up companies. You hear the success stories. But the Valley is also littered with people who have failed big-time.

When Dave met Amelia, he had a good job and a big house in Los Altos where he lived alone postdivorce. He was the hard-charging type, and Amelia was the prize. Then, a year ago, Dave sold his house to start a business. He called it an "information business," but he was coy about the details.

The business went bankrupt. Now Dave lives out of his car, a nearly-new BMW with a back seat full of clothing. Mostly he hangs out at Amelia's house.

There's nothing coy about Amelia. She says what she thinks, and what she thinks is never subtle. At this moment she's peeved at Dave for losing his house.

Dave points out that he didn't lose the house, he sold it.

Amelia says "You know what I'm talking about."

Amelia's son Lyle says, "She's talking about the fact that you're a loser."

"Hey!" Amelia says.

I hear and see everything from where I'm replacing the door to Lyle's bedroom. Amelia, Lyle, and Dave are having lunch.

Dave frowns at Amelia and says, "You're supposed to be the tone monitor."

"I am," Amelia says. "I just monitored."

Dave says, "You're too soft on him."

Amelia says, "You know, Dave, sometimes you really irritate me. I hate the way you chew food."

Dave says, "What's wrong with the way I chew food?"

Lyle says, "You smack."

"That's right," Amelia says. "That's exactly it. You smack."

Dave says, "Where's the tone monitor now?"

Amelia says, "You really are a loser, you know that? I want you out of here."

Dave drives away in the overstuffed car.

She's tough, this woman. She told me that in Catholic high school the boys all called her Amelia I Wanna Feel Ya until she pushed one of them down some concrete stairs, breaking his leg. The quarterback. For which the school expelled her.

I finish hanging the new door. Somewhat nervously—and standing far from any stairs—I tell Amelia that I've raised my rates again, now charging forty dollars an hour.

"Oh, good," Amelia says. "I always felt guilty about how little I was paying you."

Amelia is soft in good places and firm in good places where no man will hold her for long. But many will try.

Journey

Tuesday, February 10, 1987

The apartment manager calls me: "I've got this Armenian, I can't understand a word she says. Just go there and she'll point at something. Then you fix it."

She has curtains thick as carpets, lovely, shutting out the courtyard, the neighbors, society. On the floor, exquisite rugs with woven patterns of a dragon, an eagle, a serpent.

She's a gentle, bent-over woman.

She points at the baseboard heater. Folding arms over her chest, she shivers dramatically.

"Okay," I say. "I get it."

Her posture is like a question mark. Draped over her shoulders is a lovely knitted shawl. Smiling, she has to strain her neck to look up at me. A rough scar like a dried fig covers one cheek from her eye all the way to her jaw.

You get the sense that the world has run roughshod over this woman, and yet still she is sweet.

As I study the thermostat, I feel a nudge on my arm. She's pushing a tray of baklava and apricots at me. "Take," she says.

In a minute she's back again with a tiny cup of coffee. "Take," she says. The brew is so thick that if you turned the cup over, the coffee would not splash on the floor—it would shatter.

She points at a light switch. "Open," she says.

I turn on the light. She's right—now I can see what I'm doing.

An hour later, my brain is exploding with caffeine and sugar. My belly is grinding like a coffee mill. And the heater is fixed.

I kneel over the baseboard, rubbing my hands in a pantomime of heat.

She takes my hand between both of hers. Beaming, she nods her head, thanking me with her eyes.

She opens the door.

I step outside, returning to the bright sunlight of California, USA.

Atherton Okies

Monday, February 16, 1987

It's President's Day, a holiday. Not being a president, I'm working.

The house has a FOR SALE sign out front. With two stories and a wraparound porch, it looks like an old-fashioned farmhouse except that (1) it's gigantic, (2) it's in Atherton, a town of major money, and (3) access is controlled by a security gate.

The owners are Ronnie and Ron. They wear sweatshirts; they're pudgy; their hair is tousled. They are about as glamorous as the muffler on my truck. I like them instantly. While Ron, with an Okie drawl, gripes to someone on the phone about an eighty-dollar furnace repair bill, I tell Ronnie that her plans to light up her kitchen will cost several thousand dollars. "Sure thang," she says without batting an eye.

I ask, "Is this to make the house more attractive to a buyer?"

"No," she says, "it's to make it more attractive to me. We're askin' a stu-oo-pid price. Maybe we'll find a stu-oo-pid buyer. Meanwhile I'm the cook, and this kitchen is too dark."

So I begin cutting holes and running Romex. Ronnie goes outside and fertilizes the lawn from a hand-pushed spreader. Ron crawls under their Mercedes on his back, changing the oil. His other car is a baby-blue 1924 Cadillac.

The next time I return, nobody seems to be home. I'm installing fourteen recessed lights in the ceiling, plus a couple of undercabinet fluorescents. Mostly ladder work, but often it's easier to stand on the countertops.

I like working alone. Today I get into the flow of the job, singing my own words for a Hank Williams song—*my hair ain't so curly but my eyes are all blue*—daydreaming, running wires, when suddenly I have a vision of falling—of forgetting I'm standing on a countertop, taking a step to the side—cracking my head and dying, all alone among my tools in the kitchen of some hillbilly millionaires.

A moment after this vision, somebody walks into the kitchen. Teenager, female, pudgy. In a glance I can tell she's totally at ease with her body. I like her instantly. I'm still standing on the countertop wearing my tool belt. My hair and clothes are powdered with gypsum dust from cutting holes in the ceiling.

She gazes up at me. "You all right?" she asks.

"Fine. Why?"

"I was studyin' upstairs? And you were singin'? And then suddenly I thought I'd better check up on you like maybe you'd electrocuted yourself."

"Amazing! I was just thinking something like that."

"I guess you stopped singin'."

"So if I'd fallen and cracked my head and my brains were oozing out on the floor, you would have held my hand and comforted me so I wouldn't die alone?"

For a few seconds, she studies me with furrowed eyebrows. "No, actually, I would've called for an ambulance."

"I appreciate that. But I guess you won't have to."

She grins. "Maybe I should call a psychiatrist?"

Wednesday, February 20, 1991

Four years later, Ronnie calls and asks me to do some electrical work at their business, a plating company. It's a grubby-looking warehouse in the industrial section of a town that is the opposite of Atherton. The air inside reeks of chemical fumes. In one corner Ronnie and Ron have desks piled with papers and ringing telephones, surrounded by vats containing bubbling liquids of eerie colors—chartreuse, yellow, blue. Workers are dipping electrodes and shiny metal plates into those strange tubs. "Be careful what you touch," Ronnie says.

I have a vision of accidentally placing my hand in one of those brightly colored vats and having the fingers disappear in a swirl of bubbles.

I need to stop these visions.

After I repair a heater and replace a circuit breaker, Ron writes out a check. On a small table like a nightstand next to his desk, the only uncluttered space in the entire warehouse, sits an enormous Bible with Ron's name embossed in gold.

Ron sends me back to their house on the other side of the world to repair the security gate.

The FOR SALE sign has a SOLD slapped on it. They finally found a stu-oo-pid buyer. Or else inflation caught up with their price.

As I'm puzzling over the gate motor, the daughter (whose name is Ronette) drives up in a dark green Jaguar with a Stanford sticker on the window. The gate is closed with the motor disconnected, so she waits. "Cracked your head yet?" she asks.

"No. Actually, I was more worried about dissolving my hand today."

"Wouldn't dissolve. But it might get plated with silver."

I point at the sold sign. "Where will you go?"

"Mom says for what we're gettin', we can buy a whole town in Oklahoma. We've got family there."

"What about the plating business?"

"They're givin' it to the workers. It's like givin' away a headache? Then they'll tinker with cars and putter in the garden wherever they go. That's all they want."

"And what'll you do?"

"I'll get a doctorate in chemistry. Like they did." She smiles. "It's a family tradition."

Hosed

Monday, February 23, 1987

I'm eight minutes late for an 8 a.m. appointment I made weeks ago—which seems close enough to me, but Mr. Roch is outside pacing the sidewalk.

"The floor has creaky spots," Mr. Roch says. "Personally I'm not bothered, but my wife thinks the house is falling down."

Creeping on my belly through the shallow, dusty crawlspace, I check the floor and foundation. It's a big house, requiring lengthy creeping. I'm wearing a crawl suit and a headlight, but, stupidly, I forgot the dust mask.

Back in daylight, I stand up . . . and sneeze for a solid minute, sneeze after sneeze after sneeze, bent over with my hands on my knees, tears pouring from my eyes. Something under that house didn't agree with my nose. At last I can say, "Your house is fine. Tell your wife nothing is wrong. I could add some bracing if it would make her feel better, and as for the floor creaking there are some things I could—"

"Don't bother," he says. He pays me.

Back at my truck I reach for my keys—and they're gone. Oh, man. They fell from my belt clip somehow while I was creeping under the house. This time I'd definitely take a dust mask, but it's locked in the truck.

The keys, of course, turn up in the farthest corner of the crawlspace. I emerge sneezing and filthy.

While I continue sneezing, Mr. Roch sweeps me off with a long-handled broom. His wife comes out of the house. She asks me, "Are you all right?"

I can't answer. The sneezes won't stop.

To her husband she asks, "Is there anything wrong with the house?"

"No," he says, still sweeping my clothes. "It's fine."

"I told you so," Mrs. Roch says to her husband. "Are you satisfied now? How much did that cost?"

"Forty dollars."

"Forty dollars! For nothing!"

I'm still sneezing. Mrs. Roch studies me with disgust, then says to her husband, "Should we call an ambulance?"

Mr. Roch says, "Maybe we should turn the hose on him."

I hold up my hands—please, no hose. But I continue sneezing. Mrs. Roch bustles to the house and returns with a green garden hose. She squeezes the nozzle and hits me full blast: face, hair, shirt.

It works. I stop sneezing.

I take off the sweatshirt. With a towel from the truck I dry my face and arms and dab at the wet T-shirt. It's 9 a.m. on a cold day in February.

With the heater on, I drive to the next job, Pahm.

Her name is actually Pam, but she has an intimidating British accent. Pahm wants me to "soften some angles" on her garage.

I don't understand. "Can you draw it?"

"No." She waves her hand as if it's an absurd idea. "I cahn't draw."

She explains that the corners of the garage door opening are too harsh. They are the perpendicular corners of just about every garage. She wants me to construct something out of plywood and hang it at each corner of the opening, sort of an archway, and it has to be done today because the painter is coming tomorrow.

I think I get it.

My shirt's still wet. I'm outside, working in a cold wind. Carrying a silver tray, Pahm brings me a teacup of hot water on a saucer with a slice of lime, and a napkin. Very nice.

It's not easy drawing a big curve on a piece of plywood and then cutting it cleanly with hand tools. I make a prototype. The edges are a little jagged. I hang the prototype on a corner of the garage opening. As I step back to look at it, Pahm's husband, Gus, drives up in a vintage MG, jumps out, and says, "What is *that?*"

I start to explain.

"It's *ugly!*" he shouts. Actually, I agree, and I think the entire project is insane, but before I can explain he continues: "It's not just ugly. It's *unprofessional!* You didn't even sand the edges. They're *rough!* You call yourself a *carpenter?*"

"It's temporary," I say. "A prototype. Next step is for your wife to look at it, and then—"

"You call yourself a *carpenter?*"

Pahm appears. She is no longer the hot-drink-on-a-tray-with-a-napkin Pahm. In the presence of her husband, she is a different woman. "I thought you were a cahpenter," she says. "Is this up to your stahndards?" She holds up her hands as if warding me away. "I'm sorry," she says. "You should leave."

I throw my tool belt in the box, step into the cab of the truck.

Some days I feel like an actor in a slapstick comedy. And let me tell you, slapstick is hard work.

Gus is shouting: "You call yourself a *carpenter?*"

I'm out of here. No bill, no pay. Just gone.

Offerings

Sunday, May 10, 1987

Tom studied architecture at the University of Michigan. He draws house plans for people, but his first love is roofing. He says it's clean on a roof. Fresh air. Tom is not an office guy. Tom, in fact, is not like anyone I've ever worked with.

He has just reroofed a house for which he wants me to build a deck. He'd help out some with planning and nailing. We'd work together. I'd have to do all the cutting, though. Tom reveals that he's allergic to the sawdust of redwood and cedar.

"I guess you're not fond of cedar incense," I say.

"Doesn't bother me. I use it for ceremonies all the time."

Tom is a short man with a ponytail and a beard. He's part Native American. He drives a Checker station wagon when it's running. He lives simply. His time frame is less rigid than mine, less pressured—and, boy, do I envy him that—but also he's less able to meet deadlines. And make money.

I recommended Tom to one of my favorite clients. Tom duly appeared, discussed the roofing project, and never called back. They hired somebody else. Tom isn't flaky, not exactly. He simply operates in a different culture.

Though casual about time, Tom is a perfectionist about work (and I'm not). For this roofing job he rejected at least ten percent of the cedar shingles. In a regular commercial job, every shingle is used. He'll use them elsewhere—as siding, maybe. He wastes nothing.

As for the deck job he's offering, I tell Tom I'll think it over.

Tom's son and my son are friends. We've arranged a group outing with several families to the Hiker's Hut in Pescadero Creek Park. The Hiker's Hut is a cabin run by the Sierra Club. You can hike in, stay a night, hike out.

On a dirt road we rise through the redwood forest, pass a horse farm, and cross a lush meadow where the oat grass is turning golden in the sun. After dinner, from the porch of the Hiker's Hut, we watch the fog blow in through the valley as the sun sets. Paki, Tom's son, has brought a flute and is trying to learn how to play it. A park ranger stops by and asks us to be on the lookout for two runaway horses.

Suddenly the fog rises and envelops us, blotting out the nearly full moon. Then, ten minutes later, the fog is gone, still nestled snug in the valleys but leaving us clear and moon-shadowed as we take a walk through the meadow among the grazing deer. Tom is with us and without us, appearing and disappearing, carrying a sack of corn. He likes to stop and make offerings to the animals.

> You gentle mountains
> round, folded like a sleeping woman
> breathing fog
> stretching under baking sun
> curling beneath stars
> you nurture my spirit.
> Your deer comb the grass
> lizards drum in the dust
> a crow calls
> the sun falls
> a boy plays a flute
> answered by quail.

The next day we take a hike. Tom hangs back. I'm with several families in the middle of the group. Descending the Grizzly Trail, Tom, at the rear, spots two horses far off among the trees. We had all missed them.

With apples and nuts as offerings, Tom and his wife Judy approach the skittish animals, clucking, speaking horse language, until they can put their hands on the lead ropes.

Suddenly we have two quivering, beautiful beasts with us on our hike.

We descend to the bottom of the valley. The horses seem to enjoy the walk, the fresh smells, the constant, cheerful guidance from Tom and Judy, with whom they have a mutual understanding. In their eyes I see a mixture of animal instinct and kindness, a rapport of the human and the equine.

Returning up the hill, we encounter a search party that relieves us of the horses. They thank Tom and Judy as heroes of the day. They say, "The owners will give you a Coke if you drop by."

Tom is the last person I can imagine drinking a Coca Cola.

Later we pass the ranger who says, "That was twenty thousand dollars worth of horse." They had run away after being spooked by some bicycles.

Back at the cabin we encounter a bicyclist who is angry and bewildered because some horse people have just yelled at him and he doesn't know why.

We're annoyed. Thanks, horse people, for the offer of a Coke. We returned your $20,000 horses. Now stop yelling at people on $200 bicycles. And next time tether your damn horse before you leave it at the side of the trail.

Only Tom is amused. "It's been a good day," he says. He doesn't seek a reward. He bonded with two fine animals, gave them offerings, shared their journey for a few miles, and moved on.

After two days with Tom, I feel spiritually renewed. Sometimes he leads us from behind.

Back home, I tell Tom I don't want to do the deck job he's offered. I don't think I can work with him. Our paces, our approaches to jobs are too different. I admire him. Sometimes I wish I could be like him. But I'm not. We should be friends, not partners.

It's all fine with Tom.

The Good Life

Friday, November 13, 1987

In cool water I swim. In bubbly silence I view a shapely dolphin in a yellow bikini. She's surging along in the lane beside mine, passing me every third lap, which is humiliating. But at least, with each pass, I catch a glimpse of her bouncing butt.

Okay, I'm a pig, sorry, but swimming a kilometer is boring and merits whatever distractions you can find. And I cling to the belief that through constant physical labor I should already be stronger than most women, even though this one must be twenty years younger. *God,* she has power!

I'm washing out four not-unpleasant hours spent in an attic installing heat duct, breathing insulation, swallowing dust. Hard work is an odd satisfaction, but there it is. Like swimming laps.

Now I have a half-hour before picking up the kids at school. A half-hour to hang out at a fancy club that I joined only as a place to swim.

Poolside there's a bar and some tables. The bartender knows me. He pours a mug of decaf and says, "You're the only member of this club who actually works for a living."

It isn't that the other members don't have jobs, at least the ones who aren't retired. But he's saying that these venture cap dudes and corporate captains are the winners. Which makes me—and him—the losers. If you play that game.

The tables have white linen. Sipping decaf, I hear the *thwock, thwock* from the tennis courts. The bartender is right: they're all here, midafternoon, at play on a weekday. But then so am I.

From another table I hear a gray-haired couple discussing eye surgery. At yet another table I overhear two young women—could one be the dolphin of the yellow bikini? Yes, I recognize her bum, wait, I mean her features. In street clothes without goggles or a swim cap, her hair is lovely, her eyes, sharp. She is telling a joke: "Every lady should have four animals in her life. A mink on her back, a Jaguar in her garage, a tiger in her bed, and a jackass to pay for it all." From another table a man calls out: "What? No puppy to lick her feet?" Everybody laughs.

It's time to meet the kids. Parked among the Mercedes and BMWs sits a well-worn pickup. In the truck bed lies an old water heater on its way to the dump. The extended cab has jump seats, room for my three: the graceful gazelle, the mountain monkey, the joyful lark. Call me papa pig. At home, mama bear is heating soup.

The vinyl driver's seat has molded itself to my body. The motor purrs.

The Townhouse War

Friday August 12, 1988

Kit, the high-stress decorator, meets me at a townhouse in Los Altos. It's one of those planned developments with shared courtyards: clean, tidy. Very upscale. With very upscale cars. Everybody has a designated parking space—except for tradesmen. I park my truck in front of the job site, partially blocking the access road.

Kit points out all the spots where lights are to be installed. She shows me a schematic drawing, sketched by the owner, showing where electric heating panels are embedded in the ceiling. The heating elements are tiny wires woven through 4×12-foot panels of gypsum that look like regular drywall. Kit says, quoting the owner, that you can't make any holes in the heating panels because if you happen to hit a wire—any tiny wire—it ruins the entire 4×12 panel.

It's the most impractical heating system I've ever heard of. You want your heat at the floor, not the ceiling, and you want something that can't be disabled by one wayward thumbtack.

"Kit," I say, waving my hand at the ceiling, "this sucks."

"The townhouse association is suing the builder," Kit says. "They've got a whole list of complaints." She looks at me sharply. "Don't be one of them."

We're interrupted by a knocking on the door, a neighbor woman leaning on a walker. She says the carpenters who were working here yesterday left too much sawdust in the courtyard.

"Wasn't me," I say.

Kit glares at me. "We're sorry," she says. "It won't happen again."

Just as Kit is leaving, Dave the painter arrives. Kit says to me, "I know it would be better to let you finish the lights before Dave starts painting, but we're in a time crunch."

"No problem," I say.

"When I'm gone, you and Dave can talk about me. All your complaints." Beneath her hard exterior Kit is amazingly insecure.

She's also right: as soon as she's gone, we talk about her. Kit brings high-end clients and good money, but she always brings high drama, too.

Our conversation is interrupted by persistent honking from outside. A man in a black BMW is beeping at my truck.

There's room. He could pass. But oh, well. I move out of the access road. There is actually a designated spot for deliveries and tradesmen to park, but it's 300 feet from this townhouse. I'll be making constant trips back and forth, getting one part or another.

Nearby, about half the reserved parking spaces are empty. I choose one that's convenient—reserved, but empty.

I commence marking the ceiling, based on the sketch that was left by the client, outlining areas where I can drill holes, areas where I can't. Then I start hanging lights.

On a trip out to my truck, as I open one of the side-mounted toolboxes, a voice shouts, "DON'T MOVE! POLICE! KEEP YOUR HANDS WHERE THEY ARE!"

Two cops are walking toward me, guns drawn.

One of them slams me against the door of the truck.

He wants to frisk me, but I'm wearing a tool belt with a hammer and drill dangling, pouches of screws and wire nuts, slots for screwdrivers and pliers and electrical tools. Apparently this situation was never covered in cop school. Already, from the slamming, the tools have scratched the paint on my truck.

The cop tries to unfasten the tool belt, which puts his fingers in contact with an intimate section of my anatomy.

"Let me do it," I say.

"Don't move," he says.

Eventually he loosens the buckle. The belt drops. All my tools and screws and wire nuts spill onto the asphalt. The drill falls point-first, breaking the bit.

Dave the painter, in his paint-spattered overalls and painter's cap, has come out to watch. He's holding a roller. "Yeah, he looks pretty suspicious," Dave says, smiling. "You better lock him up."

"What's this all about?" I say.

The cop who isn't holding me says, "We had a call about a burglary in progress."

Looking over the roof of my truck's cab, I see the black BMW idling, lurking. The driver is watching. I shout, "*Is this your parking space?* Why didn't you just honk? I know you can do it!"

The nonrestraining cop says, "You mean this is about a parking space?"

Suddenly the driver of the BMW seems to remember an important errand. He backs up and shoots out of the parking area.

Dave, who could charm the horns off a bull, gives the cops a tour of the work we're doing. It's obvious we're not burglarizing the place. Burglars don't paint.

The cop who frisked me points at a fixture I've installed and says, "I've got a ceiling light like that one but it keeps cutting in and out."

"It's overheating," I say. "They cut out when they overheat." I explain that the newer lights contain a thermal switch—a safety feature so they don't cause a fire. The fixture is probably buried in insulation. Everybody's jamming insulation everywhere these days. You're supposed to leave an air gap around the light box so it can cool. "Go up to your attic and clear some space around the light if you can."

"I'll try that," the cop says.

"What about that black BMW?" Dave asks.

The cop closes his eyes and shakes his head, his lips compressed in a weary grin.

We're allies, now, in the endless skirmishes of the great class war.

Shane: Love and a '55 Corvette

August 1988 and August 1999

In August of 1988 Shane was fifteen years old. He had respectful Virginia manners and a somewhat troubled background. He'd recently been sent to California to live with his father after a stint in a military school and problems with his mother. He was polite, big, and strong.

I was looking for a part-time helper.

Without telling Shane what I had in mind, I asked him to come over and have a talk with me. I was working on a deck. When Shane arrived, I made some small talk while examining a pile of lumber.

I squatted to pick up one end of a heavy board.

Without asking, Shane squatted and picked up the other end.

Excellent. That was the job interview. He'd just passed.

"Shane," I said, "would you like a job?"

A helpful attitude is the quality I look for in a worker.

Shane owed his father a hundred dollars. He took the job as carpenter's helper. I showed him where to haul wood, dig holes, mix concrete. He could hammer and saw. He was sturdy, quiet, self-effacing.

After a week Shane's stepmother thanked me for hiring him. "You're better than military school," she said. "Just look at him. Upright, confident."

I don't train kids in attitude. The job does. I just try to lead by example.

Shane already knew (or said he knew) how to work on cars, though he was too young to drive. I paid him to change the oil in my truck. A few miles down the road the oil drain plug fell out, and I barely dodged an engine meltdown. Not everything works out.

Not everything was working out between Shane and his father, either, though Shane didn't talk about it. Shane paid off the hundred dollars, but then, with his sixteenth birthday, he started to drive. His father let him use a vintage Corvette, one of the family cars. Shane had to supply the gas money and make the repairs himself. The car was barely operational, and with its solid rear axle it drove like a rowboat.

With that car to support, Shane worked as my part-time helper for a year and a half. He dug ditches for an irrigation system. He mixed concrete and hauled wood for a massive driveway entry gate. He helped me tear out a roof and build a new one. Meanwhile he'd found a girlfriend and was doing poorly in school.

Shane showed me a photo of himself and Minh, his girlfriend, taken at a costume party. Shane was dressed as a priest while Minh was wearing a toga with a snake—an asp—wrapped around her arm. A lovely girl, Vietnamese.

On the last job Shane did with me, we built a backyard deck for a modest house in Mountain View. Sometimes everything clicks. I'd designed the deck to be low to the ground with hidden support so it seemed to float. I'd kept it simple and modest. It looked great. We finished the final decking on a cloudy day with intermittent showers that became more and more mittent. As I cut the final piece of wood, I got a shock from the wet electric saw.

We were both soaked, driving home in the cab of my truck. Shane told me he'd be driving his car to Virginia next week, moving back to his mother.

"You're taking the Corvette? Will it make it that far?"

"My dad's buying a bunch of spare parts for me to bring along. It's hard to find that stuff if you break down in Utah."

"And he's *paying* for it?"

"Yes, sir. He really wants me gone."

"So what's up with Minh? Is she going too?"

"No, sir."

"So is that your dad's idea? How do you feel about that?"

"It's kind of a weird situation."

"Weird in what way?"

"Nothing." Shane was never the chatty type, though he would criticize my driving if he thought I was "cheating on a corner." To Shane it was a matter of honor to stay within the lines. I don't know why it was so important to him, but sometimes I'd shade the line just to get his goat.

Shane, age seventeen, drove the '55 Corvette with a trunk full of spare parts from California to Virginia in four days. He could have made it in three, but he had to stop and replace a few items, which, fortunately, he'd brought along. I thought it a shame he didn't dawdle some, taking in a few sights. Shane, though, was always a straight-ahead kind of guy. When he had a job—digging a hole, driving across a continent—he was focused right through to the end.

A week later, Minh and her mother had a visit with Shane's father. I'm glad I wasn't there. Not for nothing was the man known as Kattila the Hun.

Minh was pregnant. Shane had known this before going East. The mother was on dialysis. They had no income. Minh planned to have the baby and drop out of high school. Shane wanted to marry her.

Of course he'd marry her. I could have predicted it from that first job interview.

Shane flew back to Minh, sans Corvette. He'd discovered which of the two he could live without.

Now, ten years later in August of 1999, I am called back to do some work at the house in Mountain View where Shane and I did our final job together. In the quiet of the backyard, the deck floats over the lawn, lovely and modest. I feel a surge of pride. It just might be the nicest thing I ever built, perfect in its proportions, so true to its surroundings, so restful. Sweet and yet strong.

And Shane has a ten-year-old child.

Shane, we built something good.

Murder of a Client

Friday, September 23, 1988

Isabella, my favorite decorator, calls and says, "I've got a strange one for you. He's an alcoholic. He's wealthy, but you never know when he'll drive off a cliff. Get your money before you leave. Are you game?"

It's a new-looking community behind a security gate in Cupertino. The units are conventional, what you get when you build tract houses with a dose of quality. Large garages, no trees. Sterile.

Bob is an old man. He smokes, shuffles around, and mumbles *God damn it* a lot. He's white. His girlfriend Lisa is fresh, young, athletic, lovely—looks about half his age. She's black. She says she's studying for the law boards. She's framed her undergraduate degree and hung it on the wall: Princeton, 1979.

Lisa lives here with her two kittens. And Bob.

The white kitten, Lisa tells me, has just been declawed, so he mustn't leave the house. Without claws he's defenseless.

"And the other?" I ask, indicating the black kitten.

"She can take care of herself," Lisa says with a meaningful look. "That little pussy has claws."

Okay, this is weird. And none of my business.

I remove a valence and install a multiglobe light over the bathroom sink. I work fast. Unfortunately, the faster I work, the less I can charge for labor—just the minimum service call. I use these small jobs as loss leaders because they often lead to bigger jobs later on.

Every time I go out to my truck for a tool or supplies, the black kitten climbs in. Mewing, purring, curling up and beseeching me with kitten eyes, she's either very friendly or desperate to escape.

When I finish, Bob is gone. Lisa inspects the work and says, "Hey. You're good."

"Good" in this case means you can't tell I've been there. She writes a check and follows me out to the truck. I roll down the window, hand her the black kitten that has nestled into a cup holder, and I drive straight to the bank as Isabella instructed.

At the bank they tell me the checking account has closed.

I call Lisa. She apologizes profusely. I return. She pays me cash. She seems like a spacehead. Maybe she's stoned. Anyway, an hour wasted.

Tuesday, October 4, 1988

Isabella sends me back for more work behind the security gate in Cupertino. Another woman is working there, hanging wallpaper. I'm installing wall sconces and an overhead track light.

While we're working, Bob and Lisa get into a shouting battle. After they cuss each other out, Bob yells, "You're a junkie!"

Lisa with a flat tone in her voice says, "That's right. I'm addicted to your lo-o-ove." Then, sharply: "If you don't quit, you're going to die of cirrhosis of the liver."

Bob: "I don't drink that much."

Lisa: "You're an alcoholic! You quit AA, you quit every treatment program."

"Junkie."

"I haven't had a joint in so long . . ."

The wallpaper lady finishes up quickly and somewhat sloppily. Outside she tells me, "I'll never go back there. Ever!"

I should probably feel the same. These people are out of control. But when I finish, as Lisa watches Bob writing me a check, a calculating look comes over her face. "Could you replace these downlights?" she asks, indicating the living room ceiling. "Is that all right with you, Bob?"

"God damn it," Bob says.

Apparently that means yes.

Lisa and I make arrangements. I give an outrageously high estimate—I'm not interested unless the money's good. She accepts.

I don't know if Lisa actually wants the lights or if it's just a domination game here. That little pussy has claws.

The robotic tone of Lisa's voice as she told Bob, "I'm addicted to your lo-o-ove," sounded as if she were reading a line, badly. As if she too were controlled by something with claws.

Tuesday, October 18, 1988

Lisa is home when I arrive; Bob is out. Good. It's easier to work when the two are apart.

Everything goes well and I work fast, but the blankety-blank electric-parts supplier short-counted me, and I have to drive to San Jose to pick up another can for the downlights, wasting an hour on a hot afternoon. Unfortunately, Bob is there when I return. He and Lisa commence fighting.

She taunts him: "In eight days you're going to jail. You got a string of DUIs. They caught you driving with a suspended license. You ready for jail? They're gonna fuck your powdery butt."

Bob throws a bowl of soup at her. He's shaky.

On the kitchen wall is a placard:

> It is better to have loved and lost.
> Much better.

I get paid and immediately drive to the bank and cash the check. I never want to see them again. Good money doesn't justify shit karma.

January 10, 1991

Isabella calls and says, "Remember Lisa? She was murdered. Isn't that awful?"

Immediately I ask, "Was it Bob?"

Apparently it wasn't. At least he was never mentioned as a suspect, though the papers described Lisa as caretaker of Bob's "upscale condo" in Cupertino (a different place from the home where I had worked for them), and she was killed in the condo, and the killing had sexual elements.

It's a gruesome story involving a drug dealer and crack cocaine. Lisa's hands had been tied behind her back. She was slashed with a knife. Her face was bound with duct tape so she couldn't breathe. She died of suffocation and knife wounds.

Could I have helped Lisa Hopewell? How do you help a junkie? How do you stop a hurricane?

I installed the lights professionally and cleanly. Got paid and got out.

A Bear and a Blue Jay

Friday, April 21, 1989

Eugene is something of a bear, hairy and gruff. He wants me to remove cork tile from a living room wall, then repair and texture the plaster. He warns me: "No fuck-ups."

First, he wants references. I give two names. One is a recent client; the other, an old friend. He hears the surnames and says, "Two Jewish women. I like that."

Whatever.

I go home.

A pair of crested Steller's jays are trying to build a nest outside my back door. The location they've selected is on a high double beam. The two boards of the beam are separated, bolted to opposite sides of a 6×6 post. For a week now the jays have brought more and more moss, twigs, bag ties, and paper scraps, most of which fall through the five-and-a-half-inch gap between the two boards and onto the entry stairs. There's enough debris on those steps to build five nests—but so far there's no nest on the beam.

As I pass under them, the birds cuss me in jay language, *cheek-cheek-cheek*. Actually, cussing is the only language a jay knows—like some carpenters I've met. The birds are incompetent builders. No, that's unfair. They need a few tips on how to bridge a gap.

Eugene calls me: "I talked to those women. They sound like your mother and your sister. You're hired."

Over the weekend, when the blue jays are out gathering moss and car-flattened plastic drinking straws, I place a few twigs across the crevice of the double beam, spanning the gap. Laying the foundation. Sometimes a bird needs a mentor.

On Monday I scrape the cork tiles from Eugene's wall, repair the drywall surface, and try skip-troweling. Badly. I've always considered skip-troweling to be the low-class solution, a cheap alternative to the skill and extra labor of creating a smooth wall, so I've never done it except in small repairs where I was matching an existing pattern. Now, in this high-class Woodside home, Eugene wants this large, prominent living room wall to be skip-troweled.

There's a first try for every task.

Needing more mud, I go to Orchard Supply Hardware where, as it happens, a man in white overalls covered with plaster is buying supplies. I ask him about skip-troweling, and he tells me to buy topping compound, not the regular joint compound, and to "mix it kinda wet." Have a light touch, let it set on the wall for a few minutes, then flatten it a bit with a second pass. "Use lotsa drop cloths because it's drippy."

When I return, Eugene greets me at the door and says the wall looks like crap. I say I'm aware of that. Then Eugene says I left a trowel in the kitchen sink. "Be professional. Don't use the kitchen sink."

Somehow I sense that he's speaking for his wife, whom I've never seen though I know she's home. He's the bear protecting his mate. And it's his mate who's upset about the sink and who is prejudging the wall.

The next day, Tuesday, I find the zone. Skipping that trowel over the wall feels oddly like conducting a symphony with a baton. Stroke, stroke, stroke, trying for a random pattern while being systematic.

When I finish, Eugene says he's happy. I'm less happy. Once you start scrutinizing a skip-troweled wall, you start seeing unintentional patterns, the repetitive strokes.

Back home, the Steller's jays have finished their nest—or perhaps, better put, they have abandoned all hope of improving it—and mama jay is now sitting on spotted green eggs. Even after my help their home is a lopsided pile of twigs.

While mama sits, papa jay tries to attack me through the window glass. He pecks. Cusses. Scratches. He will defend his imperfect nest. And who am I to sit in judgment? Maybe to him it's beautiful, like a skip-troweled wall. Or maybe next time he'll do better.

So will I.

Earthquake

October 17, 1989

Today's job was rewiring a house in Menlo Park. It was grubby crawlspace work, creeping on my belly, running Romex, lying on my back hammering staples into joists. Thinking, always, *I'd hate to be down here in an earthquake.* Now I'm swimming laps. Oddly enough, after a hard day's work there is nothing I enjoy more than swimming myself to utter exhaustion.

It's 5:04:49 p.m. Suddenly I'm surging on a wave. Like in the ocean. I'm body-surfing.

I'm swept to the side of the pool. Waves are breaking over the edge. Aluminum chairs are dancing and rattling all over the concrete deck. That was the sound of the quake for me—clattering aluminum chairs. With water splashing all over the concrete deck, there is a smell like a dusty road after a summer rain.

The pool is at a private club. My son Will, age seven, comes running to me wearing a baseball glove. He's been throwing balls on the tennis court. He says, "What happened?"

"Earthquake," I say. "You feel it?"

"I fell down."

"I was in the pool," I say. "Come to think of it, a swimming pool may be just about the safest place you can be in an earthquake. Nothing can fall on you."

"Can I get in?"

The water level is a few inches below where it was. The power is out. Otherwise everything is normal. No damage. What can I say? When you've lived in California for a long time, you get blasé about earthquakes. This one didn't seem any different, only bigger.

"Sure," I say. "Jump in."

And so for the next half-hour I finish my laps while Will dives for pennies. It will prove to be my last half-hour of calm in the next few weeks.

Two boys also jump in the pool—with their clothes on. Later their mother arrives. "We fell in," they say. "The earthquake made us fall."

"I hope your shoes aren't in there," she says.

"No, we took them off," they say. "Then we fell in."

After I shower and change, as I'm getting a cup of coffee, the bartender tells me that a section of the Nimitz Freeway collapsed.

Hmm.

Will and I drive to the Portola Valley Town Center, where my older son, Jesse, is just finishing soccer practice, which also continued as normal. A soccer field—like Will on the tennis court and me in the pool—was a safe place to be. The town center sits exactly, literally, right smack-dab on top of the San Andreas Fault. My twelve-year-old son had been standing on it. He said he fell down, then stayed perched on his knees watching waves move through the grass.

None of us have any idea how big the quake was. But as I drive to pick up my daughter, Ruth, on the radio we hear that a section of the Bay Bridge collapsed.

In my truck we follow the route of the San Andreas Fault along Portola Road, crossing back and forth over the fault line, then continue on Sand Hill Road to the gymnasium where Ruth has gymnastics.

She's waiting for us in the parking lot. Everyone else has already been picked up. Her class had to leave the building because ceiling tiles were falling down, so she's been waiting outside. "Where *were* you?" she asks. She was bored.

We drive home. Many radio stations are off the air. KNBR is on. They say the Bay Bridge and the Nimitz collapsed and fires are breaking out.

On the way home we see a small barn that has collapsed.

I stop in front of our house and hear voices and falling brick. The La Honda Fire Brigade is dismantling our chimney, which is on the verge of collapse. My wife Rose is holding a flashlight for them. Our power is out.

The house is a shambles. The shockwaves have tossed books, records, and cassette tapes all over the living room. Food fell, glass smashed all over the kitchen—molasses, peanut butter, vinegar, sugar, wineglasses, heirloom china. And it's now dark. I find flashlights and light lanterns and loan a Coleman lantern to the neighbors. Their house has a huge hole in the wall where the chimney collapsed.

I inspect our house. Sheetrock came loose on the walls. Papers and books flew around, but the computer didn't budge. The bathroom medicine cabinets have burst open. The sink is full of pills and Band-Aids. The back porch detached itself from the house.

So we start cleaning up. I bring in a garbage can, and we fill it up. Ruth tends to her stuffed animals, who are traumatized by the quake. Will and Jesse clean up the living room. Rose tackles the kitchen. I reshelve the bathroom supplies. We replant some potted flowers that crashed. We mop the kitchen floor several times, which seems to have no effect. It's still sticky, smelling of vinegar and molasses.

The phone works, but you have to wait for a dial tone. I call a friend whose husband is out of town. "Are you all right?" I ask.

"I'm fine," she says. "Don't worry about me."

Several days later I learn that this woman was standing in the rubble of her collapsed fireplace, an entire corner of her house suddenly missing, telling me she's fine and not to worry. She thought I should help somebody who might really need it. This attitude of altruism will show up again and again among practically everybody in the days to come.

We listen to the radio a bit, but its tone is basically one of panic—saying, "DON'T PANIC!!!" and giving a lot of foolish and contradictory advice such as, "Stay out of your house!" and then a minute later: "Don't go outside!" So we turn it off and deal with the real.

We light candles.

I leave a window open. Some instinct tells me that if there is any danger, I'll hear it coming.

The kids and the dog sleep on the floor in our bedroom, which is how we respond to disasters, and we've had a few: storms, falling trees.

The night is silent. Maybe all wildlife is traumatized. Not even the owls are hooting.

We feel aftershocks, little trembles. The candle shakes, so I blow it out. Can't risk a fire.

When my eyes adjust, they find light even in the darkest night. I see a shadowy spread of bodies and blankets, a slight radiance of flesh—or so I imagine.

The dog snores.

Near dawn, an owl starts to hoot. Watch out, mice. Nature can't be stopped.

Plenty

The Karma of Plumbing

May 1979 to November 1989

Greg is a rich man. He has a tennis court, pool, brick walkways. He has a lovely wife, two blond munchkins, a golden retriever. He lives in a mansion covered with ivy. Greg is a Xerox salesman, and he must sell those copiers by the truckload.

In May of 1979 Greg hires me to extend a gas pipe the entire length of his house through the crawlspace. When I finish, late in the day, Greg asks me to double-check all the fittings because his wife is terrified of leaks.

I'm charging by the hour, so the longer the job lasts, the more I earn. But . . . "I already double-checked," I lie.

Unforgivable.

I never lie.

And yet I lied. Crawling the length of that house was like doing sixty-two pushups. On the first pass I'd already connected each joint firmly and tightly.

Exhaustion is no excuse.

Half a year later, in October of 1979, I get a call from Greg. He's furious. After continually smelling a faint odor of gas, he called a plumber named Bruno to check it out. "Bruno said you did it all wrong."

"Could I talk to Bruno?"

Greg gives me the number. I call Bruno and ask what I did wrong.

Bruno has a German accent: "One of the joints was wrapped in Teflon tape. You can't use Teflon on gas pipe."

"I know I can't do that. Just one joint?"

"That's right."

"You told him I did everything wrong."

"I may have exaggerated."

I *never* use Teflon tape, so I don't know how I happened to use it there, but Bruno charged more to fix that one mistake than I charged to plumb the entire line. Greg hasn't asked for reimbursement—I think he just wanted to yell at me—but I send him a refund check: a day's pay. A day of crawling, for *nothing*.

Could've been worse. At least I didn't blow up the place.

Eight years later, in 1987, I remodel a kitchen for a depressed—and depressing—woman named Jacqueline. Even in her gloom Jacqueline is a gourmet French cook. She treats me to exquisite pastries. Always stiff and formal, she sits straight-backed in a chair, flipping through cookbooks, pouting and moping and watching me work. Maybe I'm flattering myself, but she seems to entertain a fantasy of boinking the plumber.

Unfortunately for Jacqueline I have no such fantasy about her. She just seems so *sad*.

A few weeks after the job Jacqueline calls and tells me that her kitchen flooded. The plumber she called, a man named Bruno, said I'd kinked a drain line on the dishwasher, causing it to overflow and ruin her floor.

"Did he say I did it all wrong?"

"No, just the one kink. He said otherwise everything looked great."

Her insurance will cover it, so she isn't asking for anything. She just thought I'd want to know. She doesn't seem angry. Or sad. Maybe Bruno has fulfilled her fantasy. At least he isn't badmouthing me anymore.

Two years later it's 1989. On the Monday before Thanksgiving I get a call from a woman named Ingrid for some plumbing repair. She says I was recommended by her friend Jacqueline. (Which makes me wonder: Are they enemies?) Ingrid has the same address, and the same last name, as Greg. Oh, my gosh.

I take the job. What will happen when her husband sees me? Will he attack? Will he send me away?

When I show up, men with jackhammers are removing concrete around the swimming pool. There are soccer balls in the ivy and cleats by the door. The munchkins have grown.

Greg isn't there.

Ingrid is a touchy, bouncy type. She says a man was working on their plumbing this week, and then the shower and sink faucets stopped dead.

Jokingly I say, "What was his name? Bruno?"

"Yes. That was the man, Bruno."

Plumbing is a small world. I say, "You should make him fix this."

"I don't want him back. He said something indiscreet. About a friend."

About Jacqueline? Did they boink?

As a plumber, you don't just enter people's houses. You enter under the sink, behind the toilet, over the tub. You enter their lives.

Bruno entered. Then he blabbered. What an asshole.

Ingrid's shower and faucets are clogged with debris. Bruno should have flushed the line after making his repair. I say nothing about his fundamental mistake. No badmouthing. This circle is now complete.

Ingrid is delighted. She bounces up and down. "I can wash my hair!" (She already looks great.)

I leave a bill and a business card. Will her husband recognize and remember my name? We'll see. This is Tuesday.

Wednesday night I get a call from Ingrid. The men with jackhammers shut off the water to work on the pool, and now the water won't go back on. The valve is stuck and the handle broke off. Could I come back on Friday?

Certainly.

On Friday Greg greets me at the door. I say hello. Greg says, "I had seventeen guests yesterday for Thanksgiving dinner, and no water."

He shows not a flicker of recognition. To him I'm just a generic tradesman. Which is how it is with most people. I'm the invisible plumber.

The problem is in the main shutoff, a gate valve. A brick walkway surrounds the base of the valve, leaving no space to attach a wrench. I show Greg. He runs off and returns with a jackhammer borrowed from the pool workers. He doesn't ask one of the workers to do it for him. He just grabs the jackhammer and blasts away. I see the key to Greg's success as a salesman: he is a man who doesn't blink at denial. He gets results. He turns his own front entry into rubble. Then he watches as I solder a ball valve into place with painstaking care.

As we stand among the wreckage, the dirt, the fragments of brick, when I turn the new handle, the sound of rushing water makes him shout: "Thank you! Thank you!" Then he looks at me closely. "Do I know you from somewhere?"

I tell him about our previous encounter ten years ago.

He's surprised: "That was *you*? That son of a bitch? He had a beard. He had hair down his ass."

I'm clean-shaven at the moment. Short-haired. I'm in disguise.

Then Greg laughs. So much time has passed. "I remember now—you sent me a *refund*. I was amazed."

We part on good terms. Another circle, complete.

There are lessons to be learned.

Don't lie. Don't badmouth. Don't blabber.

Double-check your gas lines.

Watch the karma.

Plenty

November 1989 to January 1990

In the mail comes a handwritten letter on lined paper, careful script, like a school assignment. The letter is from a woman in Honolulu I've never met. I imagine a trim desk, elegant pen, a pot of tea.

> Dear Mr. Cottonwood,
>
> You repaired a bathroom for my daughter in Portola Valley. By her report, you do excellent work. I own a condominium in Palo Alto which is rented by a nice young doctor who desires to make some changes. Please do whatever he wishes and send me the bill.
>
> Victoria S

I find a meandering complex of condos behind a Beacon gas station. When I meet the "nice young doctor," he introduces himself as Doctor Strimwick and calls me by my first name. Strike one. He looks to be about seventeen years old. Strike two. He wants to divide a room. Okay.

He's an orthopedic surgeon and a friendly guy. Already having an MD, he's now taking classes at Stanford for an MBA.

I mail an estimate to Honolulu, since Victoria hasn't provided a phone number. A week later I receive a handwritten letter on lined paper, careful script:

> Dear Mr. Cottonwood,
> Please proceed.
> Victoria S

The day after Thanksgiving, when I show up to begin the job, there is a note taped to the steel security gate:

> Joe—Get in as best you can.
> Dr. Strimwick

Strike three. But I'm committed.

The gate is six feet high. I climb over. As my feet touch the ground, a man's voice says "What the *hell* are you doing?" I show the note, which seems to placate the man. It's from a doctor, after all.

Opening the gate from the inside, I start moving all my tools, 2×4s, chop saw, drywall, and a bucket of mud down the long passageway, into an elevator, and down another hallway to Strimwick's unit on the third floor.

Young Dr. Strimwick seems to be hot property in the marriage marketplace. While I'm working, six different women leave messages on his answering machine. It's Friday. The kid will have a busy weekend.

When I return on Saturday, Strimwick is home. I install two doors and trim while he rearranges all his belongings, which seem to consist mainly of shirts, medical texts, and a stack of *Playboy* magazines— "Anatomy manuals," he says with a boyish grin. Watching as I drill holes and drive screws, he says, "I do the same thing in my job." He studies my chop saw. "Brutal," he says, shaking his head.

Strimwick leaves to meet a woman. He says, "I hope you won't be working into the evening."

"Shall I leave my tools?" I ask. "The chop saw, perhaps?"

"I won't be cutting anything tonight." He laughs. "Just screwing."

A tenant from downstairs comes to complain about the noise but loses his nerve. Maybe I'm intimidating, standing at the entry cradling a 22-ounce Vaughan framing hammer and a Makita 6-amp drill with a 2⅛-inch hole saw, plus, probably, a demeanor of taking-no-shit, while my clothes are coated with gypsum dust. Yeah, I've got attitude.

The doors take hours longer than I expected, and the doorknob doesn't fit. Lugging all my tools back to the truck, I prop the gate open with a scrap of wood. When I return, another tenant is waiting, holding the scrap. "I removed it," he says. "For security reasons."

He actually says "for security reasons" in normal conversation. I find this abnormal. The whole condo complex gives me the creeps. Too tidy. No children.

I can't return for a few weeks, overbooked, making good money but missing time with my kids. I like being so busy in December that I don't notice the short days, the goddamn darkness. When I finally return on a Friday, December 22, day after solstice, I'm all alone. More messages pile up on the answering machine, smiley voices—you can almost smell the perfume and feel the powder. I install the doorknob, paint the walls, doors, and trim, which takes all day. Painting is meditative, and I have a backlog of contemplation to catch up on. I wonder about Dr. Strimwick's seeking an MBA: Doesn't he have enough? Is orthopedic work unsatisfying, sawing off limbs, putting screws in shoulder joints? One thing is clear: a young man with an MD, seeking an MBA, is powerful bait for the female sex.

By evening I'm mellow and the job is done. All jobs are done. As I drive my truck past the pond near my house, a young coyote runs across the headlight beams. Home, parking, I step out under swaying redwood trees, the rush of wind in the branches. There's the scent of rain, the chill of a big storm approaching from Alaska.

Inside I write out a bill and lick the envelope addressed to Honolulu. My father-in-law calls and advises me to incorporate. He wants me to run the business like a business. Two of my children are setting up Christmas decorations, while the oldest, age thirteen, needs help hanging a hammock in his bedroom. Hot mulled cider is brewing.

Two weeks later, daylight now increasing, the quince in front of my house already in bloom, there's a check from Hawaii. A hand-written note on lined paper:

> Dear Mr. Cottonwood,
> Perfect. Thank you.
> Victoria S

Just that. Which is plenty.

Kattila the Hun

July 1990

Sometimes you're blindsided. Sometimes the right thing turns out to be wrong. Sometimes a client goes berserk—cracks, like the earth beneath your feet. In October 1989, the so-called World Series Earthquake shook La Honda hard. My house sustained damage, but I felt lucky compared to one of my neighbors. One rock-walled side of his house peeled open and fell off, leaving it exposed like a dollhouse.

I was suddenly in demand as a contractor. After a few weeks dealing with emergencies all over town, I settled into a long-term job rebuilding my neighbor's house.

Kal, my neighbor, was a small man with a competitive instinct. If you jogged with Kal—which I did—he would run slightly faster than you. If you played tennis with him, even if you were a better player—which I was—he'd find a way to beat you. Kal was a vice president at a big corporation. His coworkers called him Kattila the Hun.

Kal had a teenage son named Shane. Kal bet his son that he couldn't beat his father in a three-mile race. The bet was for a hundred dollars. Shane was already a big, strapping boy. Shane trained every day for a month. Shane was taller, legs longer, heart younger—and yet Kal won the race. "It's about desire," Kal said. And he made Shane pay him a hundred dollars.

The money didn't come easily to Shane. Kal wouldn't give his son an allowance. Shane ended up working for me on a couple of jobs—digging ditches, carrying lumber—to pay off the bet.

Kal had a vivacious wife, a southern gal. She was his third wife and, he said, his last. He told her with a straight face that he would never divorce her because he had been through two already. Murder, he said, was the only option.

The earthquake work went well enough. After seven months I'd exceeded my estimate by about fifty percent, but I'd uncovered extra damage and Kal had added several changes. The house looked better than ever. He paid without a problem.

A couple months later, in July, Kal asks me to install a new kitchen door. He selects—rightly—a 1¾-inch exterior door to replace the old 1⅜-inch model. After discussing the options, we decide not to replace the existing jamb but rather to rout it to accommodate the thicker door.

On a pleasant, sunny day I do the job while nobody is home. There's a special pleasure in carefully performing an exacting task, knowing it's hard but knowing you can do it well. Kal is a stickler for details. I work cautiously, slowly, exactly. The router throws wood chips all over the place, so I sweep the porch and walkway, leaving a tidy site.

A few hours later, Kal pounds on my door. He says he wants to have a word with me.

The words are many and foul. "You got sawdust in the fucking garden."

It never occurred to me to worry about that. "It's good mulch," I say. Perhaps not the most useful comment.

He's shouting: "Look at that! White sawdust on dark soil! It looks like sugar on shit!"

"I could wet it down with a hose. It'll darken. I could rake it, mix it in."

"No! You have to spread topsoil over it."

"Okay, I'll do that."

"No! I'll have to do it myself!"

"I'll buy the topsoil."

"No!"

At this point, I realize we've gone beyond reasoning. The encounter is building like a thunderhead over the Kansas plain. There's the rapid, boiling rise, the ominous dark. Now comes the blast of wind. Lightning. Hail.

"*You're a fucking slob!*" He's in my face now, shouting jaw to jaw. "I've been picking up after you for *nine fucking months!*"

"I wish you'd said something earlier if you think I'm not cleaning up. This is the first I've heard about—"

"FUCK YOU! FUCK YOUR FAMILY! FUCK YOUR FUCKING DOG!"

Now he's totally lost it. He likes my dog. He's offered to buy that dog from me several times. (Which, by the way, shows utter cluelessness about family values: my kids love that dog.)

So far, somehow I've retained my composure. This is my first experience with the military drill-sergeant break-down approach—with Kattila the Hun. He's glaring into my eyes, drooling slightly, bouncing on his feet like a boxer.

"Kal," I say, "I wish you were handling this with a little more maturity."

"BULLSHIT ON MATURITY! YOU'RE A FUCKING *SLOB!* NOW WHAT ARE YOU GONNA DO ABOUT IT?"

"Jeez, Kal."

"*WHAT!?*" There's a look of eager anticipation on his face.

"No wonder Shane hates you."

Oops.

Kal breaks into a crooked smile. "Nice try," he says. He turns and marches into his house.

I wish I hadn't said that. It's a true statement, and it's exactly what I was thinking at that moment, but my saying it . . . he'd won. He'd broken me down.

I was shaking. All evening.

And I'd lost.

Kal always wins.

The Big Freeze

December 1990

There's an unspoken bargain struck between residents of coastal California and residents of most of the USA: we get the quakes; you get the freeze.

Occasionally there are exceptions. Sometimes there's a shaker on the East Coast or in the Midwest. Here in La Honda we have a few frosty nights every winter. For the most part, though, the bargain is kept.

And then there is December of 1990. This is just a year after the big World Series earthquake, so it seems we're getting the worst of both sides of the bargain. We're still patching our houses from the quake, and now the pond at the center of La Honda freezes over. Ducks are wandering around in a state of bewilderment until my neighbor empties bags of grain on the ice for them.

Everybody's pipes are cracking. Nobody has ever bothered to insulate their exposed water pipes because it has never been necessary. When a pipe freezes, of course, the water inside the pipe expands. The pipe bursts.

Readers who live in Ohio or Maine—or Canada or Russia—are probably laughing at our naiveté, imagining a town of stoned hippies standing around in paisley shorts and sandals, shivering and saying, "Wow, man, my pipes are shattered!" Despite La Honda's public image, we're not exactly like that.

Saturday, December 22

I get so many broken-pipe calls that I disconnect the answering machine. We need to prepare the house for our annual Christmas party— with thirty guests invited—coming this evening. We have no water. Our outdoor hose bibbs have frozen, so I've shut off the main valve. I make emergency patches, then cut and cap the exposed pipe along an outside wall that extends to a hose outlet.

With my own water restored, while my wife and kids deal with party prep, I repair a pipe for the nuclear physicist who lives down the street and another for an old friend who lives nearby. I arrive home an hour late for my own party. In spite of the cold, we build a fire outdoors in an old metal wash tub and gather around, singing and toasting.

Sunday, December 23

I try not to work on Sundays, but today, postparty, I repair frozen pipes in a yurt owned by a nice man who happened to inherit a fortune. His swimming pool has frozen over, though we won't be addressing that damage today. Meanwhile his fourteen-year-old daughter is driving his new minivan up and down the driveway, up and down, up and down.

Then I go to the house of a musician, a happy-go-lucky guy who plays keyboards in a popular band. While I solder patches onto his pipes, I chat with his new girlfriend, a woman who has moved from house to house in La Honda, wrecking one home after another. She's a coke-head. Doesn't he know? More is about to burst in his life than just water pipes.

Then, back home, I note that many of our plants are dying. The water meter across the street from our house has blown up. It simply exploded.

Monday, December 24

On Christmas Eve I begin the day by repairing another broken pipe, inside the wall this time, for the nuclear physicist who lives below us. He'd gone away for the weekend and turned off the heat in his house. When I present the bill, he gives me a check and a bottle of wine. Good man.

Then I repair pipes for Ezra at his vacation house at the end of three mountainous miles of dirt road. The house is both modern and rustic, set now in a frozen Shangri-La. The outdoor hot tub overlooks the ocean and the sunset. Fortunately the tub had been drained.

Ezra uses the house as a summer retreat but holds an annual Hanukkah party. This year it will be on December 26. There is also a geodesic dome on the property where Kilo, the caretaker, lives. Ezra is a psychiatrist, and I suspect that Kilo is one of his clients. Clearly, Kilo needs to live in isolation at the end of three miles of bad road. In fact, as you might judge from his name, Kilo is only half present even when he is standing right in front of you. Anyway, Kilo shows me around.

A pet peacock follows my every move. I'm wearing gloves with the fingertips cut off, which seems to fascinate the bird, as do my hooded sweatshirt and propane torch. Each repair I make leads to a new break— utterly frustrating, a plumber's nightmare.

I work ten hours. It's night; it's freezing; it's Christmas Eve. I have to leave Kilo and peacock with no hot and limited cold water.

Ezra, with wife and daughter, arrives as I depart. He is clearly disappointed at the state of things—his wife more so and quite vocal about it. From the trunk of the Bentley, Ezra's grown daughter extracts a bottle of wine—a fine one, which is the only kind Ezra would have—and hands it to me with a thank you. The wife frowns. Ezra scowls.

Two jobs, two bottles of wine—one given gratefully, one with mixed feelings. But given.

Back home my kids have stayed up late, so I catch them in time to sing a few Christmas carols, have an eggnog, hang up stockings, and help put them to bed. I haven't even had a chance to clean myself up. Spatters of solder cling to my sweatshirt as I tuck them in. The kids all sleep together in one room on Christmas Eve, a tradition in our house, bundled on the carpet with blankets and dogs. All this emergency plumbing has kept me from finishing the presents I was building—trophy cases—in time for Christmas, but that's okay.

Tuesday, December 25

Most of our gifts are low-key this year: home-baked goods, baskets of plants, handmade books and drawings, coupons for massages or trips to the beach. And some partially built trophy cases, which I will finish today for my trophy-winning children. Only my youngest son is disappointed. He isn't being selfish or greedy, but at age eight he wants that old magic of Christmas as a seemingly endless unfolding of delights. Now he is learning that Christmas is finite. Part of the problem is that we had to cut back on gifts this year because we simply couldn't afford them. Another part is that Grampa was recently hospitalized and had no time to order presents, though they'll come later. Otherwise, though, the day is delightful, freezing outside but a warm fire burning within, fresh bread, cookies, and the special pleasure of staying home together, making things for each other.

Wednesday, December 26

I repair a pipe for Danny, my jeweler neighbor, and then spend another ten hours at Ezra's house while they have a party. A brunch. His daughter brings me lox, a bagel, a cup of tea, and several cookies while I crouch under the floor joists soldering pipe and discovering more problems. By late evening I've restored most of the hot water. When I finally get home the kids are in bed. They spent most of the day home alone so my wife could also go to work. We really need the money.

Monday, December 31

For a few days the temperature rises above freezing, and I catch up on a number of nonemergency broken pipes for a number of my favorite clients. Today, New Year's Eve, it's turned cold again. I return to Ezra's house, where everyone still seems to be cleaning up from the Hanukkah party. While the peacock follows me about, kibitzing, I restore water service to the nonurgent parts of the house. At one point, as I'm taking a break, Ezra smashes a telephone against a post and then explains to me: his fourteen-year-old adopted son just got kicked out of school and hopped a train. Now Ezra is sending the kid to a three-week, $3,400 wilderness survival school. Tonight the kid will sleep where it's thirty degrees below, on rocks that were warmed in a fire and buried in a pit. Ezra says, "He tests limits." Ezra narrows his eyes and asks me, "How much are you charging me?"

I tell him my standard rate, which he already knows.

"That's unconscionable," he says.

I've never heard that word from a client before. "I told you my rate before I started."

"Yes, but that's when we both thought it would be a small job. You've been here for days. Shouldn't I get a discount?"

For a moment I just stare at Ezra. Those days include Christmas Eve, the day after Christmas, and now here I am after dark on New Year's Eve at the end of a dirt road in the mountains that he and I both know wouldn't be visited by most plumbers. And most plumbers charge more than I do. "What's your hourly rate?" I ask.

"That has nothing to do with this," Ezra says.

"I'm sorry, but I can't give you a discount," I say.

"I don't have my business checks here. I'll have to mail it to you."

So he's claiming my work on his second home as a business expense to his psychiatry practice. At current tax rates he'll only pay half of my bill. Uncle Sam will pay the rest.

Talk about unconscionable.

I make it home in time to spend New Year's Eve with my youngest son. The two older kids, ages fourteen and twelve, are with friends where they are safe. My wife, our youngest, and I watch the movie *Lassie Come Home*, which proves to be too intense for the lad. Plenty of eight-year-olds could watch the slaughter of armies without a flinch. Not my son, who can't handle seeing a dog in jeopardy. We "guess" the ending for him and let him sit on our laps. A sensitive kid, like the other two. We've sheltered them from a cold and crazy world. I would have it no other way.

The Secret Value of Junk

Saturday, March 28, 1992

It's Saturday morning in Half Moon Bay, California. Before a Little League baseball game, I'm cruising a few garage sales with my son Will, who is almost ten years old. Will is wearing a dark blue uniform with a cap that says SIMMS PLUMBING. Simms and I are competitors for plumbing business, but I'm coaching their team.

This being Half Moon Bay, the weather is foggy and cool. Everything you touch is damp.

At one driveway I linger, checking out a stereo receiver, sorely tempted, but eventually I pass. Now where's Will?

I find him at a table of crap: common rocks, used nails, rusty cans, scraps of chain. An old guy with stubble beard and wool cap is watching Will's every move.

The boy fingers each item, frowning, pondering, curious. The old man's face reacts to each touch. The boy fondles a bedspring; the old man smiles. The boy rattles a coffee can filled with screws; the old man listens. The boy disdainfully drops a dirty hinge; the old man flinches.

Like everyone else at the sale, I gave the offerings only a glance—but my son and the old guy are on exactly the same wavelength. No prices are marked.

After a good fifteen minutes of study, Will selects four springs from ballpoint-pen size to bedspring size, and one thin chain.

The old guy gives thought to the price, rubbing his chin, clearly not wanting to take advantage of the boy but also not wanting to give away what might be his only sale of the day. Finally with a gruff voice he says, "A buck. That's two bits each for the springs, and I'll throw in the chain for free."

I hand the man a dollar.

The springs and chain will never be used. I think we all know that. What I am paying for is what I am too practical to understand—a dollar for the great mystery of hardware, for the encounter between two minds, one old and one young, who share a magic bond: they know the secret value of junk.

Big Game Hunter

January 1993

Tommy is about twenty-five years old and still looks like the all-American college boy. He's just bought a modest two-bedroom bungalow in Menlo Park, not a bad start for a kid.

Yes, Tommy's a kid in my mind. He was born a few years after John F. Kennedy was assassinated. The draft, the war in Vietnam are just history to him, something old people argue about—old folks like me, age forty-five.

Tommy's got rumpled hair, dimples, a winning smile. He could star in a movie as the romantic interest of Julia Roberts. Tommy would play the good "friend" whose interest she doesn't recognize as she throws herself at one bastard after another until finally she realizes . . .

I'm there because Isabella, my favorite decorator, is revamping Tommy's house. I'm installing new lights in every room, which requires an entire day of crawling through his insulated attic wrestling in the dust with Romex cable.

At some point, up in the attic, I must have slashed my finger. By the time I notice, the finger is filthy and swollen from knuckle to tip.

The next day I arrive at Tommy's house at 8 a.m. and Isabella lets me in. Tommy sleeps until nine, makes himself a cup of coffee, and hands me a pair of white slippers. "You have to wear these in the house," he says. "Leave your shoes at the door."

"I'm sorry," I say. "Did I make a mess?"

"No. Nothing like that. My wife called from Japan and told me to tell you to wear them. It's a Japanese thing. She's Japanese."

"Okay. No problem."

"The Japanese are insane about dirt. In fact they're insane about everything."

"Um . . ." I don't know what to say. He's talking about his wife. Can this marriage be saved? He's also talking about several of my friends and also my brother-in-law and my three half-Japanese nieces, all wonderful people.

"Okay, Tommy," Isabella breaks in. "I'll make sure he wears the slippers."

Isabella, I notice, is barefoot.

Tommy goes to work. The sink is full of dirty dishes.

"Have you met his wife?" I ask.

"No," Isabella says. "I'm decorating her house and I've never seen her."

"Who does the dishes?"

Isabella laughs. "For him? The dish fairy."

I work a ten-hour day wearing white slippers.

Isabella says Tommy designs computer games. He's just joined a new company. "The house was a stretch. Money's a little tight."

On Tommy's desk I notice a sketch pad full of combat drawings with circles that—I'm guessing—indicate where software buttons will be placed. A man's arm pierced by a knife; a button on his ring finger with the notation, *Escape*. No blood whatsoever. This is sanitized war.

My finger hurts.

I'm expecting the next work day to be short, just a few details to clean up, but Isabella meets me at the door with a whole new plan for the kitchen. Tommy's listening, fixing coffee. I say, "It'll cost another three hundred dollars." I smile at Tommy and say jokingly, "But with stock options you'll soon be a megamillionaire, right?"

Seriously, Tommy nods. "Uh huh." And he's out the door.

Isabella is glaring at me. "What are you doing?" she asks.

"I was just joking."

"Never talk about that. It's bad manners."

"Sorry. Does he really have stock options?"

"Of course. He'll make jillions."

That night I go to a party, a gathering of my friends and neighbors in La Honda. To my surprise my little infected finger draws a lot of interest. Today it's bright red. A circle gathers around me. A friend who is a dentist says I should soak it. Another friend says I should rub it with a marijuana poultice.

The circle dissipates, and I'm talking to Zeke, a neighbor. Zeke says: "My finger got infected like that in 'Nam. Red like that, then it got worms." He holds up his right hand: three fingers. The hand trembles. Zeke's hands always tremble.

"You get a Purple Heart for that?"

"Nope." He laughs, which ends in a hiccup.

"What did you do in 'Nam?"

"Survived."

"But really—what did you do?"

He glances over his shoulder, then in a low voice says, "I did what you do in a war. I mean, come on." He looks again at my finger. "See a doctor, will ya?"

But I never do. My finger heals. Some things, the body can fix.

Over the next years, Tommy does well with his combat games. Not jillions, but—yes—megamillions.

Zeke does less well. The hand still trembles.

Filthy Mother

Thursday, April 28, 1993

You work with construction workers, you end up talking like a construction worker. In a hardware store I'm buying springs for a garage door. Hefting one in my hands, I remark, "Wow. That's a heavy mother."

The salesman looks shocked. "No, it isn't a heavy mother. What a *filthy* thing to say. It's a heavy *spring*."

All I said was "mother." But words have roots. I'd forgotten I was speaking in code. This salesman knew the code and reacted to it.

I'm sorry I upset him but, honestly if he's that sensitive, he's in the wrong line of work.

My next stop is Men's Wearhouse, where I tell the salesman I need something dress-up. Suit and tie. I have nothing.

"*Nothing?*"

"Nothing formal."

"Is this for any particular occasion?"

"I'm receiving an award tonight."

"Ah. And you want to show a little respect."

Respect. Exactly. The salesman recommends a blue blazer. "That's your basic starter set." He fits me out in a light blue shirt, dark blue necktie, tan pants. I store them in the cab of my truck, a shopping bag full of respect.

Next stop is a house in Woodside where I meet a goddess, a woman blessed with the striking beauty that bestows special privileges, like a birthright. For the gorgeous goddess I scrape sprayed-on popcorn glitter from a ceiling, overhead work that sprinkles me with hopefully nontoxic chemical flakes. Then I re-mud the ceiling to make it smooth, more overhead work. Shoulders, neck, arms all dead by the end of the afternoon.

At a friend's house I shower the glitter off my body. In San Francisco, wearing the blue blazer and blue tie, watched by hundreds of the best and brightest, I receive the BABRA Award (from the Bay Area Book Reviewers Association) for children's literature.

I give a little speech about the power a writer is granted by readers, especially by children—a power to be used wisely. Make careful choices in the stories you tell—and in the words that you use.

After the awards, an elegant man says he likes the glitter in my hair. He means it as a compliment and sees it as part of my attire. I don't tell him how it got there. I'm glad I dressed up. It's an evening of honor, something every writer should have at least once in his life. Bless you, BABRA. Thank you.

Sometimes I cuss too much. But on this evening of BABRA I'm not even tempted.

As it happens, I got stiffed for scraping that glitter. The goddess woman never explained—she simply never paid. That's how the beautiful behave sometimes.

As for calling a piece of hardware a mother, I've never used that expression again. Though I might call it a goddess.

Wall Phone

Tuesday, July 13, 1993

I'm pissed at Katerina, a strikingly beautiful woman who has owed me $455 since April for a tough job at her expensive home in Woodside. I removed popcorn from her ceiling, then repaired and replastered. I ought to charge extra for overhead work—if you've ever had to reach over your head all day, you'll know what I mean. But I charged my regular rate, and she's stiffing me. Won't answer her phone. No communication. Nothing.

Today I'm doing some earthquake retrofit on my own home, cutting plywood panels to brace the inside framing of the crawl space, which with its low clearance ought to be called the creep space. I worm-wriggle under the house, measure, worm-wriggle out, cut the panel, worm-wriggle back in, dragging the panel.

In the darkness, I'm wearing a headlamp. The beam moves as I turn my head. I must lie awkwardly on my side. My fingers grope for nail and hammer. From this horizontal position I fasten the plywood to the knee wall. I've got a cordless phone in the pouch of my tool belt because I'm expecting a call from my son.

Lying sideways as I'm nailing one panel, I hear the phone ring.

My fingers fumble, searching. There's no phone in the tool belt.

Still ringing. Where?

There! Somehow—I'll never figure exactly how it happened—the phone got nailed to the wall through one corner of the plywood. Nailed solid. Upside down.

I crucified the cordless Panasonic.

It still works, and it's still ringing.

I can't miss this call from my son. I press the Talk button, then place my head against the wall, stretching my neck clumsily with my ear to the receiver.

"Hello, Jesse?"

A woman's voice: "I'm not Jesse. This is Katerina. Do I owe you some money?"

"Yes."

"Oh."

"Is there a problem?"

"Um . . ." A pause. "No."

That pause is a sign. Here's where I need to be sensitive and fully communicative and encourage her to be the same. I need to say, "I thought I heard a hesitation in your voice. Is there something I did that was unsatisfactory? Let's try to work this out."

I don't say it. On my hands and knees contorting my neck—which aches already—pressing my ear to an upside down phone that I've just nailed to the wall, I say, "So can I expect a payment?"

She hangs up.

How could there be a problem? I'm a careful worker. What could possibly give her the idea that I'm incompetent?

With difficulty I pry the phone from the wall, trying—unsuccessfully—not to crack the plastic casing.

She'll never pay.

A Raw Vintage

Monday, January 24, 1994

On the coffee table are glossy magazines about wine. On a shelf, carefully arranged like a little shrine, are empty bottles: 1989 Château Clinet, 1985 Château Gruaud Larose, and so on. It's a lovely house with a backed-up drain. My snake goes about ten feet, then hits a solid blockage.

In the crawl space I find a 2-inch steel drain pipe. Following it for ten feet, I find an old rubber no-hub joint. Gotta be the problem. Lying on my back I reach up to touch the no-hub—and it breaks just from the touch of my hand. Worse, the pipe sags downward and pours a stream of sewer water onto my face and into my open mouth.

My immediate impression is a vintage of poor clarity, attacking the nose with a barnyard bouquet that is earthy and complex. A brawny presence on the tongue, an intense structure, robust and chewy with a lingering finish, strongly metallic, leaving an unforgettable aftertaste.

I crawl out sputtering. My clothes are soaked. I stink.

Back home I gargle, change my clothes, gargle, wash my hair, gargle, wash again, gargle, scrub, gargle. Not one molecule of sewer water could possibly remain in my mouth, yet still I taste it. Dr. Wisler returns my call: "I hear you had a surprise shower." He says I need a tetanus shot and I might as well get a hepatitis shot too. Otherwise, no worries.

After the shots, now in the evening of that same day, I return to the lovely house, fix the drain, leave a bill.

No response. A month later I phone them, ask them to pay. A caretaker answers. The homeowners have gone to Tuscany.

They never return to their lovely house. And they never pay.

Me, I prefer beer.

There But for the Grace of God

Wednesday, February 2, 1994

Religious quotations cover the walls; open Bibles appear on every table. I'm here to install a drop-down ladder to the attic and then add a few lights.

I'd better watch my mouth, I'm thinking. *No cussing today.* So first thing, I drop an 8-foot ladder that bangs my shin and puts a dent in her oak floor, and I shout: "Fucking shit!"

I'm hopping on one foot, holding my shin with both hands, as Dottie rushes into the hallway. "Are you all right?"

Dottie is a perky blonde, cute, chipmunk cheeks. Her chunky black eyeglasses, combined with a bit of extra body weight, almost disguise the fact that she is still a great-looking woman. I've known her for years—fourteen years, in fact—since our kids were in a playgroup together in La Honda. She and her husband recently moved to Palo Alto. This is my first time inside her new house.

"I'm not broken," I say, still hopping, "but it hurts like, um, heck and now there's a dent in the floor. Sorry about the cussing."

"Forget the floor," Dottie says. "Let me look at your leg."

I stop hopping. She leans close. Already a bruise is visible. To my amazement, she leans even closer and kisses the bruise.

She stands up straight. "Did that hurt? Or help? It always worked on my kids."

"It helped." I'm not kidding. Awesome, the amazing healing power of lips and spit. Temporary pain relief, at least.

"My kids didn't have so much hair," Dottie says, wiping her mouth.

"Sorry," I say.

"You can't help it if you're a grown-up," Dottie says.

The conversation has taken an odd turn, and we both know it. Dottie walks to another part of the house. I return to work.

Dottie's impulsive. She plunges into things, and it's usually for the best. She's the one who started a preschool playgroup in La Honda, which is how I met her. It was quickly obvious to me—and everyone else—that she had no idea how to run a playgroup, so other parents soon took charge, and Dottie bowed out. You could say she failed as a leader, but in fact she created a group that became a La Honda institution.

My second involvement with Dottie came when I volunteered to supervise the La Honda swimming pool. Dottie had been running it for the last six years and was delighted to hand it over. "Do you know anything about swimming pools?" she asked.

"No. Nothing."

"Me neither. But somebody has to do it. You'll find yourself making decisions you are totally incompetent to make. You'll look to the sky and say, 'Why me, Lord?' but nobody will help, and you'll just have to decide."

She was absolutely right. I ended up taking charge of remodeling the entire pool and rebuilding the filter plant because it simply had to be done.

Both Dottie and I served on the guild board of directors, which was La Honda's town government. At one point I wanted to allow kids from the Glenwood Camp to swim in the town pool as a reward for their help in cleaning the place up. To my surprise the board of directors was opposed to the idea. La Honda had always been an outlaw town, former headquarters of Ken Kesey and the Merry Pranksters, frequent gathering spot for Hells Angels, and long ago a hideout for the Jesse James gang— but in 1983 La Honda was run by a conservative group of old farts. "We don't want those kids in our town," they said. *Those kids*, of course, were juvenile delinquents and—worse—most of them were nonwhite.

"I know those kids," I said. "I grew up among people like that. There but for fortune go you or I."

"Amen," Dottie said.

We were outvoted, seven to two. (That was the last gasp of the old guard.)

Somebody told me that Dottie and her husband, both devout Christians, had experimented with wife-swapping in the 1970s. I didn't know what to make of that, and I wasn't going to ask.

Dottie told me that she had met her husband doing missionary work in Africa. Her husband was Chinese, not African. He was on a medical mission; she was founding schools. "We didn't preach or anything," she explained. "We led by example."

I'm installing a pull-down ladder in the ceiling of a hallway that connects two sides of the house with a sort of vestibule/laundry room in between. In the vestibule are a hot tub, washer, and dryer. Now, with the ladder installed, I have to keep going up and down as I run wires in the attic for new lighting.

Near the end of the day I come down the ladder to find a young man squatting, naked, stuffing his clothes into the washing machine. It's Ben, Dottie's son, who played soccer with my son back in the day. Now Ben is a college student. We nod hello to each other, and then Ben climbs into the hot tub. Ben, an Asian-American hybrid, is a gorgeous human being.

223

After another trip to the attic I find Jack, Dottie's husband, also naked, standing in the hot tub with his son. Jack is a surgeon at Stanford Hospital. He's smoking a joint. Jack and I nod hello, and then Jack holds out the joint to me.

"No, thanks," I say. "I'm working."

"Good for you," Jack says. "I take it for my arthritis. I hope you don't have that problem yet." (In 1994 this is long before medical marijuana has been legalized or even entered mainstream discussion.)

Jack does not share the joint with his son, nor does Ben seem interested.

After an extended trip to the attic I come down the ladder to find that Dottie has joined husband and son in the tub. She's wearing a bikini bottom, no top. She's pinned up her hair, which gives her a sloppy elegance, exposing the curve of her neck and shoulders. Her fair flesh is mottled red from the heat. Without eyeglasses, she squints. "Are you about done?" she asks.

"All done," I say.

Jack isn't sharing the joint with Dottie either. Apparently it is purely medicinal.

"I'll write you a check," Dottie says, and she climbs out of the tub. Shrugging into a bathrobe, she pads into the living room and finds the checkbook in her purse. Dripping onto the carpet, squinting, she says, "I hope we don't shock you. Over the years we've found the hot tub is the best place to talk family matters with the kids. I'd rather it was at the dinner table, but you have to grab these moments. And," she laughs, "everybody's more honest when they're naked. Ben wants to drop out of college and do missionary work in Mississippi setting up health clinics. We support his ideals but we wish he'd finish school first. Don't you think?"

"I'd better not take sides on this," I say.

"You're so smart. You've always been smart. It was always so great to work with you. Sometimes I—" She breaks off.

The top flap of her bathrobe is hanging open. I can't help but notice. Her breasts are literally steaming. A small silver cross nestles above them. There's the scent of chlorine as the water evaporates.

For a moment, she squints at me.

Then she hands me the check. "There but for the grace of God." She flashes a smile.

Maybe I should say *amen*, but I don't. I like her; she admires me; but we're separated by the Christian thing, and, anyway, neither of us is looking for adventure of that kind. I think. I'll never know.

Dottie walks back toward the hot tub. "Thanks for the good work," she says.

I came out of the 1960s: pot-smoking war protester, hairy hippie, no church. Dottie the devout makes me feel straight.

A few months later a friend tells me that Dottie and Jack have sold their house. With the inflated price of Palo Alto real estate they could retire. Instead they've put all their possessions in storage and gone to some South Pacific island to do missionary work: Jack the surgeon-with-arthritis, Dottie who will start schools and then not know how to run them. They'll do more good than harm, guided by their love and their God.

Melody

August 1995 to August 2002

When I arrive, Melody is in front of the cabin with a hand saw, cutting a pile of branches. She greets me with a smile. She's fresh, freckled, with big, friendly eyes.

Melody is wearing leather gloves and sweating from the work of sawing. We're by a creek in a redwood grove, deep in a canyon. Fallen needles bury the roof like drifts of brown snow.

Parked by the cabin is a yellow 1958 Volkswagen Beetle—I know it's a '58 because I used to have one myself. Mine was white and died in 1967. Now it's August 1995. Her yellow Beetle is older than she is.

All this I take in before we've spoken a word. Already I like her.

"Got to do something with all these branches," she says. "So I cut them for the stove. For next winter."

"Looks like you'll never have to buy wood," I say.

"Haven't yet." She looks around. The scent is fresh. The shade is cool, even in the midst of a heat wave. Here the sun rarely penetrates the towering redwood canopy. The creek babbles. "I love this place."

I hadn't asked. But I can see it's true.

My job on this quiet day in this peaceful forest is to unstick a door, replace deck stairs, and patch the roof where a branch shot through. All the time I'm working, Melody keeps sawing, by hand, limbs that have fallen into her yard. In winter storms this rotten little cabin is pelted by plummeting missiles.

We chat a bit. I learn that she moved to this cabin as a newlywed ten years ago; that in return for absurdly low rent Melody pays for all the maintenance. She teaches history at De Anza Community College, commuting three days a week in the yellow Beetle. She's a widow.

All this branch-sawing seems obsessive—and unnecessary. With a cheap power saw the work would go faster, more easily. Something tells me not to mention this—or to ask any details about her husband. There's a gentle friendliness about Melody, but her manner tells you to mind your own business.

I return many times over the years. Melody's cabin has endless needs. Even with my frequent repairs, the general condition declines as trees bomb from above while fungus enters from below.

On one visit Melody apologizes for her frugality and says that she is still paying off "large medical bills" from her husband. On another visit when Melody is absent, a neighbor stops by to make sure I'm supposed to be there and then, rolling her eyes, says "That woman would be a fine wife for some lucky husband—if she'd ever get over the last one."

Melody will not complain; she will not be pitied. If my schedule is inconvenient, Melody says, "Oh, it's no trouble at all." If my working will disturb, Melody says, "Oh, it doesn't bother me." One winter storm blows down a fir tree that clips a corner of the house, tearing out half the kitchen and crushing her electrical entry. This happens on a Friday night. She waits until Monday morning to call me. She says, "I didn't want to disturb you over the weekend."

There's a well-thumbed Bible on her nightstand.

In 2001, after I've been maintaining that wretched little cabin for six years, Melody calls and says, "The floor is falling."

A corner of her bedroom has collapsed. The understructure at one end of the cabin, plus the attached deck, is rotten.

Melody confesses that she can't afford to replace the deck because she has her own "large medical bills" to pay. She can't avoid the need to brace one end of the shack with a beam set on new concrete piers. I come up with an elegant solution for both reinforcing her house and supporting the new deck all in one strong yet economical beam.

I'm proud of the plan. I'm less proud of the deck, which is simply cheap, though it meets her modest expectations. I build it at cost, taking no profit. Melody has that effect on a person.

I perform my last job for Melody in August of 2002. Some kid with a cherry bomb blew up her mailbox out by the road. She apologizes for not replacing it herself: "I'm a little too weak right now with the radiation therapy."

Melody is too pathologically upbeat to say it, so I'll speak for her: Cancer is evil. Certain people—good, wonderful people—seem like magnets to evil. Why, Lord?

Melody's God works in mysterious ways. Two years later, at a Chevron station where I'm pumping gas into my truck, a yellow '58 Volkswagen Beetle pulls up behind me. It's Melody!

I honestly thought she'd be dead.

Melody says she met a "very kind" man, and they're married and living in San Mateo. She has a baby boy. She still teaches. Her husband is a minister.

Her son has Down syndrome.

She looks radiantly happy.

Everybody Lives Somewhere

A Boy on a Bike

Friday, October 11, 1996

In the truck loaded with plumbing equipment I'm driving Will, my youngest child, to school—a wealthy private school where he's the scholarship kid. He feels he doesn't belong there. He's playing in a rock band that is gaining local notoriety.

We've argued about marijuana. We've argued about unchaperoned parties. Today Will is questioning why he should go to high school. *Any* high school. He wants to play music.

Since he's only fourteen, the law is on my side. But I'm thinking ahead: "I want you to go to college."

"Why?"

"Because it's okay with me if your career plan is to be a rock star, but I don't want you to be an *ignorant* rock star."

Which ends the conversation. It's a twenty-five mile drive to the high school. The remaining twenty miles pass in silence, Will fuming.

When you decide to have children, you're aware of how much work it is to take care of a baby. If you aren't aware, people will tell you. But nobody warns you that eventually you'll be dealing with a fourteen-year-old. Will is my third (and final) pass at this dealing, so at least I bring some experience to the task.

I spend the day repairing a shower stall.

> Building a shower
> all day getting dirty so
> people can wash.

Driving home, I take note of six boys in the bike lane ahead, single file, pedaling hard, apparently racing. Just as I catch up with them, one of the boys loses control. His front wheel wobbles.

Suddenly boy and bike shoot into the road directly in front of my truck.

I hit the brakes. The wheels lock.

The bike topples. On his side but still on the bike, the boy scrapes a half circle in the road and comes to a stop.

My truck is in a skid. The tires screech. The boy looks up at me in naked terror.

Our eyes meet. And hold.

The truck jerks to a stop with its front bumper just inches shy of the boy's head as I hear the toolboxes in the bed crash against the back of the cab.

Then there's absolute silence.

I can smell the smoke of my tires.

The kid stands up. He's wearing a helmet. Road burn on one arm.

For a moment, the kid and I are staring at each other, separated by a windshield, not a word spoken. The kid has blue eyes. Fair hair. His fixed gaze transforms into a glare. He seems angry as if it's all my fault. No apologies and no thanks. He hops onto his bike and pedals furiously away.

For a minute I can't move. I'm shaking. Cars come up behind me, honk, then pass.

Now I can move.

Slowly, I drive home, reexamining my life.

What am I hustling for? Two kids in college, one starting high school. I'm writing huge checks and working harder than ever. Does it all come to this? I'd been driving five or ten miles per hour over the limit, pushing the edge on speed just as I'm pushing the edge on my career. That boy I almost killed will soon be fourteen himself, angry, confused. I caught a glimpse of it in his eyes.

A thought is crystallizing, and it isn't coming from my brain. Something, some One, has spoken.

Back home, when I walk into the kitchen my wife sees it right away. I'm forty-nine; Rose is forty-eight. Our bodies, beginning to expire.

"What's wrong?" Rose asks.

"I want to have another child. Is it too late? Can we do that?"

"Wow." She checks my face for signs of a mental breakdown. None there. Water is boiling on the stove. She shuts off the burner. She's thinking. At my request she's actually suddenly giving serious consideration to bringing another soul onto this planet.

The air tingles.

Miracles happen in moments like these.

Softly, with a look in her eyes as if she's questioning her own sanity, she says, "Okay."

This is the essence of love.

It'll be a boy. I just know it.

She reads my mind. "You'd better not die," she says, "before that boy turns eighteen."

The stove remains off. There's a boy to be made.

Or not.

It takes more than love to create a child. Just as the truck stopped right before impact, so, in a sense, did the ovaries. But what audacity that we would even try.

Almost eighteen years have passed.

I miss that boy who never was.

Linda, Phase One

October 1996

Edie leans over my body and crunches her shoulder into my spine. I feel vertebrae realigning, ribs relocating. "Can you handle a client who is a horrible human being?" Edie asks. She crunches me again, higher.

Edie is my chiropractor. Edie is also a wonderful source of referrals.

"Horrible in what way?" I ask.

"Pathologically honest. And totally without warmth."

"Autistic?"

Edie shrugs. "The first time I met her, she told me my teeth were yellow. Then she asked me, 'Where'd you get that sweater—Goodwill?'"

I take the referral. Edie loves to recommend me to her well-to-do clients, not only because I'll do a good job, but also because the more work I do, the more often I have to return for chiropractic adjustments. It's a symbiotic relationship.

The job is an old farmhouse with a wrap-around porch surrounded by an acre of fruit trees. I love it: a relic in a bustling suburb. Given its age, the house could be an ongoing source of employment.

The client greets me with a cold handshake. "I'm Linda," she says. "You're on time." She speaks without a flicker of emotion. She's fortyish. Maybe high thirties. She's impeccably dressed. There's something awkward in her bearing, no matter the clothes.

"Yes," I say, "I try to be punctual."

"I had to file a lawsuit against my previous contractor."

"Because he wasn't punctual?" I smile, trying to set a light tone.

No reaction. "My husband is in intensive care," Linda says. "I want to get this done before he comes home next week." She then shows me a month's worth of projects.

This job comes wrapped in warning flags, but I take it. I tell her she'll have to prioritize because I can't finish everything in a week.

"Work hard," she says.

She's so graceless that I actually like her. If the face weren't frozen, she'd be lovely. Counterbalancing her personality, she has two goofy English sheep dogs who slobber on my power tools and stick their noses in my armpits.

I repair a shower stall, replace a double-hung window, rebuild one side of the porch. From her garden Linda comes carrying a bowl. As she passes, she hands me a yellow heirloom tomato and says, "You should trim your nose hair. Hasn't anybody complained?"

On my fourth day Linda asks me to "hammer quietly." Her husband is upstairs, resting. "Don't you dare disturb him."

I tell her I can't hammer quietly, but I can switch to screws instead of nails. "Okay," she says. "Keep working hard."

The next morning before work I see Edie. She crunches my spine and says, "I hear you're a hard worker."

"Did Linda say that?"

"Yes. She likes you." Edie laughs. "Can't you tell?"

"How could I tell?"

"That's the joke."

Edie and I often swap stories about our well-heeled clients. Their sense of entitlement. Their unshakable belief that they *earned* it. As we make our livings catering to the whims of the wealthy, we need a sense of humor—and someone to share it with.

But Linda is a mystery. No sense of entitlement. I admire her tomato garden, her farmhouse, her two loopy dogs. I admire how she protects her husband. There's something behind that stony facade.

From Edie's office I move on to Linda's house. When I arrive, Linda isn't home. A nurse answers the door. "You from the church?" she asks.

"Contractor," I say. I'm wearing a tool belt and carrying a pry bar.

The nurse lets me into the house.

"Is it okay if I repair the floor in the dining room?" I ask. "It'll be noisy."

"Why don't you ask him," the nurse says, indicating that I should go upstairs.

In the bedroom he's half-upright in a hospital bed. He looks old and awful. Even if he weren't sick, he's thirty years older than Linda. He founded and runs a Silicon Valley company. There's a smell of urine and antiseptic. "Make all the racket you want," he says. "I've got endless morphine."

I'm fitting the last board into the patch of hardwood floor when Linda comes home. She drops five shopping bags onto a kitchen table and says in a monotone: "There's sawdust all over the kitchen. I wish you'd told somebody you were going to do this."

"I told your husband."

She frowns. An actual ripple of feeling. She's not totally catatonic.

One of the bags sags, spilling a pile of white brassieres onto the floor. Into the sawdust. "Shit," she says in a flat voice.

Immediately the sheep dogs snuffle their noses into the pile.

I reach for the animals, which she mistakes as my reaching for the underwear.

"Stop," Linda says. "I don't think my carpenter should handle my lingerie."

"I'll hold the dogs."

"Okay." She plucks bras from the floor, shakes them, stuffs them back into the bag. They're plain, nothing frilly. "It's so difficult finding a good fit," she says. "So when I find it, I buy a dozen. One of my breasts is bigger than the other. I'm the same as you."

I must have looked surprised.

"Not your breasts," she explains. "One of your shoulders is higher than the other. We're both lopsided."

It's true about my shoulders. It's an effect of my scoliosis. Few people notice. Or at least few people comment.

By lopsided, she means ugly. Linda is telling me we're both ugly. Edie was right: this woman is pathologically honest. But also, I think, pathologically self-critical. Without a filter.

"I never had children." Linda shakes the last bra and stuffs it into the bag. "If I got pregnant, maybe my breasts would've matched. They fill out, you know."

Is this some kind of flirting? Or just random, inappropriate intimacy? Her deadpan delivery is tough to decode. I don't tell her what I'm thinking: *It's not the breasts, whatever size. You'd be splendid if only you smiled.*

High school must have been hell for her.

"I'll clean up," I say after a moment.

"You did a crappy job," she says. "Can you make your patch look less like a pimple?"

So I rip out the oak strips I've just installed, plus a few more, changing the straight border of the repair into a staggered edge that seems to blend in. And Linda is right. It looks better now.

The next week I'm working in an outbuilding. There's one big breezy room lined with windows, and then there's a crummy little bathroom on the side. I'm upgrading the electrical power from 15 amps to 60 while tearing out all the old knob-and-tube. Linda wants to turn it into an art studio. She tells me she's a painter. She never shows her work to anybody. "Except," she says, "the self-portrait on the staircase. I did it for my husband a long time ago."

Later I study that painting on the staircase. The art is inelegant, the work of a student. In it her face is neither warm nor cold nor happy nor sad. Expressionless. The painted Linda is younger, wearing a shawl that exposes a bit of cleavage. Of course I compare the left to the right, and maybe, just possibly, one side is slightly smaller. Difficult to say.

Now that she's informed me, I can't help but notice her chest, whatever she's wearing. Wondering . . .

And then there's the trash incident. I'm unloading lumber from my truck in the driveway when a muscular little man marches up to me and points at his garbage truck. "I can reject!" he's shouting at me. "I don't have to eat your dust!"

It takes me a few seconds to figure out that he's mad about the pile of loose sawdust atop the household trash in the garbage can. You're supposed to bag it.

Suddenly Linda appears with a five-dollar bill. Without a word she hands it to the garbage man. Without another word he takes it, then marches out the driveway with the metal can and empties it into his truck.

"Garbage with attitude," Linda says. "I guess I didn't warn you. Sorry."

I pull out my wallet and find a five-dollar bill. "My bad," I say, offering the bill.

Linda glances at the money in my hand but makes no move to take it. "My treat," she says. She's standing close to me, gazing at me, eye to eye. Her face is unreadable as usual but her heat is not. There is a force to a woman's flirtation, a flush of the flesh, a scent, a bearing of the body. She says, "Is that dandruff in your hair? Or sawdust?" Then she walks away.

From then on there is a push/pull in my interactions with Linda. We both wear wedding rings; nothing will happen. We speak only of the job at hand. Anything extra would be in the eyes, the posture. Maybe I'm just imagining. I notice that she's left-handed: another reason she's slightly askew. Meanwhile she guards her husband, screening visitors—of whom there are many—while monitoring the nurses. She seems an implacable boss but a loyal wife. I ask how her husband is doing and she says, "It's hospice care. No intervention."

"Oh! I didn't know. I'm so sorry."

"He wanted a mansion." She waves her hand in a circle indicating the farmhouse, the orchard, the little estate. "Instead, he bought this for me." She puts the hand to her throat. "Only now he regrets it."

I'm nailing V-rustic redwood 1×6s to the outside of the art studio when I see cars pulling up at the farmhouse. A big, black limo. A couple of sedans. Then another big, black limo. Men wearing serious suits file into the house carrying briefcases. The sheep dogs, sensing trouble, slink to my side and settle in the grass, panting.

I complete the siding. Back inside the studio I get involved installing the electrical duplexes, seventeen outlets connecting 126 wires. Yes, I counted. Mindless work. Black, white, ground wire. Meanwhile, with all the crouching, a hole in the fragile, ancient fabric of my blue jeans widens until my entire knee is exposed. In a moment of frustration I wrench off the rest of the fabric and cut the seam with my utility knife, so now I'm working in cut-offs on my right leg, a full length on the left.

As I'm cleaning up, the door opens. Linda steps inside. "Are you working hard?" she asks.

"Finished," I say. "This phase."

It's the first time I've seen her as anything less than perfectly coiffed. Her hair is down. She's wearing a black sweatshirt: CORNELL. She says, "We'd better suspend operations for a while. Before Phase Two."

"Is something wrong?"

"I'm afraid I'm having a bad day. I shouldn't make any decisions for a while. That's what I'm told."

"Your husband. Is he—?"

"He's all right. I mean he's at death's door, but he's comfortable. He's sleeping. Oblivious."

"I'm so sorry."

She is silent.

After a few moments I ask, "Is there anything I can do?"

"I'd like to show you my paintings."

"Now?"

"No. I'm a little upset. Don't listen to me." She stands rigid, hands flat against the side of her hips. Utterly alone. "There are people at the house. I think I'm supposed to entertain them. It seems insane."

I don't want to do this, but I say, "Would you like me to go to the house and tell all the people to leave?"

"No." She shakes her head. "They'd laugh at you. You look ridiculous in those pants."

"Sorry."

"They all hate me." She gestured toward the darkness outside the windows. "Somebody's probably watching us right now."

"Why?"

"It's about money."

"Are you okay?"

"Yes. I'll be fine. I can't pay you for a few days. Will you give me an invoice?"

"Of course."

"He wasn't able to father children. In the beginning I thought it wouldn't matter."

I say nothing. To this day, I wonder what would have happened if I'd said, "I can."

She inhales, deeply. "I should be at his bedside." She drops her eyes. She turns to leave. "Your blue jeans are hilarious," she says without a hint of joy. The sheep dogs follow her to the house.

A few days later I receive an envelope in the mail. On the bottom of the check she has written: "Phase One. Now buy Levis."

There is no Phase Two.

I buy some pants—Lees, not Levis. At my next chiropractic adjustment Edie says, "The lawyers will be fighting for years. There's millions and millions of dollars. Linda should get it, but she probably won't."

"Why not?"

"The guy was a bastard. Overseas bank accounts. Chicanery." Edie chews on that last word, relishing it. Edie loves this stuff. *Chicanery.*

I say, "I wonder if millions of dollars would make her happy."

Edie laughs. "She needs marijuana and a good lover. Light up and get laid. But, oh, my God. She'd be hard work for any lover."

"I hope at least she gets to keep the farmhouse," I say. "And maybe she'll find a hard worker."

"Not you?"

"Not me."

I wish I'd seen her paintings. I bet they were honest. Aching, lonely, lopsided. And honest.

Breaking Waves

Friday, February 13, 1997

Mike is an engineer at a company that makes disk drives. He's a big guy, ex-football player, square of jaw and wide of shoulder. He bought a townhouse in Santa Clara and hired a decorator, Isabella, who hired me to spiff the place up a bit.

Isabella told Mike he needed a work of art to "energize" the dining room. She then made the mistake of letting Mike choose the art. He bought a gigantic painting of waves breaking over rocks under a moody sky. Framed, it weighed eighty pounds. My job was to hang it and install low-voltage lighting to show it off. Dramatic lighting.

I was just cleaning up when Mike came home accompanied by a splendid young woman who, you knew in a glance, was fresh and smart and smitten. She gazed at the breaking waves while Mike set the table with a bottle of wine, a sourdough baguette, a bowl of cherries, and a dark chocolate cake. "How do you like the painting?" Mike asked.

"Nice lighting," she said.

Today Mike calls me back to the townhouse. A couple of years have passed. The painting, still nicely lighted, remains on the wall. The home seems clean and barely lived in, with no sign of female habitation. Mike, looking more than two years older, meets me in a rush and tells me he's working eighteen-hour days. He says, "I should have noticed sooner, but there's water running down the inside of the kitchen wall whenever it rains. Find the source. Fix it. Okay?"

On a ladder I have to remove long strips of Masonite siding. A two-man job. I'm working alone.

I trace the water back to some bad flashing around second-floor windows. There's rot. Worse than rot. Termites are everywhere. I call Mike. "I can fix the flashing," I say, "but you need an exterminator."

"Who do you recommend?"

"It depends on what you want. There are a lot of environmentally friendly companies that use different techniques. Like, there's one that uses microwaves, and there's one that—"

"I want lethal poison. Toxic, high-hazard, nuclear waste would be okay. I want them *dead*."

In less than an hour I've got Izzie the exterminator out there to take a look. Izzie says, "Santa Clara used to have the greatest fruit orchards in the world. And you know what lived under those fruit trees? Termites.

Now the farms are gone, but the termites are still underground, just waiting."

Tomorrow Izzie will come back, dig trenches around the perimeter of the house, fill the trenches with lethal, toxic, industrial-strength poison, and cover them. Mike will be happy.

I soak a couple of rotten 2×4s with Copper Green (deadly stuff), install sister studs beside the rotten ones, redo the flashing, flick termites off with my fingers, and spread bounteous caulk around the window. During intermittent sprinkles of rain I re-nail the siding. Gusts of wet wind try to whip the long strips of Masonite out of my hands. Again I'm doing a two-man job, working alone, enjoying the rhythm: lift, whack a nail, whack another. Move the ladder, lift, whack, whack.

A physical challenge. A test of strength and skill. Ladder work can exhaust you.

I finish in darkness. Sore, tired, the muscles tremble with exhaustion in my arms, legs, shoulders. I feel good about this day, the same satisfied feeling you get after climbing a mountain.

Mike returns. Standing together in the back yard amid concrete-and-Masonite suburbia, we stare at the completed wall. Rushes of wind flap our clothing and roar in our ears. Raindrops strike our skin like pebbles. Wet, moody clouds are blowing overhead, playing hide-and-seek with the moon.

Through the window, inside where it is cozy and quiet, I see the painting bathed in warm light. The art may be a cliché, but clichés come from truth, from trying to express the inexpressible, the relentless force of nature.

"Good job," Mike says. "So I'll have no more problems?"

"For a while."

Summer Snapshots

June 1997

This fresh young couple, the Bebes, just half my age, want me to convert an atrium into a home office. Lucy Bebe is pregnant, expecting twins, and wants the work completed before the due date in September. Her husband needs the office because his company is growing so fast that they can't provide space for everybody.

"What's the company?" I ask.

"It's called Enron," Lucy says.

"Never heard of it."

"That's what everybody says." Lucy smiles. "But you will."

My own family numbers five, and for the summer we are all working. My older son, Jesse, age twenty, is a counselor at Plantation Farm Camp, teaching kids to milk cows and smash machines. My daughter, Ruth, age eighteen, found herself a job at Walgreens in Palo Alto. My younger son, Will, age fifteen, is working for me.

This is to be my summer of Will. We've been drifting apart. I hope to mend that. Will smokes marijuana and plays in a rock band. He hangs out with older kids, dropouts. He hates his high school, which is full of rich kids who don't need summer jobs.

It's been a tough school year for both of us. I'm newly, stridently antidrug, which is a tough position to advocate when Will knows I used to smoke pot myself. I tell him that thirty years ago the stuff I smoked was only one-tenth the potency of what they sell now. I know because I recently tried it, and it knocked me flat. This amuses Will. I also remind him that the girl next door, who we've known since she was a toddler, is now strung out on heroin. What a waste. What a fucking waste.

I take a test in *Newsweek* that calculates I'll live to age seventy-eight. As the summer begins, I'm forty-nine. Just twenty-nine to go.

In Ruth's second day working a checkout register at Walgreens, a customer calls her an idiot. "Thank you. Idiot." The woman in line behind leaps to Ruth's defense, saying "You must be a really unhappy person."

I have more construction jobs than I could handle in two summers. With a headful of details hanging, with the atrium conversion about to begin, I decide to do what's right: I take Will backpacking for three days on the Skyline-to-the-Sea Trail. On the second night some raccoons steal our remaining food, so we hike out to the ocean on our third day without breakfast or lunch. Meanwhile Will and I heal our differences the guy way: we don't talk about them. After three days with no mention of drugs, we're ready to work together.

July 1997

At the Bebe job Will digs dirt, drills holes in concrete, and tears out drywall. He's a good worker. I give him a raise.

Ruth makes friends with workers of all nationalities at Walgreens, especially some Filipina women who keep giving her food.

At the end of each day Will and I drive home together in the truck, listening to blues music without talking. Most days we are filthy, sweaty, tired. Each day as we step in the house, Will is buried by dogs—just two, but they're big—and he lies on the floor accepting their waggy, licky love. Welcome home.

After a couple of weeks of hard work, falling behind schedule, Will suggests we take a few days off and backpack in the Sierra, just the two of us. I jump on it.

In the high country for five days and four nights of wonderfulness, we speculate if anything has happened while we've been away from society. Will says, "For all we know, L.A. may have been invaded by aliens and we haven't heard the news."

I point out, "L.A. was invaded by aliens years ago. They took over, and nobody noticed."

This amuses him.

We descend along a beautiful, rushing creek, patches of snow in midsummer, a meadow, little lakes. All is glory. Will starts talking about another student at his high school who took a summer job. She took a life-guarding gig not to make money but to meet guys. Will imitates her Valley-speak: "Oh my God there's a guy who's like totally drowning and he's so cute!"

This is how we talk about high school and drugs. Avoidance. A few jokes. And bonding. We're tired, dusty, sun-burnt—and satisfied. Nearing the lot where the truck is parked, crossing the San Joaquin on a footbridge, we encounter a group of men and women who are naked except for flip-flops, hiking on the trail to Rainbow Falls. We are back in California.

Back home I discover I've lost three pounds—an inch of waistline.

With Will I frame walls, floor, ceiling. By now Will is a terrific helper. He looks for ways to be useful, has good craft skills and attitude. We put in ceiling joists, a skylight, roof sheathing. I make Will do the tasks that are up top in the heat. After work I drop him off for band practice or, once, at a Further Festival at Shoreline Amphitheater.

Ruth spends most of her evenings on the phone. Her Filipina coworkers need constant help—evictions, boyfriends who beat them. She is the sympathetic ear, the calm voice amid storms of drama.

August 1997

Will and I lay the subfloor and then hang drywall. I measure and cut; he glues and screws.

In the back of my truck are drywall tools, 2×4s, fiberglass batts—and a drum set. The band is getting notice. After work Will often has a practice or a gig.

I arrive home at 8:30 or so, stopping at the La Honda post office, where I step out into twilight, mountain stillness, dark silhouette of redwoods, and the sound of bluegrass from the patio of the Merry Prankster Cafe—so nice and clean and fresh after a day in the valley. At home Ruth is on the phone. One of her coworkers attempted suicide. She's up most of the night, talking. Often she comes home with gifts: orchids or plates of exotic food.

Will now has a learner's permit from the DMV. After a few lessons getting the feel of the clutch, I let him take the wheel of the truck for the drive home. He almost runs a red light, skids, stalls out, restarts the motor and says, "Thank you for being calm." Calm is a deliberate choice of mine—a survival tactic.

One day Will stays home while I run electrical wires at the atrium/office. I tell Lucy, "I'm so glad for this job this summer. Will and I had been growing estranged, but working together was perfect. It's been great for us."

To my surprise, she starts crying. And smiling.

If you want to melt the heart of a pregnant woman, tell her she's helped a father bond with his son.

One of Ruth's coworkers just had $10,000 stolen by her lesbian lover who, when confronted, tried to kill her. Ruth is right there, helping her friend sort it out. I warn Ruth about people with endless needs who suck you in and drown you. She listens but is not concerned. She thrives on what I see as underground, third-world soap opera.

In August I turn fifty. Just twenty-eight to go. Ruth turns nineteen. She's decided she wants to major in English and philosophy, then go to grad school in psych with a specialty in cultural differences. At nineteen she's found a talent and a passion.

By the end of August my Summer of Will is over. I carry lasting images: Will thanking me for being calm; tears flowing after he hammered his thumb; strolling with his backpack at 9,000 feet. The atrium is now an office. We've made good money.

September 1997

In early September I repair somebody's fence and build a gate. It's pleasant, sweaty carpentry with good results. After work I drive the pickup to Will's high school, where a teacher tells me tradesmen are supposed to park in the rear lot. I'm wearing what I call my cruddies — cut-off jeans speckled with sawdust.

I watch the last minutes of Will's varsity soccer practice. Well-dressed mothers gather in a group, casting glances at me. Will is not the only one who doesn't fit in here.

After practice, Will brings a couple of his teammates over. "This is my dad," he says. No shame. In fact, he says it with pride.

In the mail I receive a final check from Lucy Bebe along with a photo of the twin girls and a note:

> Thank you and Will both for all your good work! ☺
> Guess what? We've been transferred to Seattle! ☹

A few years later when Enron unravels, it occurs to me that the company was paying for that atrium-to-office conversion. I should've charged double. I can't complain, though: I may be one of the few people who actually walked away from Enron with a profit. And it was more than money.

The Chewing Gum Teacher

Friday, May 29, 1998

Zeke has that gift with children. Rapport. Leadership. Empathy. Especially with boys. He has a boyish face himself—I doubt he could grow a beard if he tried. He used to coach my son's AYSO soccer team and managed to keep it fun and noncompetitive. He has three children of his own, all boys.

When you meet Zeke, he offers you a stick of gum. He's got several packs in his pocket. He's a salesman for Wrigley's, so he's well-supplied. Cynically, you might think it's like a drug dealer offering free samples—and I tease him about this—but with Zeke it honestly seems like a friendly offer. Zeke's a friendly guy.

Zeke's wife has hired me to install a hot tub. Today it will be delivered. Zeke is here to help. A truck with a crane will have to lift the heavy tub to their second-floor deck.

While we wait for the truck, Zeke and I chat. I ask how he came to be in the chewing gum business.

"I didn't exactly plan for it," Zeke says. "I got a degree in education. When I got back from 'Nam, I looked at the starting salary of a teacher. And you know what happens."

"It's a waste, Zeke. You have such a natural talent with children. You should teach. You selling gum is like Michelangelo selling paint at Home Depot."

"Michelangelo never went to 'Nam."

"What was it like?"

I've asked this before, and Zeke has always been evasive. Today, though, he opens up: "I was on a PBR. You know about them?"

"Yes. My cousin—he served on one." PBR stood for patrol boat, river. The boats had a two-foot draft and could go up shallow rivers through weeds without getting stuck. They had machine guns, a grenade launcher, and they were speedy. They were also sitting ducks for Viet Cong snipers hiding in trees along the shore.

Zeke is frowning. "Your cousin died?"

"No. He came through."

"Drinks a little too much? Wakes up in a sweat? Maybe some drugs?"

"I don't know about sweat."

"I never did the drugs," Zeke says. "Half my unit used heroin. Can't blame them, but my one and only goal was to survive. Drugs always

244

seemed like another way to die. Casualties for river patrol were eleven percent a month. That's each month, eleven percent. In twelve months, not good odds. Got a little better after they started dropping Agent Orange. It cleared some space around the river's edge."

"Sounds like you could teach math."

"You want kids to hear that?"

"Yes."

Zeke shows me his arm. Little spots, like mini-boils. "I get these. Hundreds of them. Little fatty growths under my skin."

"Agent Orange?"

"Can't prove it."

A truck arrives with a crane. Zeke and I go out to meet it at the head of the driveway. As we walk, Zeke says, "I wouldn't want to scare them. If I taught."

"Maybe they *should* be scared."

"Maybe. I just want to forget."

"Can you?" It's been almost thirty years.

"Not yet." Zeke smiles. Turning to greet the driver of the hot tub truck, Zeke offers him a piece of gum.

Fixing an Outlet

Wednesday, May 4, 1999

His name is Ken. He says a neighbor recommended me. He wants me to replace an electrical outlet. He says the outlet broke when he plugged an old lamp into it.

First thing as I arrive, I ask to see the old lamp.

"It's the outlet," Ken says. "That's what I called you for."

"The lamp probably has a short. May I see it?"

"I unplugged the lamp and the outlet was still dead. It's the outlet."

"May I please see the lamp?"

"No. Aren't you going to do the job?"

When I remove the outlet, there's no power coming to the box. "The outlet isn't the problem," I say. "Where's your circuit-breaker box?"

"It isn't the circuit breakers," Ken says, "it's the outlet. It's dead."

"The circuit breaker was tripped by the faulty lamp. The outlet's dead because it has no power."

"Of course it has no power. It's dead. That's why I called you."

"Then where is the circuit-breaker box?"

"You don't need the circuit-breaker box. The problem is the outlet."

"Ken, why did you call me?"

"Because the outlet is dead. I want you to fix it."

"But why aren't you doing it yourself?"

"Because I'm not an electrician. I thought you were an electrician."

"Then why are you arguing with me?"

"I'm not arguing. I just want you to fix the outlet."

"Please show me the circuit-breaker box."

This goes on for a good ten minutes. Finally, he leads me to the breaker box. I reset the breaker. Then I return to the outlet, which is now working.

"Aren't you going to replace it?" Ken asks.

"It doesn't need to be replaced. It wasn't the problem."

"I called you here to replace the outlet."

All right. What the heck. No harm in it. I replace the outlet.

"Don't plug that lamp into anything," I say.

"It wasn't the lamp. It was the outlet."

"May I see the lamp?"

"I threw it away. It caught on fire when the outlet broke."

In the street, as I pack my tool belt into the truck, a neighbor says, "How's Ken doing? Still crazy?"

Mrs. Roper's Lover

July 1999

On the phone she says, "My name is Mrs. Roper." In my experience the only women who introduce themselves as "Mrs." are old-style ladies of wealth. Mrs. Roper, however, lives in Redwood Terrace, a motley collection of dwellings that would never be mistaken for an outpost of the upper class.

She says, "My lover was celebrating and went through the screen door. Could you fix it?"

I drop by and take a look. It's a plain two-room cabin with a big screened porch facing the highway. In the yard there's a roofless '57 Chevy Bel Air on blocks, a sapling growing from the front seat.

Mrs. Roper is a thin woman with gray hair. She wears no ring. She's spry and lively. As I examine the door she says, "Can you beef it up a little? For the next time he celebrates?"

"Sure. I could add a cross-bar at least. Or more. Does your husband celebrate a lot?"

"He's not my husband."

A man shuffles onto the screen porch, scratching an armpit. It's 11 a.m. and he's clearly just awoken. He has tired eyes and a curly gray beard.

"Good morning," I say.

The man consults his watch. Like Mrs. Roper he's thin, sixtyish, weatherworn, a bit stiff. "I'll concede that it's morning," he says. "But I don't see much good about it."

It's a gorgeous day.

I decide I'd better build a major reinforcement for the door.

The man steps into the sunlight, grimacing. "Mrs. Roper," he says, "your coffee's so weak I could read a newspaper through it."

Mrs. Roper squints at him, not giving a reply.

I squint at him too. What I see is a grizzled old fart in a white T-shirt. And something more. My quick read of Mrs. Roper and her lover is that they are educated people. It's in the vocabulary, the grammar and articulation, a certain quickness of mind. But they live like hillbillies, and that's the mystery.

"I'm going up to AJ's," he says, and he sets out walking with a slight limp. "AJ's" is what we call Apple Jack's, our local bar. From Redwood Terrace it's a hike of more than a mile.

For half a minute Mrs. Roper watches him go shambling along the roadside. "I guess I'll keep him," she says, jutting out her chin as if expecting me to argue. "We've been living together for forty-two years." She smiles quickly, then recomposes her stern face.

In 1957 she ran off with her lover. She wants me to know: she'd do it again.

Fridays with Denny

October 2000

The kid starts following me around. He's skinny, a teenager with a sweet face.

"See that?" I say. I point with the beam of the flashlight. "That's a termite tunnel." It looks like an ivy root snaking over the concrete footing. Touching it with a screwdriver, I break a hole in the sculpted mud. Immediately, grubby fat termites start tumbling out.

The kid squats, studying. Suddenly he tucks his head toward his shoulder, brings one arm up and swats his hair as if he's being attacked by hornets. Then he resumes studying the tunnel.

Tapping a band joist with the screwdriver, I find a soft spot and pry it open, exposing a nest of squirmy, white bodies.

I hate termites. Gut reaction. They bring out a murderous kernel hidden deep in my personality. I resist the urge to smash the nest with my hammer while the kid studies. He's fascinated. His name is Denny.

"How'd you know they'd be right there?" Denny asks.

"I heard them." I show Denny how you can hold your ear to a board and detect the tiny legs scuttling around inside.

He holds his ear to the joist and says, "It's like Rice Krispies. Snap, crackle, and pop!" He's delighted. His feelings are naked, like a puppy's.

He runs to fetch his dad and his stepmom. "Listen," he tells them. "It's like Rice Krispies!"

I say, "Don't get too attached to them, Denny. You know I have to kill them, right?"

"Can I help?"

"Are you a carpenter?"

"I make models."

"Like, model airplanes?"

"Airplanes are my dad. I make tanks."

"Out of wood?"

"Mostly plastic."

Dad and stepmom are exchanging a look. "Let's talk," the dad says, and he motions for me to follow into the back yard, where we can be alone.

Denny, he tells me, has Tourette syndrome.

"You mean," I asked, "he breaks out cussing?" It's the only thing I know about Tourette's.

"No, only a small percentage of people do that. Mostly he has tics."

"What's a tic?"

"Did you see him swatting his hair? That's one. He's never had a job because the tics can freak people out. Working for you would be fantastic. If you can handle it."

I can use an extra pair of hands on the job, even unskilled. I like training teens. I like Denny. Win, win, win.

Denny lives with his mother in San Jose and only visits his dad in La Honda once a week. We make an agreement that Denny will help me for half a day every Friday. The repair on his father's house will proceed slowly on that schedule, but everybody is happy with the plan. We'll begin next Friday.

During the following week I try to learn as much as I can about Tourette syndrome. I'm worried about the tics, which are like little spasms. It is a safety issue. If Denny holds one end of a board, will he suddenly drop it?

It's amazing how difficult it used to be to find information that is now at our fingertips. I find some books in the library, and I try that wild and wooly new thing called the internet. Fortunately I find an online forum where I get some reassuring advice. Denny, they say, won't drop his end of the board. There are airline pilots and surgeons who have Tourette's. They can suppress it when they're concentrating on a critical task.

There is also a belief that people with Tourette's have an "intense" personality. With Denny, how would you know? He's a teenager. Intensity is a given.

Some of what I learn is worrisome. Tourette's is often accompanied by obsessive-compulsive behavior. Will Denny be willing to get dirty? It's a job requirement for a carpenter.

The next Friday, Denny kneels in the dirt without hesitation to help me remove a rotten beam. Also on the plus side, I give him the chore of tightening up some bolts with a wrench, which he does okay. And he gets the hang of holding a spirit level against a post or beam and steadying it at level while I attach it. So he's useful in an elementary way as long as I supply the tool (he has none) and show him exactly what to do and how to do it.

Though willing to kneel in the dirt, Denny isn't strong enough to hold a beam as I cut it, so it drops painfully onto my knee. He can't hammer a 16-penny nail more than halfway into a 2×4 of Douglas fir. Beyond halfway, the nail won't budge no matter how many times he taps. So I give him the job of starting the nails, then I whack them home.

Wanting to start a conversation with a safe topic, I ask Denny about school. He says he's taking psychology and art at the community college.

I ask, "You going somewhere with that?"

"Psych is for self-preservation. Art, maybe I'd like it to go somewhere."

His tics, I notice, come more frequently when I'm cutting. If he holds the board while I saw, he controls himself until I finish the cut. Then he has a hornet attack. He tucks his head toward his shoulder, brings one arm up, and swats his hair. Sometimes both arms.

"What's that like?" I asked him.

"Sorry," he says.

"I'm not complaining or criticizing. I'm just curious. That thing where you hit your head. What does it feel like when you do that?"

Denny studies me for a long moment, looking defensive. He says, "It's like sneezing."

"Like, your body tells you to do it, and you've just gotta do it, and then it's over?"

"Like that." He relaxes. He brushes some sawdust from his jeans, has a tic attack, then studies me again. He says, "I get therapy but it isn't something you fix. You just have it. I could take drugs, but it feels like somebody put styrofoam in my head. I won't do it. They can't make me."

In half a day we've repaired the termite damage, torn out an old deck, and started a framework for the new deck. The work is basic, easy-to-grasp, and soulfully satisfying. Denny is happy. Construction meets a deep need in guys.

So I think it's going well.

The next Friday I arrive before Denny. Justine, the stepmother, tells me Denny had problems last week after I left. He'd been suppressing his tics, which always results in a storm of tics later on. He hadn't slept well. He banged around the house during the night. Screaming. Crying.

I ask, "What did I do wrong?"

"Nothing," she says. "He's just so anxious to please you."

"I asked him about his tics. Was that a bad idea?"

"No. It's definitely a sensitive topic, but it's a part of life he has to learn to deal with. Just be mellow, okay?"

Justine and I share a long, friendly history. She's a smart hippie, a lovely woman, an artist whose paintings could have been created by Frida Kahlo on drugs.

She'd had no use for men in her life except for hiring me as her on-call handyman. She commissioned me once to build an elegant indoor sandbox. What a fun job. Then, after years of living alone, she suddenly, inexplicably fell in love with Joshua, Denny's father, a good-natured man who sells war toys. Joshua moved in practically the moment he met her, bringing his own bed and hanging model military aircraft by strings from the ceiling to mingle with Justine's psychedelic feminist paintings. When I noticed the separate bedrooms, Justine told me, giggling, that she wouldn't sleep with Joshua because he snored.

Joshua arrives in his van, bringing Denny, who's acting shy today. A mist is starting to fall. Rain is predicted.

"You should work," Justine says. "I threw the tarot and it looked pretty good."

Joshua laughs. "That's great!" Miming talking on a telephone, he says, "Hello, Al? Hey, man, sorry, I can't come to work today—I drew the Fear card."

Justine glares at him.

I hesitate, studying the darkening clouds.

"You guys better get to work," Joshua tells Denny and me. "If she doesn't get her way, she'll be stomping and slamming doors all day."

"Denny?" I ask. "You want to get a little wet?"

"Fuck the wet," Denny says.

So we continue framing the deck outside while, from inside the house, I hear angry words. Stomping. Doors slamming.

"It wasn't coprolalia," Denny says.

"Copro-what?" I say.

"Uncontrollable cussing. I just meant, 'fuck.'"

"This is carpentry," I say. "You're *supposed* to cuss."

Denny smiles. Then he tics.

One thing I notice is that Denny hates sawdust. It makes him tic.

Eventually Joshua comes out and watches us work.

I don't know if it's the wet, or so much sawdust, or the argument inside, or the effect of having his father watching, but Denny is having an endless string of tic attacks, and the more he has them, the more they seem to stress him. Then he makes a bonehead mistake measuring and marking a 4×4 post—and I make the bonehead mistake of not checking his mark. As a result, I cut the post six inches too short.

I don't blame Denny, but I'm disgusted with myself for allowing it to happen. Maybe I look angry. "We've gotta quit," I say. "It's too wet."

"Fuck this shit," Denny says. He rushes into the house.

Joshua stays with me while I gather tools.

"It's hard on him," Joshua says. "His mother didn't want him working with you. She wants him on drugs." Rancor is coming into his voice. "The irony is that she's a nurse. You'd think she'd know better." Hearing himself, Joshua softens the tone. "We try to keep it private, but he knows we fight about him. And then with me and Justine today . . ." He shakes his head. "He's gonna have a bad night."

"I'm not helping," I say.

"Yes, you are. He's trying so hard. He was looking forward to this all week. He worships you, man." Joshua squints. "Don't you dare hurt him."

Folks, don't ever hire me as a psychotherapist. I have no clue.

Over the weekend I call Justine and ask her what to do. I tell her I feel as though I've stumbled into the middle of a marital war, joining Denny in the crossfire. Did the kid have a bad night?

"Terrible," she says. "The worst ever."

"What should I do?"

"Don't quit. You're his escape."

"Uh, Justine, I've gotta tell you, the kid will never be a carpenter."

"That's not what you're doing. I don't care if you build the world's crappiest deck. Don't worry about it. Just stay with him. *Please.*"

The following Friday is warm and sunny. In La Honda we have some of our best weather in October. Denny and I set to work.

We're repairing the 4×4 post that I'd cut too short. I draw a diagram, explaining every step, and then mark the cut lines on the 4×4s.

"Hold it tight," I say. "I know you hate sawdust, but I've got to make a straight cut or it'll look awful." Working alone I could clamp the board myself, but I want Denny involved.

He never flinches, even when I shoot a plume of sawdust at his arm. Afterward, though, he has a hornet attack. A lengthy one.

We cut half laps at one end of each of the two boards, which I finish with a chisel. Then we place the two ends together, overlapping. I guide Denny through drilling three-eighths-inch holes and tapping the carriage bolts into place. He tightens them with my socket wrench.

The result isn't too ugly.

"It's called a splice joint," I say.

Denny looks serious. "What's it called when you just stick the two ends together?"

"A butt joint. It's weak. This splice joint, what we made, is plenty strong."

"Okay," he says. There are no tics for a while.

And then out of nowhere it comes to me: a tide of memories like breaking waves. Holy shit. Should I tell him? Why not? I say, "You know what, Denny? I just remembered this. I had twitches as a kid. I mean it was nothing like you, but I had facial stuff. Around my eyes. And the corner of my mouth. Sometimes I wondered if I was cracking up."

Denny furrows his brow. "What did you do about it?"

"Nothing. I never told anybody. Not even my mother—not that she was paying attention. That was part of the problem—*nobody* was paying attention."

"Nobody ever noticed?"

"I was one of those invisible kids. There were two thousand students in my school. I was the kind of kid nobody could remember I was in their class. I'd cover the twitches with my hand. Usually I could hold it off when I was with people. Which was weird because when I was alone, I didn't seem to have any control over it. I just twitched, man. Wow. I'd completely forgotten."

"So it just stopped? You outgrew it?"

"I'm not comparing myself to you. I don't think I had any particular syndrome—other than the simple hell of puberty. So anyway, yeah, I outgrew it. That, and I met a girl. Somebody who paid attention. And I paid attention to her."

Denny probes: "And you *forgot* you had twitches?"

"Yeah." I reflect a moment, wondering how it could happen. And what else have I forgotten about my childhood? Plenty, I hope. Because even what I do remember isn't pretty.

To Denny I say, "I think maybe there's a merciful memory gland in the brain. It erases things. Or at least it hides them, if you let it. Anyway, it was forty years ago. And I had it *easy* compared to you. Except in one way you've got an advantage I didn't have—three parents who love you maybe a little too much. Who pay attention. I don't envy your condition, but I do envy that."

"So you think I just need to get laid?"

"No! I didn't say that. And let me repeat this one more time: I had it so much easier than you."

Denny kicks at some dirt. "That's what I'm gonna do. Outgrow this shit. My long-term plan. And also get laid. I'll tell my parents you recommend it."

"I never said—"

"Oh, yeah." Denny taps his head with his finger. It wasn't a tic this time. "I forgot. My memory gland at work."

Okay, he can mock me. Tease me. A good sign.

We carry some 2×6s from my truck. Then I ask Denny, "What do you think of Justine's art?"

Denny frowns. "Honestly?" But he says no more. Credit him with some common sense.

With the frame complete, it's an easy matter to lay the decking. Normally I'd use screws, but in this case I drill starter holes and give Denny the job of nailing, which he accomplishes, improving somewhat as he goes along. Instead of the 22-ounce framer I give him my 16-ounce finish hammer, which is less powerful but easier to guide.

"Looks good," I say.

Denny steps back, regarding the deck with a critical eye. "I kind of suck," he says. "I know that."

Denny's father has come out of the house and is walking toward us. Immediately Denny has a hornet attack. Then he says, "Dad, we made a splice joint."

"What's that?" Joshua asks.

Denny points. "You cut part away. Then you overlap." He's staring coldly at his father. "It's better than a butt joint. A splice is stronger."

"That's good to know," Joshua says.

"A splice, Dad. Not a butt."

"I get it."

Denny commences a series of tics. His father and I watch helplessly. Eventually the hornets pass. Denny helps me gather tools and load the truck.

I pay him, peeling off twenties into his hand. "Thanks, Denny, for the help."

"Yeah, um, thanks," Denny says, and he walks away, a skinny kid staring at his toes. The sky is a deep purple with the barest crescent of a new moon.

I watch Denny pass under the glowing porch lamp and go into the kitchen. The screen door slams. He makes no effort to soften it.

The way life works out, soon Justine and Joshua move up north. I never see Denny again. My last view of him is through the kitchen window that Friday evening, swatting a suspended Fokker triplane out of the way like one more hornet, then bending to sniff a pot of steaming soup. I have a feeling he'll be okay.

You Fix the Toilet

You Fix the Toilet; You Prop the Porch

Tuesday, June 4, 2002

I'm deeply worried about my brother, Ed. He didn't show up last week for my daughter's wedding. He doesn't answer his phone or return calls. He lives alone.

As I think about it, I realize I haven't seen him since January, when he'd seemed confused and excessively salivary. Now five months have passed, and as I call around I learn that *nobody* has seen Ed since January. Nobody has spoken with him.

It's completely out of character for my brother to miss my daughter's wedding. He can be a pain in the rear (it isn't by accident that he lives alone), but he's a family guy. Something's wrong.

He has an answering machine. With a little work I manage to hack into it from my home phone in La Honda, sixty miles away. Allstate Insurance is calling to warn that the homeowner's policy will be canceled for nonpayment in five days. The dentist calls to remind of an appointment, then calls back to tell Ed he owes for a missed appointment. These messages are three months old. More recently, Mr. Lee the gardener calls to say Ed hasn't left a check for the last two months.

Apparently, sometime in the month of March Ed ceased contact with the outside world.

He could be dead.

With a strange mixture of dread and adventure, with no idea what I will find, I drive an hour and a half over the mountain, up the peninsula and across the bay to Albany, the feisty little town just north of Berkeley. Though fully prepared to break into the house, I find the back door unlocked. Shouting halloos, I walk in. There's a steady sound of water running through pipes; otherwise, silence.

Dust and dirt are everywhere. Potted plants are dead or dying. The lath and plaster ceiling in the kitchen has partially collapsed. The toilet is running, flushing at full blast.

I find Ed in the rear bedroom, undressed, on stinking, soiled sheets, lying with his hands folded over his belly, eyes closed. Is he alive?

I touch his neck. Warm. At my touch, he opens his eyes. "Hello, Ed," I say.

He studies me, confused. Then he smiles. With effort, he sits up in bed. Looking down at the sheets, he says, "Shit." Which is literally true. Then for some reason he says, "It's not clear."

I help him stand. He shuffles to the bathroom. I hand him fresh clothes. He washes himself absent-mindedly and emerges roughly clean, somewhat smelly, wild hair and beard looking like the Unabomber.

It's 3 p.m. He's obviously been lying on that bed for days. He must be dehydrated, hungry.

I ask, "You want some tea?"

In the kitchen he sits amidst fallen plaster. There are dishes in the sink from last Christmas. A bin of stinking compost has decomposed without ever being taken out, flies buzzing around.

I boil water on the stove. The first tea I have to throw out because bugs are floating in it. I should have washed the mugs I took from his cabinet.

I water plants. We drink green tea. His hands are shaky. Tea spills. With the spot of hydration, Ed seems to sit up a little straighter, to come more alive, like a potted plant.

"What day is it?" Ed asks.

"Tuesday."

"What month?"

"June."

He blinks, shakes his head. "I'm not clear."

I make more tea. When I refill the mugs, I leave about a one-inch gap below the brim because of how he shakes. In the closest Ed comes to full engagement, he asks me to fill his mug to the brim—as if in great need of this little nourishment. It's a B&O mug. Ed and I grew up in Maryland, where the B&O coal trains were a constant fact of life. He's had a lifelong love of railroads.

He keeps saying, "I'm not clear," and, "It's not clear." He hands me an invitation to my daughter's wedding—a shortcut around forming the thoughts and words to discuss how he will get there. I say, "The wedding was last week. You weren't there. That's why I came today—to check on your health."

"I'm not clear."

"Do you have health insurance?"

"No."

He hasn't had a job in two years. A brilliant man, he always worked as a highly paid computer programmer, though without passion. Instead, his fire has always been for leading Sierra Club hikes, learning foreign languages, and singing in amateur opera. Covering the walls are railroad posters and photos of his daughter, whom he adores but rarely sees. She lives near Santa Cruz.

I ask, "Would you let me take you to a doctor?"

"No."

"A doctor might help."

"No."

"It might clear your head."

"You think so?"

"Yes."

"If you think it's a good idea, I'll go."

In retrospect, I see this as the moment of transference. He'd always been the big brother, the one I followed and respected. Now he's placed me in charge—at least until he "clears his head," something that obviously troubles him.

I make some phone calls. I'm no health expert, but I have friends who are: an emergency-room doctor, a therapist, a psychiatric social worker. The consensus is that Ed probably has massive clinical depression exacerbated by isolation and possibly by malnutrition and dehydration. And a history of alcohol abuse.

This consensus, the preliminary telephone diagnosis, will turn out to be wrong, but at least it's a start. A plan is formed: tomorrow I will bring Ed to the emergency room at Highland Hospital in Oakland. That's where indigent people go in the East Bay. I have no idea whether Ed has any money—and neither does he. The subject of money, or anything involving numbers, seems to bewilder him.

My friend John, who is an emergency-room doctor, though not at Highland, believes timing is everything: "Don't go now. Go first thing tomorrow morning. By then they should have cleaned up all the gunshot wounds from the night before. It shouldn't be too bad—it's not a full moon." John hates to work on nights of a full moon. He says it's crazy busy.

Ed starts eating a bowl of dry Cheerios. In the refrigerator I find some cheese and seven bottles of beer. I tell Ed I'll go out and get some milk and some fruit. He gets angry: "No! I can do that."

"Do you have money?"

"Of course I have money."

"Where's your wallet?"

"I don't know."

I put two twenty-dollar bills on the table. Angrily, Ed crumples them and throws them at me. I leave them, crumpled green balls, on the kitchen floor.

I change the sheets on the bed. I open the toilet tank and see it needs new everything: flapper, ballcock, maybe a whole new flush valve. As a plumber, I hate the sound of running water. It sets my nerves on edge. This crapper has probably been gushing for months, acre-feet of Sierra snowmelt flushing into the bay.

I'm emotionally exhausted. I have an overwhelming desire to flee, to go home and hug everybody I love.

By now it's evening. Ed is clearly feeling better—from social contact and perhaps from tea. Tomorrow I'll take Ed to the emergency room, and then we'll come back and I'll fix the toilet. I also need to shore up his front porch, which is on the verge of collapse, swaying under my feet. A 4×6 beam has rotted and fallen off. The porch is stucco, semi-enclosed, with lovely arched openings and a Spanish tile roof. It would be a huge job to replace it, but I can prop it temporarily from the bottom.

I'll bring my plumbing tools, toilet parts, new posts for the porch, new beams. These things I can do. It's a plan.

Wednesday, June 5, 2002

Before rush hour it's an easy drive to Albany as the dawn breaks. On San Pablo Avenue I pick up coffee and cinnamon rolls at Happy Donuts. At 6:30 a.m. I shake Ed awake in his bed. He's surprised to see me. "Why are you here?"

"I've got coffee and cinnamon rolls in the truck. We're going to the doctor."

"What's wrong with you?"

I don't answer, which works to my advantage. Instinctively, wordlessly, in his confusion Ed gets up and gets dressed, thinking he's going to help take me to the doctor. He's a good brother.

The two crumpled twenty-dollar bills are no longer on the kitchen floor. In the refrigerator are twenty-three bottles of Coors and a can of Reddi-wip.

We arrive at Highland Hospital in Oakland at 7:30. We have to park a couple of blocks away. Ed has the shuffling walk of an old guy. Last year he was leading hiking groups in the Sierra high country. "Why are we here?" Ed asks.

"You're seeing a doctor. To get your head clear."

"I don't want that."

"You said you would."

"Oh. Okay."

Ed can't tell the registrar his social security number, his phone number, his ZIP code. He remembers his birthday but not the year. He doesn't have his wallet. He says he has a checking account but doesn't remember the bank. The registrar asks, "How much money is in your checking account?"

"Fifteen."

"Fifteen hundred? Fifteen thousand?"

"No."

"Fifteen dollars?"

"What fifteen dollars?"

"How much money is in your checking account?"

"Some hundred."

"Some hundred dollars?"

"What hundred?"

"I think I get it." She fills out some forms.

We see a triage nurse. Then we wait in chairs in a hallway among gurneys where men and women are lying strapped in place, moaning or babbling.

Around noon we finally see a doctor, and she is a gem: Dr. Frances Herb, who "used to hang out" in La Honda in the '60s, not with Ken Kesey but "nearly with" him, whatever that means. While giving Ed a physical exam she asks him to remember three words, then repeat them back to her.

Ed succeeds.

"Now spell 'world' backward."

To my surprise Ed succeeds (better than me).

"Now count backward from one hundred by sevens."

This one Ed flunks. With anything about numbers—or money—Ed draws blanks. "What day is today? What year is it?" He has no idea.

Dr. Herb asks, "Can you tell me who is president?"

"That jerk. That asshole."

Dr. Herb smiles. "Which one? What's his name?"

"He's an idiot."

"What's his name?"

No answer.

She asks about lifestyle. When Ed is incoherent, I interpret the answer for her. Ed and I are telepathic in the way you become when you share history, blood. I add what I know. Yes, he drank a lot. He also led an active outdoor life. For a while he took Antabuse. He has a genius IQ. He has episodes of horrible anger.

He's fifty-nine years old.

Her diagnosis: hypertension, mild diabetes, and the big one—dementia from alcohol abuse. Not depression. Not reversible.

This diagnosis will prove to be correct as far as it goes, but incomplete. Later it will become apparent that Ed has had—and will continue to have—ischemic attacks, both transient (TIAs, or ministrokes) and cerebral infarcts (strokes), with a significant stroke back in March when he began his retreat from the outside world. Knowing this, however, won't change Ed's treatment or outcome.

A medical social worker joins us and talks about Ed as if he weren't there. She and Dr. Herb seem more concerned about me and my reaction. They talk of Adult Protective Services, probate conservatorship, selling Ed's house and putting him in a care facility, Meals on Wheels . . .

Dr. Herb asks Ed what he eats. He says he walks to a bakery two blocks from his house and gets a loaf of fresh bread. He eats it with peanut butter. How does he pay? Ed says, "They'll always give it to me. They're my *friends*."

Dr. Herb asks, "How much alcohol do you drink?"

"Beer."

"You have to stop drinking alcohol."

"No."

"Ed, your problems are caused by a history of heavy drinking."

Ed laughs. "It was worth every penny."

At the hospital we fill a prescription of enalapril maleate for blood pressure, which requires waiting in a line of crazy people who aren't shy about acting out their problems or demonstrating their need for drugs. Then I take Ed home.

Ed has been processed through the public health system and, unexpectedly, so have I. It took an entire morning of waiting and patience to get in, but once in, the system worked well enough. The fabulous Dr. Herb spent an hour and a half with Ed. The blood tests, urine test, social worker, the prescription were all free.

The focus of Dr. Herb and the social worker was not on how to fix Ed, who is unfixable, but on how to prepare me for the long decline to come. They both said to me at various points, "You're a good brother." Have I a choice?

I repair Ed's toilet, a great relief to me, though it never bothered him. Another message from Allstate on Ed's answering machine. By phone I pay from my own credit card to resume coverage, pushing the card to the max. With a couple hours of sawing and banging, I throw together a temporary support under the sagging front porch.

I'm beat, physically and emotionally. Driving home, the view from I-80 over the Emeryville mud flats—the bay, Alcatraz Island, Mount Tamalpais—is outlined by the golden rays of the setting sun.

What do you do when you're losing your brother? You love him. You fix the toilet; you prop the porch. You do what you can.

She Doesn't Do People

Saturday, June 22, 2002

Maggie has hairy legs and a Hells Angels personality. She works graveyard shift at an animal hospital. At best you could describe her personality as prickly. Somebody got close to her once though: she has a teenage daughter. The girl is your average fresh-faced, phone-chatting, slightly awkward teenager.

Mother and daughter live in a rotten little shack by a creek, under trees, where it is always damp and dark. To get there I have to drive my truck across a shaky wooden bridge, then weave among redwoods on a dirt road.

In August of 2000 I wired a tool shed behind Maggie's shack, converting it to a laundry room.

In June of 2002 Maggie asks me to find the cause of some dead electrical outlets. She isn't home when I arrive at her shack, but her daughter Annie is there.

"Where's the problem?" I ask.

Annie shows me some outlets in various damp, smelly rooms and then says, "As long as you're here, could you find out what's wrong with the dryer outlet in the shed? It never worked."

"Never? It was working when I installed it."

"It quit, first time she used it."

"That was two years ago! Why didn't she call me?"

"She was afraid you'd charge more money to fix it."

"I guarantee my work."

"Yeah, I thought so. She didn't want to call. She doesn't do people."

Most teens are mortified by their parents. Annie has better-than-average reasons. She seems remarkably level-headed though. She is blessed with resilience—and enough good looks to soon take her out of this isolation.

The circuit breaker I'd installed for the dryer is defective. I replace it. The other dead outlets turn out to be caused by a rat who fried himself in an open junction box.

Maggie comes home. Stepping out of her old pickup with a bag of groceries, she gapes at me and shouts, *"What's the matter with your face?"*

Annie rolls her eyes.

"I guess I got a little acne," I say. "Sometimes it still happens."

"That's not fair," Maggie says. "You must be eighty years old. Pretty soon you're going to die, and then you'll have acne in your *coffin*."

264

"Mom," Annie says. "That's inappropriate."

"I'm fifty-four," I say.

"Really?" Maggie says. "Then maybe you won't die yet. How much do I owe you?"

"Nothing. I'm sorry about the dryer. You should have called."

"Okay, I should've," Maggie says. She frowns at me. "I'm not stupid like you think."

"I never thought— "

"I'm smart with dogs. They say what they mean. I think in my last life I was a dog. Wish I'd stayed there. I was a guard dog for a paranoid man in Johnstown, Pennsylvania. He beat me some, but mostly he was nice. I used to lie under his porch gnawing on steak bones. You believe that? Don't answer. Anyway, it would explain a lot, don't you think?"

"How do you know you were a guard dog in Johnstown, Pennsylvania?"

"I passed through there on a motorcycle ride and it just hit me. I knew that place." She squints, studying me. "Can acne kill people?"

"*Mom!*" Annie shouts.

Maggie trudges to the house with her bag of groceries.

Annie smiles at me. "Thanks," she says.

"No problem."

The acne will clear up. Stuff comes and goes.

A Lifetime Job

Friday, November 22, 2002

Dr. Gonzales, a lovely young woman, is examining my brother, Ed. We are in Highland Hospital, Oakland, Emergency Room Number Two. I've brought Ed here because he is acting strangely—that is, more strangely than usual—and because his left side is weak. When Ed undresses for the doctor, I see the left leg is much thinner—atrophied—so this left-side weakness is nothing new.

The lovely young woman stands before my naked older brother and listens to his heart and lungs. She tells him to bend over, and she gives him a rectal exam. Ed shouts a string of obscenities.

Matter-of-factly, Dr. Gonzales peels off her gloves and says, "You didn't like that?"

"*No!*"

She sends Ed off on a gurney to get a CT scan. When he returns, he and I wait for the results. We are sharing Emergency Room Number Two with a woman who attempted suicide via overdose. Unlike Ed, nobody is with her. Also unlike Ed, she is held by restraints.

We wait from 4 p.m. until 8:15 p.m. There are bodies unattended on gurneys in hallways, looking like they've been there for days.

Ed is in the early stages of dementia. He denies that there is anything wrong with him, and he gets angry at me when I try to help him. Still, I'm here.

If you ever met my brother—even in his dementia—you would describe him as one of the smartest people you ever met. And at the moments you least expect, funny.

Ed lies on the bed, staring at the ceiling. I talk with him about London, the Rolling Stones, Italy, Prague—about all of which he is lucid—but he can't remember what happened earlier today, how the neighbors were worried, how they called me, how I brought him here in my pickup truck.

Dr. Gonzales returns at last. Speaking to me, not Ed, she says the CT scan shows no new stroke, just a bunch of old strokes. There's no hemorrhagic bleeding. An illness such as a cold or bladder infection can cause the reappearance of previous stroke symptoms.

Now Dr. Gonzales speaks directly to Ed: "I'd like to ask you some questions."

Ed nods.

"Do you know what year this is?"

"Um. Nineteen eighty-eight."

"It's two thousand and two. Do you know what month it is?"

"December?"

"It's November. November twenty-second."

"They shot him."

"Who shot who?"

"The president. They shot him."

I feel a chill. On November 22, 1963, John F. Kennedy was shot. I was sixteen years old, idealistic, hopeful. Ed was twenty. I can tell you exactly where I was standing the moment I heard the news. So can Ed. Dr. Gonzales hadn't even been born yet.

Like any sane person of the time, Ed never believed that the assassination was the work of one man. "They shot him," he says again.

"Okay." Dr. Gonzales asks Ed some simple arithmetic questions and some memorization questions. After Ed has flunked every test, she says, "You see, Ed, this is why people think you are confused. It's very common for people in your condition not to recognize it themselves."

The words seem to sink in, and Ed looks surprised and sad.

In a moment, though, he'll forget. That's the beauty of dementia.

Dr. Gonzales leaves the room, and a nurse comes in. "I can discharge you," she says to Ed. "I just have to make sure you aren't too disoriented."

Ed stares at her blankly.

The nurse says, "Can you tell me who is president of the United States?"

Ed frowns.

Again the nurse asks, "Who is president?"

"That turd," Ed says.

"Does that turd have a name?"

"Uh . . ."

The nurse makes a note on a chart and says, "It's Bush. George Bush."

"That's what I said."

"Hmm. Do you know where you are now?"

"Yes."

"Where?"

"I'm in the *fucking hospital!*"

The nurse smiles. "Okay. You can go home now."

Family is a job, and it lasts for a lifetime. For both Ed and me.

Back home, I help Ed climb the steps to his front door.

As I unlock the deadbolt, he asks, "Where did we go?"

"The hospital."

"Oh, no." He studies me with a gaze of brotherly concern. "Are you all right?"

Dee Ann and Decor

Friday, May 16, 2003

Isabella the decorator calls: "I try to be flexible. I try to give people what they want—only slightly better in taste than what they *think* they want. That's my job. But I can't even *begin* at that house. I give you Dee Ann. And she is truly a gift. I told her to call you for some downlights. You'll like her. It comes with benefits if you want. She owns a mortuary."

"Benefits? You mean I get a free burial?"

"I mean she enjoys life. She works with death."

It's a ranch house in a neighborhood of 1960s ranch houses. There's a big new Cadillac in the driveway. You don't see many of these land yachts in Silicon Valley. They just aren't fashionable here.

Dee Ann is a heavily decorated woman with a heavily decorated house protected by steel security gates. Not one wrinkle breaks the surface of her face.

Indoors it's a jungle of expensive kitsch. There are angels, ceramic kittens, gaudy clocks, and about a dozen statues of Aphrodite. There's jaunty Muzak piped into every room. In the back yard there is more Muzak—along with ceramic turtles, a hot tub, and an Aphrodite fountain with twin streams of water jetting from the marble breasts.

Dee Ann has removed her silk jacket to reveal a semitransparent, gauzy blouse with nothing underneath except gravity-defying, sculpted body parts. Another stone-solid Aphrodite. In Dee Ann's business restoring bodies is the norm.

She has mixed herself some kind of neon-green cocktail that would likely glow in the dark. She sips and watches as I cut holes in her ceiling.

"Don't worry when you go in the attic," she says. "We don't keep our skeletons up there."

"That's a relief."

"Want a drink?" she asks. "Take a break?"

"I really can't," I say. And I won't. "I've got jobs lined up. I can't take the time."

"If you don't take time," Dee Ann says, "time takes you."

Alfredo

Tuesday, February 17, 2004

At 7 a.m. on a cold morning I meet Alfredo. We stand on the narrow road, looking up at a hillside. I explain what I need: a trench, twenty feet long, four feet deep, sixteen inches wide. The trench must follow the contour of the hillside. I need it today. Then, tomorrow, I need the trench filled with drain rock.

There's no practical access for a tractor, and the hill is too steep for one anyway. The trench must be dug by hand.

"How much you want to pay?" Alfredo asks.

Alfredo is a big man with a couple of gold teeth. In my town (La Honda), he's the go-to guy for a job like this. Sometimes he does the work himself. For digging he says he'll "get some people." We settle on a price, then I leave.

At 5 p.m. I return. There is a perfect ditch in the hillside. I check the measurements, and it is exactly right. The sides of the ditch go straight down with no narrowing toward the bottom. Somebody—probably several somebodies, working with shovels on a slippery hillside—has lifted and moved all that water-soaked clay, leaving edges slick and precise as if cut with a knife.

Sometimes hiring Alfredo is like pushing a button.

The next morning I assemble drainage pipe in mucky mud. A dump truck drops four yards of drain rock in a pile at the side of the road. Now the pile must be carried fifteen feet up the hill.

Alfredo arrives with two men in his truck. He speaks to the men in Spanish. They use two shovels to fill one wheelbarrow and begin hauling the rock up the hill.

Alfredo can round men up on a moment's notice even if they don't have telephones or permanent addresses, and he will make sure they do the work promptly and well.

A few hours later I return. The men are gone; the ditch is filled. Alfredo, alone this time, drives up in his truck, a nearly new Ford F150. I count out $400. I could have negotiated a lower price but didn't try. At this price Alfredo will make a fair profit and the diggers will receive a fair wage. Families will be fed.

Alfredo has a wife who cleans houses. They have raised three children who have married and moved away. They are honest, friendly, hard-working people.

"Nice truck," I say.

Alfredo pats the fender. He smiles with pride, gold teeth sparkling. "In Mexico," he says, "all I had was a burro."

269

Breaking your heart.
Or at least your plumbing.

Tuesday, April 13, 2004

Jemma, the live-in caretaker, calls. Ed has lost bladder and bowel control. She's upset. "I've grown attached to old Ed," she says.

I'm attached to him too. He's my big brother. He's slowly dying of dementia. It's hell to watch. Jemma's been threatening to quit because it's hell for her too.

I'm Ed's guardian. It's a ninety-minute drive to his house, so I try to manage crises by phone whenever possible. Jemma says Ed is weak and slow to respond. I suspect he's overmedicated. I call the new nurse. She says she'll check him out.

To calm myself I take my dog for a walk. I happen to meet Lulu walking her dog. She's a young woman with a well-behaved Australian shepherd. I'm an older guy with a rambunctious mutt. We often meet because we both like to walk our dogs at sunset, following a trail to the top of the watershed in La Honda, where there's a sweeping view of mountains, ocean, sky. Over several years of occasional walks, Lulu and I have come to know each other pretty well. Without direct discussion we've evolved a sort of unacknowledged relationship-with-boundaries: walk together if we should meet. Enjoy the chat, the fresh air, the sunset, the dogs. Never prearrange—walking together should only happen by chance. Never touch, even by accident. And never examine how we feel about each other because something might be smoldering and we don't want to know about it. We're both happily married. At least I'm happy. Friendship with a woman is complicated.

A year ago Lulu's husband helped my son find a summer job.

Today Lulu asks why I'm so pensive, and I tell her about my brother. Lulu works for a senior center, so she understands. Then, smart woman, she tells me to think about something good that's coming. I say my youngest son is about to graduate from college.

Lulu studies my face. "If that's good, why do you look sad?"

"It *is* good. I'm proud of him. I'm proud of all my children for graduating from college and finding their lives outside the nest. But it also makes me feel lonely."

Lulu's a pretty woman, tall, athletic, about twenty years younger than me, childless, married to a great guy. As we stand at the top of the hill gazing at orange and purple clouds while fingers of fog fill the shadows of the valleys, she says, "Can I ask you something?" She waits.

"Sure. Ask anything."

"Why did you have children?"

That's one of those questions for which there's no final answer, like asking why you believe in God. "It's kind of like faith," I say. "Faith in the future."

In twilight we walk with dogs down the trail. Lulu says she's been thinking a lot about whether to have children. She has some issues with her own mother. Lulu says she's set herself a deadline of making up her mind by her fortieth birthday, and it's almost here.

I find myself urging her to have children. She's a warm and giving person. She'd be a great mother, and I know her husband would be the soccer-coaching, let's-all-go-camping model of a great father.

"Having children seems so selfish," Lulu says.

I'm shocked. And I guess I've just learned something about Lulu's relationship with her mother, who lives in Connecticut, about as far away as Lulu could go. "No, it's the exact opposite of selfish," I say. "It's an act of idealism. All you do is give."

Lulu thinks that over for a few minutes. Then she asks, "But don't they break your heart?"

"Sometimes. They break everything. But that isn't the point."

"What is the point?"

"Accepting that you're part of the great flow of life. Embracing it. Loving it. We call sex *making love*, and sometimes it is, but having sex isn't the only way of making love. Raising children, if you're lucky—and you do need luck—and if you do it right, you *make* more love in the world. In your life. You get to love more people."

I spoke passionately. I think I surprised her. I certainly surprised myself. Again, Lulu thinks it over for a few minutes.

Sunset's over. We're walking down the trail now, and it's nearly dark. Her face is a shadow as she says, "I'm kind of embarrassed to ask this, but don't children ruin your sex life?"

This conversation has already gone farther than I would have expected. So here goes: "Well, yeah, it gets complicated. But it still happens. And I tell you this—on the subject of not being selfish—creating children, knowing you're trying to create them, is the best sex you'll ever have. Because it has a whole different meaning."

"Wow," she says. There's no eye contact here. Nor should there be.

Friday, April 16, 2004

Three days later Jemma calls again. It's not Ed this time, it's the plumbing. Ed's house, in a manner of speaking, is losing bladder and bowel control, big time.

I can't fix Ed, but I can fix his bathroom. I drive across the bay to Ed's house. Arriving at noon, I find Ed lying awake in bed. He says pleasantly, coherently, "I'm just finishing a nap." Reducing the meds was a good idea.

Despite Jemma's description of massive broken pipes in walls and attics, the problem is simply the bathroom faucet and drain. In a fit of demented anger Ed had kicked the P-trap into the wall. The entire sink needed replacing years ago, so I buy a new one and begin installing. Meanwhile I play Ed a CD of a concert my son Will just performed as a final project at college—ten songs he composed.

There are three ways to cheer Ed up. Visit him, play music, or talk about family. Here he's got all three. He's having a great day.

Late in the afternoon I take Ed to see Dr. Wu. Ed can barely walk. We go shoulder to shoulder, very slowly, with Ed balanced and supported by my arm. It's like moving a 200-pound bag of sand.

Dr. Wu reminds me that the goal here isn't to find a cure but to provide comfort and a graceful exit. And as far as he's concerned, Ed can stay home until the end.

Jemma and I work together to guide and partially lift Ed up his front stairs to the door. She asks what the doctor said, and I tell her.

"I don't want to see Ed go to a home," Jemma says. "I'll stay with him to the end."

As it turns out, she doesn't. She has the heart but not the training as Ed's needs increase. Many an adventure will come in the up-and-down saga of Ed.

Meanwhile Lulu's husband suddenly gets a promotion to a new location. They move to Fremont, across San Francisco Bay.

About six months later Lulu calls my house, something she's never done. "Hi! It's Lulu!" At first I can't even place her because I'm an idiot with names. She's offended but gets over it. Then she says, "Guess what? I'm pregnant!"

I feel like an uncle. Or a godfather. I feel like this baby was conceived by our conversation that day, watching the sunset with the dogs.

Lulu remembers too. "Now maybe you have something good to think about."

It's a boy.

The Graduate

Sunday, June 13, 2004

Yesterday my son graduated from college. Today we hike up a hill and sit on a granite bench. A meadow of wildflowers surrounds us as we look out over the Connecticut River Valley. From a backpack we remove a whole wheat baguette, gorgonzola and gouda cheese, hummus, apples—a feast. Tent caterpillars are devouring entire trees and crawling everywhere, even up our legs.

Will, the graduate, after some hemming and hawing, says he wants to ask me something: "Do you regret the way you lived your life?"

Fathers and mothers, be warned: someday your children, too, will be ready to step into a world of endless possibilities while staring back with puzzlement at the choices you made. And you can't fudge. They know you better.

Will now has a college degree in geography—cum laude, for Pete's sake—and meanwhile has always loved making music.

I have a college degree—not cum laude—and a love of writing stories. Will has worked with me mixing concrete and lifting drywall. He knows the satisfaction of construction work, but he also knows firsthand how hard it is. I haven't complained, but Will knows I'd rather be a full-time writer if only it paid all the bills.

Substitute music for writing, urban planning for construction, and you see the frame of Will's question.

"No regrets," I say. "My life had to come out this way, given who I was and who I am."

"Do you ever wish you could change anything?"

"Sure."

"Could you have done better?"

Ow. My son knows that I have never been a blazing star as a writer.

"I might have done better," I say. "If I hadn't met your mother I might've been a better writer."

"Why?"

"Because great art comes out of loneliness and pain. But I have absolutely no regret that I didn't live in loneliness and pain. And I might've turned out mediocre anyway."

We've opened beers now, local brew. Will knows I gave up a career in computers just before the internet revolution—gave it up because it didn't leave enough time for writing. Gave it up to start as a carpenter on a construction crew. I might have been rich.

He asks, "Are you happy? With your writing?"

I have to think a minute. I wish I'd written more books. I wish I'd had more time. But . . . "Yes," I say, "because I succeeded. What's tragic is if you make the choices I made and then realize you can't do it."

To my surprise, under Will's questioning I've just defined myself as a successful mediocre writer. I suppose it's on the low end of success, but I've published eight books. Via e-mail I hear from readers who appreciate what I've published—not many, but enough—readers all over the planet.

"What about you, Will? What would make you a successful musician? Radio airplay? Sold-out arenas? What?"

He thinks about it. Finally he answers: "Being good."

"How do you know if you're good? Is Preacher Shoeshine good?"

Preacher Shoeshine is a somewhat crazy man we both know who plays small venues—bookstores, restaurants, street corners—for small money, but who has lived his life as a musician. Technically he is a mediocre player, not as good as Will.

The question gives my son pause. "Yes, he's good," Will says at last. "Because even if he's not a great player, he achieves what he sets out to do and connects emotionally with people."

On that hill in New Hampshire with a view of the Connecticut River Valley, we have a view of my son's future. He'll struggle sometimes; he'll question his ability and wonder about his goals. He'll work day jobs; he may choose an all-consuming professional career as an urban planner. One way or another, full time or as a hobby, making music will always be part of his life.

He'll be good.

Laura, 15

Thursday, July 15, 2004

A girl appears at the bathroom door. "Oh cripes!" she says.

She's sweaty, hair bedraggled, wearing an athletic T-shirt and running shorts.

I'm installing bathroom lights. "You must be Laura," I say. Her mother had left a note asking me to "make way" if I could for her daughter, who would be coming home after a track-team workout at St. Francis High School.

"Give me a minute," I say, "and you can have the bathroom."

"I'll give you a minute if you can give me the sink," she says, and without waiting for an answer she steps in and starts splashing cold water on her face.

There is nothing—*nothing*—as quickening to the senses as the presence of a fifteen-year-old. At no other age are we as fully alive. Laura has mousy hair, freckles, a sweaty shirt clinging to her back and outlining the knobs of her spine. She smells like an old sock.

While working in the kitchen, I hear a shower running. An hour passes.

Laura comes down the stairs looking like a fox—a twenty-one-year-old fox. Her face shines. Her hair is gathered in a sweep over her head. That's the beauty of this age. In a flash they switch from kid to adult.

"Do I look like Ohio?" she says.

"What do you mean?"

"I'm flying to Ohio tonight. Visiting family. I've already been to New Jersey and Connecticut." She laughs. "That's my summer. Not exactly Paris and Rome, but oh well."

"You look fine," I say.

She looks surprised. "Thanks! Nice to meet you!" And she's gone out the front door.

That was the only time I ever saw Laura. I'm sure she has no memory of me whatsoever.

Always keep a teenager around. Even better, two or three. They're like sparklers on a dark night. So bright. Then gone.

Act Like an Electrician

Tuesday, February 8, 2005

I've worked with a lot of decorators over the years, but Isabella is the only one I've stayed with long term. I respect her. She's blonde and cute and sometimes, when she goofs up, she says, "I'm having a blonde day." But she's no bimbo. We've worked together off and on for twenty years.

Today I meet Isabella at a spiffy new house in Cupertino to discuss some lighting. Isabella prepares me: "It's an unusual situation. The wife works and makes millions. The hubby stays home and plays with toys."

The front of the house is divided into two large rooms, one containing a billiard table and giant model trains, the other a formal room with leather furniture and a fireplace. Featured on the mantle over the fireplace is an oil painting, a landscape in the old English style. Cows, a creek, fluffy clouds, peasant girls with creamy skin and ringlet hair. Engraved on a brass plate at the bottom of the frame is:

Ex Coll. Edward G Bulwer-Lytton

E. J. Niemann 1842

Wearing my tool belt over raggedy shorts, I study the painting and say, "I didn't know Bulwer-Lytton was a painter."

Hubby gives an amused little chuckle and asks, "What did you think he was?" Hubby has a British accent.

"A writer, of course. That's why he's known."

"Are you quite sure?"

"Absolutely. It has to be him. How many Edward G. Bulwer-Lyttons could there be in England in 1842?"

"What did he write?"

"A bunch of crappy novels. He's remembered for his style. He was the "dark and stormy night" guy. But here you have a painting by Bulwer-Lytton in the style of Gainsborough. I've always loved Gainsborough."

"Who was Gainsborough?"

"Thomas Gainsborough. You know—the English painter? He did those wonderful romantic old landscapes in the eighteenth century. And here a hundred years later is Bulwer-Lytton, a writer, imitating—"

Isabella coughs.

I stop, look around, and realize that Hubby is frowning.

Outside, Isabella says, "You blew that job. You showed him up."

"I'm sorry. I was excited. I liked the painting."

"Stay here. I'll go in and do damage control."

Isabella is a charmer. I wait in my truck.

Isabella returns. "You got the job. In the future, act like an electrician. Okay?"

"As long as you act like a decorator."

"Okay."

Isabella has no filter. It's part of her charm. We are an odd team. I always wonder what clients make of us. Being British, this client in particular might have a problem getting used to Isabella—and to California culture in general, where no topic is too personal to share.

We return to the house and take measurements for the lights. Isabella chats with the husband for a few minutes. He has the sniffles. Blowing his nose, apologizing, he says he hopes he won't infect anybody. Isabella says she won't catch it—she never comes down with a cold because she gargles with hydrogen peroxide. Every day.

Even after twenty years of collaboration, Isabella constantly surprises me. I ask, "Does gargling with peroxide work against other diseases, too?"

"Like what?"

"Oh, I don't know, bubonic plague maybe?"

"I've never caught it." Isabella laughs. "So I guess it works."

Hubby observes with a proper, British, stiff-lipped smile.

Which somehow reminds me: I mention to Isabella that a mutual acquaintance, very dear to both of us, just found out she has breast cancer. A workaholic, she quit her job, had surgery, and is now undergoing radiation.

"That's what happens," Isabella says. "Cancer gets your attention real fast. I should know."

Hubby says, "Oh, no! Oh dear. I hope you're all right."

"Oh, it's not me. I'm fine. George—my husband—has prostate cancer."

"I'm so sorry," Hubby says.

"All men get it. You will too. Maybe peroxide would help." Isabella goes inward for a moment, closing her eyes, shaking her blonde curly hair. She opens her eyes. "George had the seed treatment, you know, where they plant radioactive seeds. Now he's radioactive down there. It kind of makes me think twice about having sex."

It's my turn to cough.

Isabella puts her hand to her mouth. "We've got our measurements," she says. "We'll be in touch."

"I'm sure you will," Hubby says.

Back home, a little research reveals the obvious: the painter is E. J. Niemann. The "Ex. Coll." means *from the collection of* Edward G. Bulwer-Lytton. I'd mistaken the collector for the painter. But then so had the husband.

Isabella is right. I should act like an electrician.

I never meet the wife who makes millions. I install lights over the billiard table and the giant model trains. Two low-voltage spot lights bring out the painting of cows and creek, the milkmaids with creamy skin. Hubby seems pleased.

In his bathroom I notice a large new bottle of hydrogen peroxide.

Plattsburgh Hillbillies

September 2005

At the end of summer I sometimes spend a few weeks at a friend's cabin on Silver Lake in the Adirondack Mountains of New York state. It's heaven. I don't pay rent but I try to be useful.

For years, right after Labor Day I disassembled the wooden dock and the "big float," which is basically a raft on barrels. I lifted the sections, some weighing over a hundred pounds, into the boathouse where they would spend the winter. Every year it killed my back.

In 2005 I finally got smart and hired a kid named Virgil to do the heavy work. He lived in Plattsburgh, an hour away. In the relaxed, rustic, genteel environment of Silver Lake, Virgil stood out. He was a city boy — if Plattsburgh, New York, constitutes a city. He looked like a skinhead. He had, indeed, a shaved head, but he informed me that he was a hillbilly. He was the first hillbilly I ever met who spoke with a New York accent.

Virgil was a high-school dropout living with an older woman and her four children, none of whom he had fathered. Or maybe one was his. It was hard for me to follow. Virgil talked fast, and his mind wandered. ADD would be my nonprofessional diagnosis. ADD with a side order of violent upbringing. He grew up in the foster-care system after his father had run over his mother with a car. On purpose. Virgil had seen it.

Surprisingly, Virgil maintained a high degree of personal responsibility. He was working at two jobs plus picking up a few extra dollars on one-day chores such as removing my dock so as to support his older, unwed partner and her four kids.

Virgil was baby-faced, with some milk fat in his cheeks and absolutely no facial hair. He also had the worst-looking mouth I'd ever seen, as if he'd grown up chewing on chains. Actually, a lifetime diet of king-size Mountain Dew had rotted all his teeth.

Virgil was supposed to bring a helper named Jules, but Virgil arrived alone. "Jules is in jail," Virgil said. "He only hit the guy once, but he was already on probation." Looking around as if he didn't want anyone to overhear, Virgil confided: "Jules has an anger management problem."

I liked Virgil up to a point, but his politics were appalling. It was N-word this and N-word that. From growing up in Maryland in the Jim Crow era, I'd learned to compartmentalize people's racial attitudes from their other behavior, as there seemed to be little relationship. Also from growing up in Maryland, I had always been drawn to the Appalachians, so I was comfortable with hill people. I accepted Virgil—cautiously—on those terms.

September 2006

The next year, 2006, Virgil brought Jules. As they disassembled the big float and the dock, we talked. Virgil said he was leaving his wife. I said, "I didn't know you were married."

"Whatever. I'm gone. She can't do that."

"What did she do?"

"I saw her dancing with a nigger." Virgil spoke without anger, simply stating an unacceptable fact.

While Virgil was sweet-faced and light-haired, Jules had gaunt cheeks with a dark shadow. There was an air of menace about him. He'd just finished a year in prison. "I could've been out in six months with five years probation. Fuck that. I went the whole year so I didn't have no probation."

It made sense, actually. The just-completed one-year sentence was for a probation violation. Jules didn't strike me as somebody who was likely to go five years without another violation. He had, as he admitted, an anger problem. The one-year came about this way: "I was on a balcony with two friends. I hear something, so I look down and there's this nigger on a balcony below with two friends and he was taking a leak off the balcony. I told him to put it away and he didn't, so we had to go down there. I mean, it was a challenge. He disrespected and we had to. His two friends take off, but he puts up his fists, and you don't do that unless you expect something, so I had to. Then they called it a hate crime."

"Uh, Jules," Virgil said, "you had a choice."

"No I didn't."

"You and your buds beat the living shit out of him," Virgil said.

"Had to."

When they finished the dock, Jules surveyed some of the lakefront with a metal detector. It was his hobby, collecting old coins.

I asked Jules, "You ever think about joining the army?"

"Why would I want to do that?"

"They'd help you with that anger thing. They're good at that. They need you. You need them. Perfect match."

"Yeah," Virgil chimed in. "Because they could beat the crap out of you."

"Really," I said, "you'd get training. You might pick up a skill. And you could find some foreign coins." Also—though I didn't say so—he might learn a little racial tolerance.

Listen to me. The old hippie war protester and draft resister is now recommending the army to troubled kids. But the military can be a good deal to young men who otherwise face a pretty bleak life.

September 2008

Two years passed. Once again in need of help with the dock and big float, I called around and learned that Virgil was in jail. He'd been caught with one dose of oxycodone, which he was taking because his teeth gave him constant pain. He bought it on the street—at a cost of thirty dollars per day—because he couldn't get a prescription because he couldn't afford to go to a doctor. Or so he said. Math—and strategic planning—didn't seem to be among Virgil's strong suits.

As for Jules, he'd joined the marines.

September 2010

Two more years passed. It was now 2010 and again I needed help with the big float and the dock. Virgil had just gotten out of jail after another bust with oxycodone. He'd lost weight. You could see he was in pain. Besides the agony of his teeth, he said he had a cyst in his butt. Hurt going in, hurt coming out. Without oxy he couldn't chew. Most of the time, he said, he simply didn't eat. "The good news," Virgil told me, "is I just qualified for Medicaid. Next week I get my teeth removed and surgery on my ass."

"How many teeth will they remove?"

"All of them."

"And then they'll take out your ass?"

He laughed. "Not all of it."

Virgil's third child—of three different women—had just been born, a daughter. The mother, who at twenty-nine was six years older than Virgil, already had several children, the oldest being sixteen. Yes, sixteen. "I keep fucking old ladies," Virgil said. He showed me a photo of his dark-skinned newborn daughter.

I couldn't help but laugh.

"Yeah," Virgil said, "how 'bout that?"

I'd seen a bumper sticker on a Lincoln Town Car in Lake Placid that read: God. America. Ford. A friend had joined me on the dock, so as Virgil worked, my friend and I speculated what we would say if we had to summarize our values in three words on a bumper sticker. I couldn't do it. My friend came up with: "Family, kindness, education."

Virgil called out, "I only need one word: Unlucky."

"You ever hear from Jules?"

"His word is lucky. At least he ain't blown up."

"Still in the marines?"

"He'll stay forever. He found home, man."

281

After Virgil departed, the old couple in the neighboring cabin came over and told me they'd heard my conversation with Virgil. The old man, shaking his head, asked, "How can you talk to him?"

"What do you mean?"

"I mean I wouldn't know what to say to somebody like that."

"I just talk." I was used to dealing with carpenters like Virgil. The old man, though, had lived his life in a different stratum of society. He couldn't imagine how to function at any other level. I couldn't imagine cutting myself off from that much of the world.

July 2011

A year later it's July of 2011. I don't need any work done, but Virgil drops by just to chat.

"I'm in the chef business," he says.

"The what?"

"I got a job. Starts tomorrow. I'll be a chef."

"Where'd you learn to be a chef?"

"They'll train me. Anyway, I done McDonald's. Now I'll be at Denny's."

"Hey! Great! You'll be a cook."

"Cook. Chef." He shrugs.

"How's Jules?"

"He lost some weight. Left leg, below the knee. Some fingers. Both eyes."

"Oh, no! I'm so sorry. It's all my fault."

"Nope."

"I told him to enlist."

"I bet he don't remember. Anyway, ain't your fault. He enlisted after he got in some trouble. They gave him the choice: prison or military. I never saw him so happy. Marines was the best years of his life."

Virgil shows me his mouth. Just gums. "Another month," he says. "You have to wait a year for false teeth."

"What do you eat?"

"Soups 'n' shakes."

"You off the drugs?"

"Absolutely. I was never an addict. I got no pain. I'm clean for my kids."

"How many now?"

"Three are mine. Three hers. That's all. She got the tubes tied."

"That's enough, huh?"

"She says she's too old for that shit. Not me. I love kids. We'll be okay now." He smiles with pride. "I'm a chef."

Drilling for Water

August 2006, Adirondack Mountains

The truck, a drilling rig on wheels, creaks slowly down the narrow driveway, striking branches off a few maple trees. Daniel Barton, the driver, maneuvers to the chosen spot twenty feet uphill from the old house.

I greet Daniel. We shake hands and, with the quick glances of construction people we size each other up. In Daniel I see a proud man with a firm handshake and not a flicker of self-doubt. Just backing that truck down the overgrown dirt trail of a driveway took plenty of skill.

What Daniel sees—or what I'm sure he's prepared to see—is the hippie surfer insufferable contractor from California, here to look over his shoulder and protect the owner's interests. It takes him about two seconds, the duration of a handshake, to get over that.

"Nice rig," I say.

"Yeah," he says.

We'll be fine.

For a New Englander Daniel Barton is, in fact, a chatty man. Over the next two days I receive a gruff seminar on drilling in the Adirondacks.

Daniel gives me a tour of the machinery. Next, with his assistant Bob, he starts drilling. A river of sandy foam starts spewing from the hole, spilling over the lawn like glacial debris.

The drill quickly drops through sandy soil and then stops, chattering and grinding.

"Boulder," Daniel says. "Boulders are a driller's worst nightmare." He concentrates on the drilling, fingertips on the controls, watching and listening to subtle changes in the progress of the drilling rod.

Suddenly he's through it. The drill plunges quickly and then stops again. Daniel frowns. Another boulder. More fingertip control. Then he's through it—another plunge—and then a slow, steady grinding.

Daniel drills only thirty-five feet. He and assistant Bob set the casing and call it a day. "I just wanted to be sure I was in bedrock," Daniel says. They only need casing until bedrock. From here on he can penetrate bedrock at a rate of one foot every minute or minute and a half. He might have to go 200 feet or 600 feet. In any case, he wants to finish tomorrow.

"I hope it's not six hundred feet," I say.

"Yeah," Daniel says.

The next day Daniel drills steadily. Every twenty-five feet he has to stop so that Bob can add another drilling rod, like a link in a chain.

Between 180 and 200 feet down, the drill hits two fractures and gets a flow of seven gallons a minute. Pretty decent.

Daniel thinks he should go deeper. He thinks he could do better.

Is it a hunch? A distillation of years of experience? This is where you have to trust your professional. I trust Daniel.

There's sizable money involved. Drilling is billed at fifteen dollars per foot. Daniel could drill another 200 feet at a cost of $3,000 and find no more water. They've already got a workable flow.

I call the owners. After consultation they say, "Go for it."

Daniel goes another two rods, fifty feet. He hits another fracture and gets twelve gallons a minute. It's a gusher.

An inch of sticky gray sludge covers the front yard. Amazing. All that slime used to be solid bedrock.

The economics of drilling are not rational. The extra fifty feet of drilling took forty-five minutes and earned Daniel another $750. If beyond the fifty feet he'd had to drill another 150 feet, he would have earned another $2,250 for another two and a half hours of work. That's fifteen dollars a minute.

Daniel has fixed costs with each job. First, he has $900,000 in capital equipment sitting here to do the job, and it's a day's work to set it up and tear it down. He has to pay his one assistant, Bob. And yet he doesn't charge a setup fee. For the same amount of transportation and setup, he might drill 100 feet or 1,000 feet. For two or three days of work he might earn $1,500 or $15,000.

"Charging by the foot is asinine," I say upon learning all this.

"Yeah," Daniel says. He shrugs. "But that's how it's done."

Daniel extracts rock chips from the sludge on the lawn and shows them to me, a guided tour of the geology beneath our feet. First he penetrated thirty-five feet of soil and two boulders. Then he went through 150 feet of granitic gneiss, which is a metamorphic rock—that is, it contains crystals formed under high pressure. I love this stuff—I was a rock collector as a kid, and then I took some geology classes in college, not out of any career plans but just for the fun of it. Granitic gneiss, by the way, is the correct name for what we commonly call granite. True granite is something else.

Daniel shows me a black, coarsely grained rock. He says that below the 150 feet of granitic gneiss, he hit ten feet of gabbro, which is an igneous intrusion. The gabbro entered the granitic gneiss as molten rock and then cooled, shrinking as it cooled, forming fractures where water gathers.

Awesome! Mysteries below us, revealed. Molten lava, twisted and frozen. Rainwater from years, perhaps decades ago, coursing beneath immense dark masses of rock. I feel I've taken a subterranean voyage, shining light into the depths. The Adirondacks are an ancient, seething mass of volcanoes, earthquakes, sea beds, and ash, now solid stone.

Daniel crossed the first two fractures between 180 and 200 feet. The extra drilling crossed the third fracture, which brought the flow to twelve gallons a minute. Daniel says you could go 400 feet around here and get only a half gallon a minute. Just a quarter mile from here he drilled a well to 600 feet and got only one gallon a minute. What a crap shoot.

The top layer of gabbro is horizontal. There's a fracture at the top of the gabbro and another at the bottom, both yielding water. The second layer of gabbro, Daniel says, seems to be vertical. He can tell by how the drill bit behaves as it's striking the fracture. With a horizontal fracture the drill bit suddenly drops an inch or so as it crosses the water layer. With a vertical fracture the drill bit stutters as it tries to bite into an angular surface. Since it was a vertical layer of gabbro, there was no telling how far he would have had to go to punch through it, and we are getting plenty of water, so it was prudent to stop.

Daniel shows me some whitish chips. Calcite. The gabbro layer contained mineral deposits from the water. Which I suppose means it's hard water.

On the Northway (Interstate 87) near Keeseville, according to Daniel Barton, there's a road cut that exposes rock similar to what he drilled through here—dark bands of gabbro in granitic gneiss. I tell him I'll check it out.

The conversation wanders. We talk about fishing. I tell Daniel that last week a nine-year-old boy was fishing from the dock here. He caught a perch. As he watched, a bass swam along and swallowed the perch. The boy jerked the line to set the hook, as he'd been taught. The perch popped out of the mouth of the bass. The bass went swimming away, probably puzzled by the whole incident. The boy reeled in the perch. He's only nine and already he's got a great fish story.

We talk about our kids. Daniel is opposed to liberal arts college education. His daughter went to Middlebury, tried English, switched around for a while, and ended up with a major in math. Daniel says the most common phrase spoken by English majors is, "You want fries with that?" He says he took his daughter to lunch, and the waitress said exactly that: "You want fries with that?" They both broke out laughing. The waitress was a third-year English major.

I tell Daniel I served fries when I was in college and I was an English major. It's only a college job, just as it was for that waitress he was laughing at. I tell him all three of my kids majored in liberal arts and then two of them went on to professional schools—medicine, engineering—and that liberal arts will make them a better doctor and a better engineer.

Once again Daniel and I are taking each other's measure. Respectfully.

Daniel worked in Hong Kong for a while. I'm thinking, but don't say, *There's your liberal arts education.*

Daniel says he has a house in Vermont built so tight, "You can heat it with a candle." He's an environmentalist who would never use that word.

So we've met. We've sparred. I've learned something. Maybe Daniel has too.

Now Daniel rams his cumbersome truck up the driveway, snapping a few more maple branches on the way out.

Then he's gone.

A hush returns to the north woods. On the lake a loon is warbling. A house built shortly after the Civil War finally has a water well. I have a few rock chips to add to my childhood collection.

A good two days of work.

Ode to a Leather Tool Belt

Tuesday, April 26, 2011

I still wear it. Yesterday I modified a picture frame, rehung a door, and tried to reshape the couplings of wooden toy-train tracks that my dogs have chewed.

When I wear a tool belt and show up at somebody's house—or at my wife's therapy practice, where I'm the maintenance guy—any boy between the ages of two and ten thinks I'm a god. I've destroyed more than one therapy session simply by walking through the room. It's the tool belt, bristling with screwdrivers, chisel, big fat pencil, and cordless drill. It jingles when I move, nails clinking in pouches, drill slapping my leg. The boys follow me around asking, "What are you doing?" and "Can I help?" Not all of them, but many. (It seems to come with the Y chromosome; girls rarely respond.) And not over the age of ten, by which time most kids in Silicon Valley have decided that real life is on a flat screen.

The answer to, "Can I help?" is usually, "Yes." Depending on age or on my instant reading of their impulse control, boys can wield a cordless drill or at least help me select the right size of screw from a handful of miscellany.

The old leather tool belt is in sorry shape. I bought it in 1976. We've shared many an adventure, catastrophe, and triumph. I've washed those bags with saddle soap, sewn them with dental floss. The web of the belt is fraying, and I don't know how to fix that. Maybe duct tape will work.

The pockets of a tool belt tend to fill up over time. Every once in a while I remove every tool, every last screw and nail. I hold the tool belt upside down and give it a good shake. Sawdust, a dead spider, little strippings of insulated wire will fall out. And, once, my missing wedding ring. It had broken, and I was taking the ring to a jeweler for repair, but when I got there I couldn't find it.

When that belt frays out, maybe a jeweler can repair it. It's that precious.

A Full-Time Job

Thursday, June 23, 2011

I can't work today.

Due to a family emergency I'm taking care of my grandson. He's three and three-quarters years old, as he'll readily tell you. It's an impressive mouthful of numbers and sounds much older than my mere sixty-three.

For breakfast he chooses to have two slices of buttered multigrain toast with a side of bruschetta sauce, straight. I have coffee with goat milk. He likes to take one sip of my coffee.

We walk his dog, along with my two dogs, in a constant dance of tangled leashes. All three dogs successfully poop, two in the weeds at the side of the road and one that we must shove to the side with sticks, which is challenging and fun when you're of a certain age, as both of us are.

Without dogs we take an exploratory expedition on foot through the forest. We encounter banana slugs in their natural habitat, birds, squirrels, and a redwood tree you can walk through. Farther on, we find a redwood with an opening like a cave, into which somebody has thrown beer cans. We wonder why somebody would do that.

Moving on, we return to the road and find a turtle sitting peacefully in the center of the asphalt. We observe which parts are soft, which are hard, and we note that the turtle seems grouchy about being touched. I move the turtle to the weeds at the side of the road, and my grandson and I discuss the relative merit of leaving it alone versus annoying it with a relocation. The discussion covers some graphic consideration of the effect of a truck tire on a turtle shell.

At the playground we discover that at age three and three-quarters one can climb structures that one couldn't climb at age three and one-half. These milestones are duly noted.

Walking home by way of the pond, we observe that ducks tend to be drowsy at midday, while dragonflies are busy and bullfrogs are noisy.

We admire bountiful white flowers on thorny branches. We promise to return when there are berries to pick. My grandson's favorite question is "Why?" which leads to an analysis of why the berry hopes to end up as bird poop. Or bear poop.

For lunch we both have peanut butter sandwiches (uncut—very important!) and strawberries.

After lunch we play with a wooden train set, which, after an hour, ends in a spectacular wreck.

Following a quick trip to the La Honda Country Market, we return and eat a chocolate chunk muffin, or at least half of it. An unfortunate swing of the elbow, followed by a quick gulp by a dog, ends the snack and brings one of us (not me) to tears.

We watch the movie *Cars* from a DVD. For both of us it's our favorite movie, though it only brings one of us (me) to tears.

Inspired by the movie, I haul out an entire milk crate filled with tiny toy cars that accumulated in the course of raising my two sons. We play for a couple of hours.

Dinner is Ritz crackers with muenster and colby cheese, followed by a raucous bath.

In bed we read three books. He absorbs each one with wide eyes and critical commentary.

Now he sleeps.

Anyway, that's why I couldn't accomplish anything today.

The Inevitability of Ladders

Saturday, December 10, 2011

I have a painful history with ladders. Falling. Or really, as a friend pointed out, it isn't the falling that hurts, it's the landing.

1979
Descent: 8 feet
Cause: Top rung of a wooden ladder buckled
Landing: On my wrist
Result: Swollen wrist

1980
Descent: 2 feet
Cause: Base of the ladder slipped
Landing: None—grabbed hold of a beam and dangled by my thumb fourteen feet above the floor until rescued
Result: Sore thumb, amazement at my luck

1983
Descent: 10 feet
Cause: Base of the ladder slipped
Landing: Feet first
Result: Purple feet, purple ankles

2001
Descent: 6 feet
Cause: Lost my balance when the head of a bolt sheared off while I was tightening it
Landing: Caught a 2×4 halfway down and held on
Result: Bruised hip, twisted knee

2008
Descent: 12 feet
Cause: Reached too far when my judgment was clouded by stench
Landing: Soft, sideways in a pile of garbage in a garage where the client had piled about three months' worth of household trash in plastic bags because he was too cheap to pay for collection
Result: A few pokes, garbage being like a smelly pillow with a few embedded nasty things

How long could my luck hold out? I finally swore off ladders and all things dangerous.

Then one night in December of 2011 during a winter storm, I awake to a *bang!* as loud as a gunshot. Daylight reveals a clobbered rain gutter. A branch nine inches in diameter detached itself from a redwood tree.

The damage is up high.

This is why we have teenagers—to help with this crap. But my kids are grown, with lives of their own. The nest is empty.

So I decide to hire Tom, a carpenter with a lifetime of experience. Surprised, he asks, "Can't you do it?"

"I've sworn off ladders."

Tom sets up my 24-foot fiberglass ladder, then cuts the gutter and removes it. But now it's revealed: behind the gutter the fascia's rotten. So *that's* how squirrels have been getting into the ceiling and raising a ruckus somewhere above my dining table.

I happen to have a 16-foot all-heart redwood 1×6 in my garage. After thirty-five years of contracting I have a lot of odd planks and old tools.

Tom points out the obvious: to install a 16-foot board, somebody will have to hold each end. On separate ladders, sixteen feet apart.

So Tom climbs the 24-footer while I climb my 32-footer, each of us holding one end of the board. Tom nails; I nail. Here I am: climbing, twisting, reaching, hammering.

"Sorry," Tom says. "Just what you were trying to avoid."

But I couldn't say no. Because I'm a guy. I'm a semi-retired contractor.

Should something go wrong, the tally would conclude:

2011
Descent: 18 feet
Cause: Luck running out
Landing: Ugly
Result: Death (probably)

Instead, we finish the job. I climb back down. No falling, no landing.

There will always be a ladder chore. And I'll probably do it. It's who I am.

Acknowledgements

Thanks to Susan Walker, indefatigable editor, critic, and friend, without whom this sentence would probably say "without who."

Thank you, "Rose." If stories about my wife seem conspicuously few, it's because that's how she wants it. Be assured: she is the foundation on which all my castles are built.

Thanks to the folks who listen and read at La Honda Lit Night, who heard these stories in rough draft and encouraged me to go on.

Thanks to the readers of my blog *365 Jobs* for feedback that has shaped my writing, and thanks especially to Michael Taylor, the Hollywood Juicer, who graciously let me infringe on the title of his blog.

Thanks to James Adams—aficionado of old lumber, shaper of bookmarks.

Thank you, kickstarters, for your generous and enthusiastic support. Your preorders provided more than funds: you gave me the faith and spirit to complete this book. Through Kickstarter I feel a community gathering around this project—from all over the planet. Every one of you is an important member of the *99 Jobs* crew.

Master Carpenters

Beto	Michael Pye	Stevie and Bob
Sheri	Allan Turkal	James S. Huang
Jeff Baker	Terry Adams	Michael Minard
Eva Knodt	Michael Taylor	Daniel, Jodi, and Reene Paley
Mary Bordi	Cindy Roessler	Betsy Moore and Cliff Jenkins
Teri Garza	Carole A. Lugo	Edwin Hering and Marcy Steiner

Journeyman Carpenters

Neil Macneale   Georgia Stigall

Apprentice Carpenters

Adam Lauridsen	Diana	Jane Ingalls
Anneliese Agren	Dietrich P. Onnen	Jeanne Phelan
Arlene Balkan	Eugen Sasu	Jennifer Powell
Betty Nogues	Fred Barizani	Joanna Oshman
Bill	Gene Demin	Joe
Bill Kelly	George Varian	John Grobowski
Caroline Kerner	Graceann Johnson	John McAfee
Danny Meehan	Holly Love	Joshua Terp
Dave Minard	Jake Ketchum	Joyce Converse
David E. LeCount	Janak Das	Julie Z.

Kathleen Connor
L. Quinn
Liz Chapman
Marianne Schroeder
Marsha Silver
Mathias Stroers
Megan W.
Merry Gilmer
Nadine Fourt
Nausicaa and Paolo
Renée Burgard
Brad and Trebbie Thomas
Carol Lou Young-Holt
Daniel and Adam Rosas
Tomás and Alejandro Neou-Curiel

Roxanne Knutti
Sandra Bachman
Sandy Wagner
Scott Graber
Sharon L. Juliano
Sheila Golden
Sue Henkin-Haas
Susan S. Allen
Tom Dodd
Turtle Hosein
Will Fourt

The Wing Family
Therese Flanagan
Heckler
Audrey Helou
Lise Bee
Kevin Henney
R. Elena Tabachnick
Phil Hough
Sara Fortune Robison
Amy Waldhauer
Wendy Justus
Karen, David, and Ian Ehrhardt
Tom and Marilyn Utter
Tom and Patty Smeltzer